TOP **10**
SYDNEY

STEVE WOMERSLEY
RACHEL NEUSTEIN

DK
EYEWITNESS TRAVEL

Left **Mosaic at St Mary's Cathedral** Centre **Sailing on Sydney Harbour** Right **Kings Cross**

LONDON, NEW YORK,
MELBOURNE, MUNICH AND DELHI
www.dk.com

Printed and bound in China by
Leo Paper Products Ltd

First published in Great Britain in 2005
by Dorling Kindersley Limited 80 Strand, London
WC2R 0RL, UK
A Penguin Company

13 14 15 16 10 9 8 7 6 5 4 3 2 1

**Reprinted with revisions 2006, 2007,
2009, 2011, 2013**
Copyright 2005, 2013 © Dorling Kindersley
Limited, London

A CIP catalogue record is available from the
British Library.

ISBN 978 1 40937 342 1

Within each Top 10 list in this book, no hierarchy
of quality or popularity is implied. All 10 are, in
the editor's opinion, of roughly equal merit.

Floors are referred to throughout in accordance
with Australian usage; ie the "first floor" is the
floor above ground level.

MIX
Paper from
responsible sources
FSC
www.fsc.org   FSC™ C018179

Contents

Sydney's Top 10

Sydney Opera House	8
Sydney Harbour Bridge	12
Sydney Harbour	14
The Rocks & Circular Quay	18
Royal Botanic Gardens & The Domain	20
Art Gallery of NSW	24
Darling Harbour & Chinatown	28
Powerhouse Museum	30
Taronga Park Zoo	3
Bondi Beach	3
Moments in History	3
Historic Sites & Buildings	3
Writers	4
Museums	4
Art Galleries	4

All prices in this guide are in Australian dollars

Left **Beare Park** Centre **Sydney Opera House & Sydney Harbour Bridge** Right **Shelly Beach**

Contents

Architectural Highlights	46
Beaches	48
Parks & Gardens	50
Sporting Venues & Olympic Sites	52
Outdoor Activities	54
Activities for Children	56
Restaurants	58
Casual Dining	60
World Flavours	62
Performing Arts Companies	64
Nightlife & Live Music	66
Pubs & Bars	68
Gay & Lesbian Friendly	70
Festivals & Events	72

Around Town

City Centre	76
Kings Cross & Darlinghurst	84
Paddington & Surry Hills	90
Eastern Suburbs	96
Newtown & Glebe	102
Balmain & Leichhardt	108
The North Shore	114
Beyond Sydney	120

Streetsmart

Practical Information	132
Places to Stay	143
General Index	150

Left **Victorian terrace house** Right **Royal Botanic Gardens**

Key to abbreviations
Adm *admission charge* **Dis access** *disabled access*

3

SYDNEY'S TOP 10

Sydney's Highlights
6–7

Sydney Opera House
8–11

Sydney Harbour Bridge
12–13

Sydney Harbour
14–17

The Rocks &
Circular Quay
18–19

Botanic Gardens &
The Domain
20–23

Art Gallery of
New South Wales
24–27

Darling Harbour &
Chinatown
28–29

Powerhouse Museum
30–31

Taronga Park Zoo
32–33

Bondi Beach
34–35

Top Ten of everything
36–73

SYDNEY'S TOP 10

TOP10 Sydney's Highlights

Sydney is blessed with stunning ocean beaches, magnificent national parks and a wonderful subtropical climate that makes the great outdoors irresistible to its four million inhabitants. The Eora people, the Aborigines who settled around Sydney Harbour, arrived approximately 50,000 years ago, while the earliest white settlers arrived in 1788. Free settlers soon followed in the wake of the First Fleet of transported convicts, and after them several waves of migrants seeking a new life. Now, over two centuries later, the once far-flung penal colony has matured into a culturally diverse, tolerant and mesmerising city. Ideally located on the world's most beautiful harbour, Sydney is as exciting and bustling as it is laid back and relaxing.

1 Sydney Opera House

Sydney's architectural icon and world-renowned performing arts venue enjoys the most spectacular setting of any cultural institution in the world. It is the city's most popular tourist attraction *(see pp8–11).*

2 Sydney Harbour Bridge

This enormous and beautiful structure was an economic and engineering triumph. It reshaped Sydney's landscape and lifted the city's spirits during the dark days of the Great Depression *(see pp12–13).*

3 Sydney Harbour

From its pristine beaches to its working docklands, this deep-water port at the heart of this maritime city is the world's finest *(see pp14–17).*

Previous pages: **Circular Quay**

4 The Rocks & Circular Quay

Governor Phillip and the First Fleet arrived here in 1788 to lay the foundations for Australia's white settlement. Now it's an engaging historic precinct and a lively transport hub *(see pp18–19)*.

5 Royal Botanic Gardens & The Domain

This lovely green belt east of the city centre incorporates the Royal Botanic Gardens and the Art Gallery of New South Wales, and has been one of Sydney's best-loved public spaces for almost 200 years *(see pp20–23)*.

6 Art Gallery of New South Wales

Boasting one of the country's most extensive collections of Australian and international art, this striking building in The Domain is not to be missed *(see pp24–7)*.

7 Darling Harbour & Chinatown

Chinatown's authentic bustle and flavour is the perfect counterpoint to the ritzy Darling Harbour precinct. An extension of the city centre, Darling Harbour offers numerous museums, bars, cafés and tourist attractions *(see pp28–9)*.

8 Powerhouse Museum

Kooky. Challenging. Hands-on. And plenty of fun. Powerhouse's eclectic and sometimes eccentric science and design collection appeals to children and adults alike *(see pp30–31)*.

9 Taronga Zoo

The zoo's collection of Australian and exotic animals, not to mention its gorgeous setting overlooking the harbour, makes it a must-see destination for visitors *(see pp32–3)*.

10 Bondi Beach

Sydney's swimmers, surfers and sybarites all love Australia's most iconic beach. Don't leave the city without spending some time here, body surfing, walking along the clifftops or working on your tan *(see pp34–5)*.

Taronga Zoo **9**

3

Sydney Harbour

Clark Island

remorne Point

zabeth Bay

ngs ss

ushcutters Bay

addington

10 Sydney Opera House

The Opera House's magnificent harbourside location, stunning architecture and excellent programme of events make it Sydney's number one destination. The modern masterpiece reflects the genius of its architect, Jørn Utzon. In 1999, Utzon agreed to prepare a guide of design principles for future changes to the building. This was welcome news for all who marvel at his masterpiece and for the four million visitors to the site each year.

Opera Theatre

Home to The Australian Ballet, the Sydney Dance Company and Opera Australia, this lovely theatre *(above)* seats more than 1,500. It hosted the site's first performance in 1973, Prokofiev's *War and Peace*.

Opera House roof tiles

🍷 After the show, kick back to live jazz and a late supper at the Opera Bar.

🎭 A range of performance packages is available.

• Map N1
• Bennelong Point
• Open daily; Box Office open 9am–8:30pm Mon–Sat, 2 hrs prior to performances on Sun
• 9250 7777; for hearing impaired TTY users call 133677, then ask for 9250 7111
• www.sydneyopera house.com
• Essential tour: 9250 7250 (1 hour every 30 mins from 9am–5pm daily, $35); Backstage Tour (2 hours, from 7am, includes breakfast in the Green room, $155)
• Dis access, loop, infra-red hearing systems and audio description service: 9250 7777, 9250 7175
• Opera Bar: 9247 1666

Top 10 Features

1. Roof
2. Concert Hall
3. Opera Theatre
4. Drama Theatre
5. Playhouse
6. The Studio
7. High Tea
8. Forecourt & Monumental Steps
9. Northern Foyers
10. Bars & Restaurants

Opera House and the Bridge

Drama Theatre

This intimate theatre was not part of Utzon's original plan. Today, however, it is a much-loved venue and its size ensures good sightlines from every seat.

Roof

Comprised of 10 "sails", the roof *(above)* is made of over one million tiles. Designed to counter the sunlight, the ceramic tiles take on a lustrous glow at dawn and dusk.

Concert Hall

The Opera House's most impressive venue, and home to the Sydney Symphony, seats 2,679 and hosts concerts, opera and drama performances *(right)*. Its acoustics are acclaimed worldwide, and the Grand Organ took ten years to design and tune.

One of the best vantage points for Opera House photographs is Mrs Macquarie's Chair (see p20) at dawn.

5 Playhouse

This intimate venue hosts contemporary theatre productions and the popular 'Kids at the House' programme.

8 Forecourt & Monumental Steps

Framed by the Botanic Gardens and Government House, the Forecourt and the 86-m (282-ft) wide Monumental Steps *(left)* are the perfect setting for outdoor events, such as ballroom dancing or Greek folk music. A weekly arts and crafts market is also held here.

10 Bars & Restaurants

Dining at Sydney Opera House caters for all tastes, from cocktails at the Opera Bar and Theatre Bars or light meals at the Studio Café or Opera Kitchen to a night of indulgence at the award-winning Guillaume at Bennelong *(see below & p58)*.

6 The Studio

The Opera House's grooviest and most flexible venue is The Studio. Staged here are contemporary short-run productions that include gay cabaret, hip-hop theatre, world music and country and western. Comedy and dance shows are also held here.

7 High Tea

High Tea *(left)* combines a 20-minute opera recital by some of the world's greatest opera singers with cuisine prepared by renowned chef Guillaume Brahimi, in the intimate Bennelong restaurant. High Tea at the Opera House takes place every Wednesday 2–4pm.

9 Northern Foyers

Topaz-tinted glass canopies and massive girders enclose the Northern Foyers of the Concert Hall and Opera Theatre, and offer spectacular 180-degree views of the harbour.

Bennelong

Governor Arthur Phillip built a home on the headland for his Aboriginal translator, Bonnolong, and in 1792 Phillip took Bennelong back to London with him. When Bennelong returned to Australia in 1795 he found himself caught between cultures, and his drinking, womanising and violent outbursts became legendary, ending tragically in 1813. In 1817 a fort designed by Francis Greenway was built on the point named for Bennelong. It was replaced by a tram depot in 1902.

➤ The arts and crafts market at the Forecourt is held every Sunday from 9am–4pm, subject to weather.

Left **Roof in mid-construction** Center **Completed roof** Right **The Red Book**

Raising the Roof

1
1954
Eugene Goosens, the Conservatorium of Music's director, lobbies the state Labour Premier, Joseph Cahill, to construct an opera house. Cahill appoints Goosens to a committee investigating the proposal.

2
1956
Upon his return from an overseas conducting tour, customs agents mysteriously find "pornography" in Sir Eugene's luggage. He resigns and returns to Europe leaving an overwrought and self-righteous media frenzy in his wake.

3
1957
A Danish architect, Jørn Utzon, is declared the project's architect. Utzon's prize money is £5,000. Projected cost of the project: $7 million. Projected completion date: 1963.

4
1958
Demolition of the old tram sheds on Bennelong Point commences. Following an unsuccessful fund-raising venture, the government establishes the Opera House Lottery to cover the estimated costs of construction.

5
1959
Premier Cahill responds to public and media concern about project delays and rising costs. He insists that work commence. Utzon and the project engineer

Ove Arup protest, asserting their plans are incomplete. Cahill dies in October 1959. Work starts on the platform (Stage 1).

6
1960–62
Utzon resolves the dilemma of the roof's design and construction in 1961. Sir Eugene Goosens dies in 1962.

7
1963–65
Work starts on the roof (Stage 2). In 1965 a Liberal/Country Party Coalition elected to office promises to stem rising costs and construction delays.

8
1966
On 28 February, Utzon resigns after disputes with the government over designs, deadlines, fees, subcontractors, and his role as the architect. A 1,000 people march on state Parliament demanding his reinstatement. Four Australian architects are appointed to complete the project. Utzon leaves Australia.

9
1966–1973
The Northern Foyers, interiors, walkways and concourse are completed (Stage 3).

10
1973
At the Forecourt on 20 October 1973, Queen Elizabeth I formally declares the Sydney Opera House open. Final cost: $102 million. Final project duration: 14 years.

The Red Book, *submitted for the 1957 design competition, contains Utzon's original sketches for the Opera House.*

Top 10 "Performances"

1. 1960: Paul Robeson performs for construction workers.
2. 1973: A possum appears at a dress rehearsal for the House's first production.
3. 1975: Shostakovich conducts his father's Symphony Number 10 only days after his father's death.
4. 1983: Joan Sutherland and Luciano Pavarotti perform the "Concert of the Century"
5. 1986: Pope John Paul II addresses religious orders in the Hall.
6. 1990: Nelson Mandela gives a public address.
7. 1990: Joan Sutherland takes her final bow.
8. 1992: Peter Allen performs for the last time.
9. 2003: Protesters daub "No War" on the roof in protest at Australia's involvement in Iraq.
10. 2006: Queen Elizabeth II opens the Colonnade, the first exterior change to the building.

Designing the House

Jørn Utzon

Inspired by the fan-like ribs of a palm leaf, Utzon's intention was to construct a timeless, organic structure that defied convention. The roof "shells" were to float above the harbour like giant sails. Utzon's drawings were inspired, but didn't allow for cost-effective prefabrication. In partnership with the engineering firm Ove Arup & Partners, Utzon laboured for months over the issue. His elegant epiphany came in 1961. If the shells were all cast from the same sphere, thus sharing a radius, it would be possible to pre-cast the concrete ribs as segments which could then be later assembled. Work began on the roof in 1963 and, in 2003, Utzon's genius was recognised by the architecture world's equivalent of the Nobel Prize, the Pritzker Prize. Following Utzon's death in 2008, a State memorial was held in the Concert Hall.

Segmented globe   **Roof comes into view**

Utzon's Opera House Model

Utzon's original interiors and certain design features now only exist in model form. The architect donated his models and plans to the State Library of New South Wales (see p22).

Sydney Harbour Bridge

Nothing you've ever seen can prepare you for the size and beauty of the world's largest steel arch bridge, opened in 1932. Its balanced composition and the graceful sweep of its southern approach have captivated artists for years. Francis Greenway (see p23) proposed a bridge in 1815, but the logistics vexed engineers until 1911, when John Bradfield suggested a single-span bridge. By then the North Shore's rapid growth demanded a solution, the only alternative being a long road trip through the western suburbs. Most visitors can easily understand why Sydneysiders love their old "coathanger".

The Harbour Bridge

🍸 Enjoy a cocktail on the rooftop of the Harbour View Hotel, where you'll be almost level with returning bridge climbers.

🔄 For a unique perspective on the bridge, lounge at the North Sydney Olympic Pool beneath the bridge.

- Map D2
- BridgeClimb: 3 Cumberland St; The Rocks; 8274 7777; www.bridgeclimb.com; operates daily; adult/ child (minimum age: 10) $208–$228/$138–$158 (prices rise in peak season: 26 Dec–9 Jan)
- Southeast Pylon Lookout: 9240 1100; www.pylonlookout. au; open 10am–5pm daily; closed 25 Dec; adult/ children 8–12 $9.50/$4
- Harbour View Hotel: Cumberland St, The Rocks; www.harbour view.com.au
- Pedestrian path entry: Cumberland St, The Rocks; Cycle path entry: Observatory Park

Top 10 Features

1. Design
2. BridgeClimb
3. Pylon Lookout & Museum
4. Pedestrian & Cycle Paths
5. Bradfield Park
6. Dawes Point
7. Maintenance
8. Tolls
9. Famous Portraits
10. Memorial

1 Design

Engineer John Bradfield established the design parameters, completed by Dorman Long & Co. Sir John Burnet and Partners of London designed the decorative granite-clad Art Deco pylons.

2 BridgeClimb

Since BridgeClimb *(above)* opened for business in 1998, almost two million people have climbed the bridge. The 3.5-hour guided climb over the top of the arch is well organised and exhilarating, and there's no better way to appreciate the structure's enormity and beauty.

Poster for the Bridge's opening

3 Pylon Lookout & Museum

The Southeast Pylon *(below)* offers 360-degree spectacular bridge-top views of Sydney as well as three levels of exhibition space exploring the bridge's genesis.

BridgeClimb also offer an Express Climb of 2 hours and 15 minutes and a Discovery Climb through the inner arch.

4 Pedestrian & Cycle Paths

Free highlights include a pedestrian and jogging path *(above)* along the eastern side of the bridge, and a cycle path along the western side.

6 Dawes Point

Below the southern pylons is Dawes Point, where the colony's first observatory was built in 1788. The park's interpretation boards, and the excavated remains of the fort that replaced the observatory in 1791, offer an interesting perspective on the city's development.

9 Famous Portraits

Works by renowned artists such as Grace Cossington-Smith, Dorrit Black, Gwen Barringer and Henri Mallard reflect the optimism inspired by the bridge in the midst of the Great Depression, and honour the bravery of its construction workers.

10 Memorial

During the Great Depression 1,400 people *(above)* worked on the bridge while hundreds more worked for subcontractors. A plaque on the southern approach commemorates the 16 workers who lost their lives during construction.

5 Bradfield Park

Under the northern pylons, this small park commemorating John Bradfield offers unparalleled views of the Opera House and Circular Quay. Directly beneath the bridge is the bow of the original HMAS *Sydney*.

7 Maintenance

Over $14 million and 3000 litres of paint a year are needed to keep the bridge shipshape. Before establishing himself as an actor, Paul Hogan worked as a painter on the bridge.

8 Tolls

When the bridge opened in 1932, the toll for cars was 6 pence. Horse and carts cost 3 pence and sheep and pigs were a penny per head. The current toll for vehicles *(left)* is $3–$4.

"Captain" Francis de Groot

Before Premier JT Lang could cut the ceremonial ribbon at the bridge's 1932 opening, a man swept forward and slashed the ribbon. "Captain" Francis de Groot declared the bridge open in the name of "decent citizens of NSW." He belonged to the right-wing New Guard, which opposed Lang's "socialist" government and believed that only royalty should inaugurate such an achievement. He was arrested and sent to a psychiatric hospital while Lang re-cut the ribbon.

Paul Hogan's big break was the starring role in the hugely popular movie *Crocodile Dundee* (1986).

TOP 10 Sydney Harbour

Arguably the most beautiful harbour in the world, it took the Parramatta and Lane Cove Rivers thousands of years to carve it from the sandstone. Well protected from off-shore winds, the harbour is also remarkably deep in parts. From its working docklands to its pristine and secluded beaches, this harbour is a natural asset that most cities can only dream of. Over the last 200 years the harbour has seen vast real estate developments, now comprising a lively array of apartment buildings and large residences, each vying for vantage points of the gorgeous harbour views and bustling maritime life.

A harbour beacon

🧺 Pack a picnic hamper and catch a water taxi to Clark Island for an al fresco lunch. There are picnic tables along the foreshore and walking trails through the bushland. Contact NPWS for details.

☀ On a sunny day, carry your bathing gear and towel on a harbourside walk. You will surely stumble upon an inviting beach or a harbourside pool.

• Map E2
• NSW/NPWS Information line: 1300 361 967
• www.nationalparks. nsw.gov.au • Sydney Harbour Tours: Cadman's Cottage, 110 George St, The Rocks; 9247 5033; Open 9:30am–4:30pm Mon–Fri, 10am–4:30pm Sat–Sun; Closed Good Friday, 25 Dec • Sydney Harbour Federation Trust: 8969 2100 • www. harbourtrust.gov.au

Top 10 Attractions

1. Sydney Harbour National Park
2. Harbour Beaches
3. The Heads
4. The Islands
5. Harbourside Walks
6. Harbourside Mansions & Penthouses
7. Harbourside Parks
8. Harbour Wildlife
9. The Working Harbour
10. Ferry Rides

1 Sydney Harbour National Park

This remarkable national park includes 5 islands. Aboriginal rock art sites, historic buildings, secluded beaches, monuments, lookouts and bushwalks are just some of its highlights. The National Parks and Wildlife Service (NPWS) manages the park and operates several tours.

2 Harbour Beaches

Sydney's harbour beaches *(below)* are glorious and several have protective shark netting, including Shark Beach and Manly Cove *(see p118)*. Parsley Bay, Camp Cove, and Lady Bay Beach in Watsons Bay are all gems and are accessible by ferry.

Aerial view of the harbour

3 The Heads

The rugged South and North Heads *(above & p51)* mark the entrance to Sydney Harbour and offer magnificent ocean and harbour views. They are particularly popular on Boxing Day when crowds gather to cheer the start of the Sydney to Hobart yacht race *(see p73)*.

4 The Islands
Of the harbour's seven islands, Sydney Harbour Federation Trust manages Cockatoo and Snapper, and the NPWS manages Goat, Shark, Clark, Rodd and Fort Denison *(above)*.

6 Harbourside Mansions & Penthouses
Among the fabulous abodes are Boomerang *(see p86)*, built by Frank Albert, Craigend (Darling Point), originally owned by shipping magnate James Patrick), and Russell Crowe's penthouse at Woolloomooloo Finger Wharf *(see p86)*.

9 The Working Harbour
View the harbour's working history at the Australian National Maritime Museum *(see p42)*, wander Balmain's backstreets, or discover the convict and maritime history of Cockatoo Island with the Sydney Harbour Federation Trust.

10 Ferry Rides
No trip to Sydney is complete without a ferry ride *(above & pp16–17)*. A journey to Manly is the classic trip, but other popular destinations include Watsons Bay, Balmain, Mosman and Darling Harbour.

5 Harbourside Walks
Thanks to the Harbour Foreshore Vigilance Committee *(see p97)*, set up to retain harbourside and for public use, Sydney has great harbourside walks. The www.walkingcoastalsydney.com.au site has maps and information about a range of harbour walks.

7 Harbourside Parks
While some parks offer extensive walking trails, others are lovely pockets of shaded greenery. The best parks include Rushcutters Bay *(see p87)*, Balls Head Reserve *(see p115)*, the Botanic Gardens *(see pp20–21)* and Nielson Park *(see p51)*.

8 Harbour Wildlife
Sydney Harbour is remarkably healthy, home to rainbow lorikeets *(left)*, several species of shark and fish, sea horses, dolphins, the occasional whale and the only known Little Penguin breeding colony on the Australian mainland.

HMAS Kuttabul
Three Japanese midget submarines passed through Sydney Heads on 31 May 1942. One sub aimed at the US naval ship *Chicago* but its torpedo missed and sank a Sydney ferry serving as a dormitory ship for Australian and British soldiers, the HMAS *Kuttabul*. The *Kuttabul* sank within minutes and 21 soldiers died. A chase ensued: one sub escaped, one was sunk by depth charges, and one set off its own charges and sank. Two subs were recovered and their four crew members were buried with full military honours.

Left **State ferry** Centre **Water taxi** Right **Seaplane**

On the Water

Ferries
1 It's been over 135 years since the first row boats transported customers across the harbour. Now 15 ferries service 39 destinations.

Harbour & River Cats
2 If you plan to visit Sydney Olympic Park or Parramatta's historic attractions, avoid the congestion of Parramatta Road by taking one of the sleek Harbour or River Cat Ferries. If you can't wait for a swim at Manly Beach, catch the Fast Ferry for the 17-minute trip.

Spectator Ferry
3 Catch a spectator ferry which follows the famous 18 Footers Skiff racing on the harbour on weekends. ◎ *www.18footers.com.au*

Water Taxis
4 Although too expensive for daily commuting, these taxis are a fun option if you fancy a peek at the luxurious harbourside mansions or a picnic on one of the islands.

Boats of all sizes at Circular Quay

Catamarans
5 Several gigantic catamarans service the harbour tourist trade. In some cases you can enjoy an on-board BBQ, or work on your tan as you cruise the harbour.

Jet Boats
6 If you feel the urge to "burn rubber" on the harbour, the harbour's jet boats will definitely give you an adrenaline fix.

Tall Ships
7 If they're in town, enjoy a harbour voyage on either of Sydney's two tall ships, the *Svanen* or the *Bounty*, a replica of Bligh's vessel built for the film of the same name.

Boats for Hire
8 Rent anything from sea kayaks to 14-ft (4.3-m) aluminium boats to 20-ft (6-m) half-cabin cruisers. Or hire a kayak and explore Middle Harbour.

Seaplane
9 Numerous flights around Sydney Harbour offer excellent fly-and-dine packages and can also take you to the gorgeous Northern Beaches, Pittwater and Hawkesbury regions.

Helicopter
10 For a touch of *Mission Impossible*, catch a helicopter for an exciting and scenic ride over the Harbour Bridge, the Opera House, Eastern Suburbs and Manly Cove.

The traditional, slow ferry from Circular Quay to Manly is the quintessential Sydney trip.

Top 10 Famous Harbourside Residents

1. John Howard, former Prime Minister
2. John Laws, radio shock-jock
3. Craig Parry, golfer
4. Judy Davis & Colin Friels, actors
5. Ken Done, artist
6. Jimmy Barnes, singer
7. May Gibbs, author
8. Nicole Kidman, actor
9. Cate Blanchett, actor
10. Russell Crowe, actor

- Harbour & River Cats depart from Circular Quay
- Eco Hopper 2-hr Sydney Harbour Cruise or hop-on-hop-off for 24 hrs, adult/child $35/$20; www.manlyfastferry.com.au
- Jet Boats: Sydney Jet & Oz Jet Boating www.sydneyjet.com, www.ozjetboating.com
- Kayaks: Sydney Harbour Kayaks under the Spit Bridge in Mosman • Boats, yachts & cruisers: Sydney Harbour Escapes, Rose Bay (see p55)
- Seaplane companies: Rose Bay • Sydney Heli Tours: Mascot SydneyAirport
- Sydney Ferries: www.sydneyferries.info

Sailing on Sydney Harbour

Sydney Harbour is perfect for sailing, although sometimes you can't see the water for the canvas. Wednesday afternoons and weekends are popular with the more competitive old salts, especially in the the competition season which runs between September and March. Friday twilight sailing is perfect for the more laid-back yachtie. Several firms, including Sydney Harbour Escapes, hire yachts for bareboat charter and offer social sailing and sailing lessons on Fridays and Sundays. The Sailing School, Sydney by Sail, and East Sail can also teach you the ropes. Afloat is a free monthly magazine for the yachting fraternity and for those with an interest in Sydney's maritime history. It also carries a regular calendar of events, tide charts and fishing tips. Check the Crew Wanted classifieds if you fancy running away to sea; Afloat is available at all marinas and the Australian National Maritime Museum.

Sydney to Hobart Yacht Race

Sailing on the harbour

17

🔟 The Rocks & Circular Quay

Near Circular Quay, The Rocks is a sanitized precinct of narrow laneways, galleries, boutiques and restaurants. West of the Argyle Cut, the road cut through solid rock in the 1860s that links east with west, the area is mainly residential. The Rocks sprang up beside the Tank Stream following the First Fleet's arrival on 26 January 1788. Within days, Governor Phillip's prefabricated canvas and timber residence was erected and the convicts housed in tents beneath the sandstone outcrops that gave The Rocks its name. Nowadays the open sewers, drunken sailors, convicts, brothels and plague-ridden rats are long gone, and the area is ideal for a winding stroll and a cold ale at a historic hotel; try the Hero of Waterloo or the Lord Nelson.

The Hero of Waterloo pub

🍺 **The Australian Hotel at Cumberland and Gloucester Streets serves great pizzas.**

🍺 **To meet the locals, have a drink at the Mercantile Hotel on George Street.**

- Map M1
- Sailors' Home: Billich Gallery, 106 George St; 9252 1481; Open 9am–7pm Sun–Wed, 9am–9pm Thu–Sat
- Cadman's Cottage: 110 George St; Open 10am–4:30pm Mon–Fri, 10:30am–4:30pm Sat–Sun
- Garrison Church: Argyle & Lower Fort Sts; Open 9am–5pm daily
- Sydney Observatory: Watson Rd; 9921 3485; Open 10am–5pm daily; General entry free, Adm for theatre, planetarium & night viewing • Hero of Waterloo: 81 Lower Fort St • Lord Nelson Hotel: see p146

Top 10 Features

1. Circular Quay
2. Customs House
3. Tank Stream
4. George Street
5. Sailors' Home
6. Cadman's Cottage
7. Museum of Contemporary Art
8. Overseas Passenger Terminal
9. Garrison Church
10. Sydney Observatory

Circular Quay

This maritime hub is Sydney's nucleus *(right)*. Plaques in the paving along Sydney Writer's Walk record obser- vations by authors such as Umberto Eco, Mark Twain, and Germaine Greer.

Customs House

Renovations of this stately 1844 building have seen the addition of a major public library. The Union Jack on Loftus Street marks the site of European landing and settlement.

Tank Stream

The only harbourfront reminders of the tidal creek *(see p38)* that determined Sydney's location are two artworks on Alfred Street. Stephen Walker's is at the western end, and Lynne Roberts-Goodwin's *(see p47)* is at the corner of Pitt Street.

George Street

Australia's oldest street is now a busy stretch of boutiques, galleries, shops and pubs. The Rocks' market below selling crafts, jewellery and the like is held at the northern end of the street on Saturdays and Sundays from 10am–5pm.

5 Sailors' Home
Formed in 1859, the Sailors' Home ran until the 1970s providing cheap lodging to seamen. Home to the Billich Gallery, the building's original north wing is Romanesque Revival in design.

6 Cadman's Cottage
Built in 1816, this is Sydney's oldest surviving dwelling *(right)*. It contains items excavated beneath the floors and the National Park Information Centre.

10 Sydney Observatory
The 1858 Italianate building *(below)* was converted into a museum of astronomy in 1988. The tower's time-ball still drops daily at 1pm, while a cannon is fired simultaneously from Fort Denison *(see p38)*.

7 Museum of Contemporary Art
The cutting-edge MCA displays contemporary art from Australia and around the world *(see p44)*. It offers tours, exhibitions and lectures. It is also home to the National Centre for Creative Learning.

8 Overseas Passenger Terminal
A stylish glass structure containing excellent restaurants, its 1988 renovation replaced the 1950s terminal that once accommodated passenger liners. Its views of the Opera House are unparalleled.

9 Garrison Church
Australia's first military church is officially named Holy Trinity Church *(below)*. Designed by Henry Ginn in 1840, it was remodelled in 1878 by Edmund Blacket, Colonial architect of the Victorian Gothic main building at Sydney University *(see p103)*.

Lieutenant William Dawes

Lieutenant Dawes established Australia's first observatory on the point that now bears his name. In 1790 he earned Governor Phillip's displeasure when he refused to join a reprisal attack against Aborigines. His refusal sprang from his relationship with a Eora woman, Patyegarang. Dawes' journals detail his conversations with Patyegarang and document the vocabulary and grammer of the Eora. Dawes was shipped out in 1791 and spent years campaigning against slavery in the West Indies.

TOP 10 Royal Botanic Gardens & The Domain

Located around Farm Cove on the shore of Sydney Harbour is the spectacular Royal Botanic Gardens and Domain. Established in 1816, this oasis in the heart of the city occupies the land on which the first crops were planted. Australia's oldest scientific institution is home to an impressive collection of native and exotic plants and trees. The grounds also house an art gallery and music school.

Water lily at the gardens

🍽 The Poolside Café at the "Boy" Charlton Pool has baguettes and light lunches.

🕐 During the Sydney Festival, the Open Air Cinema makes for a a lovely evening.

• Map N3
• Royal Botanic Gardens: Mrs Macquarie's Rd; open 7am–sunset daily; www.rbgsyd.nsw.gov.au
• Visitor Information Centre: 9231 8125; Open 9:30am–5pm daily
• Andrew "Boy" Charlton Pool: Mrs Macquarie's Rd; 9358 6686; Open Sep–Apr: 6am–7pm daily; adult/child $5.80/$4.40; www.abcpool.org
• Sydney Tropical Centre: 9231 8104; Open 10am–4pm daily; Adm
• Conservatorium of Music: 9351 1222; Open 9am–5pm Mon–Fri, 9am–4pm Sat
• Government House: 9931 5222; House open 10:30am–3pm Fri–Sun (Tours every half hour from 10:30am), Grounds open 10am–4pm daily

Top 10 Attractions

1. Mrs Macquarie's Chair
2. Andrew "Boy" Charlton Pool
3. Wollemi Pine
4. Cadi Jam Ora: First Encounters
5. Palm House
6. Art Gallery of New South Wales
7. Sydney Tropical Centre
8. Conservatorium of Music
9. Government House
10. Walks & Tours

1 Mrs Macquarie's Chair

This sandstone bench *(above)* was carved in 1816 for the governor's wife, Elizabeth Macquarie. The landmark offers breath-taking views of the Opera House, Harbour Bridge and Fort Denison.

2 Andrew "Boy" Charlton Pool

Named for a 16-year-old Olympic winner, this glorious 50m (164-ft) pool overlooks Woolloomooloo Bay and Garden Island. Its patrons take their laps and suntans seriously, but the toddlers' pool is perfect for those who just want to dip their toes.

The lush Royal Botanic Garden

3 Wollemi Pine

Discovered in 1994 in a Blue Mountains *(below & p121)* canyon, this botanical curiosity was thought to be extinct. The Royal Botanic Garden's specimen was planted in 1998.

→ *During the Sydney Festival in January, call 1300 366 649 for details of the Open Air Cinema.*

6 Cadi Jam Ora: First Encounters

This award-winning presentation of the Eora people's story offers an intriguing look at white settlement, Sydney's environment, and the Eora's spiritual connection with their land.

7 Sydney Tropical Centre

Tropical ecosystems are recreated in the centre's two glasshouses (above), the Pyramid and the Arc. The Pyramid features Australian natives, while the Arc houses the "exotics". Follow the walkways up to the canopy level to admire plants from the tropics.

8 Conservatorium of Music

Designed by Francis Greenway (see p23), this building (below) was one of the first casualties of the enquiry into the cost of Macquarie's public works. "The Con" has been training future musicians since 1915.

10 Walks & Tours

The Royal Botanic Garden's volunteers conduct free guided walks which depart from the Garden's shop. The walks run daily at 10:30am and also at 1pm on weekdays during autumn, winter and spring except for public holidays. An Aboriginal Heritage Tour is conducted every Friday at 10am and costs $28 per person.

Mrs Biggs' Bathing Box

The Eora enjoyed the sheltered waters of Woolloomooloo Bay for thousands of years before young Andrew Charlton won the 1,500-m (1,640-yard) race at the 1924 Olympics. The colony's first public baths, The Fig Tree Baths, stood on the site of the "Boy" Charlton pool. Several establishments once catered to the delicate sensibilities of Sydney's lady bathers, including one owned by a Mrs Biggs. An artwork by Robyn Backen, The Archaeology of Bathing, recalls Mrs Biggs' 1833 Bathing Machine, designed to protect the modesty of her patrons from bothersome manly gazes as well as sharks.

5 Palm House

The Victorian era glass-house was designed by James Barnet (see p77) to display tropical plants. The plants are now in the Sydney Tropical Centre and the Palm House is used for art exhibitions.

3 Art Gallery of New South Wales

The AGNSW (right pp24–25) has a permanent collection of Australian, European, Asian and indigenous art.

9 Government House

Gipps was the first governor to occupy this Gothic Revival structure in 1845. It ceased to be the governor's residence in 1996, and the house and grounds are now open to the public.

Left **Parliament House** Centre **Entrance of Sydney Hospital** Right **Mural at St James Church**

Macquarie Street Precinct

The Astor
One of Sydney's first skyscrapers, this elegant 1920s apartment building has housed artistic notables such as artist Portia Geach and actor, writer and comic Barry Humphries.

State Library of NSW
More than five million items are held in the Library's Mitchell (1910) and Macquarie (1988) Wings (see p45). The exhibition spaces showcase this collection and the library holds a range of talks and events. ❧ Free tours 11am Tue & 2pm Thu

Parliament House
The oldest parliament house in the world began in 1816 as a wing of the "Rum Hospital", built by contractors licensed to import rum into the colony in lieu of payment. The New South Wales Legislative Council held its first meeting here in 1829.

Sydney Hospital
This structure replaced the central wing of the Rum Hospital in the 1880s. The statue of a boar, Il Porcellino, is a replica of a 1547 Florentine artwork.

Martin Place
Australia's grandest banks reside on this broad plaza (see p77). A Cenotaph near George Street commemorates Australia's war dead, and The Passage by Anne Graham celebrates Sydney's Georgian heritage.

Mint Museum
An elegant museum and home to the Historic Houses Trust, this 1816 Rum Hospital wing was converted in 1854 into a branch of London's Royal Mint. ❧ Open 9:30am–5pm Mon–Fri

Hyde Park Barracks
Perhaps Francis Greenway's finest work, these barracks were built in 1819 to house convicts. Later a hostel for immigrant women and then courtrooms, since 1979 it has been a museum of the site and its varied occupants (see p42).

Great Irish Famine Memorial
Built into a barrack wall is this memorial to the victims of the Famine (1845–48). This catastrophe forced 30,000 Irish women and over 4,000 orphans to migrate to Australia; some were housed at the barracks.

St James Church
Another Greenway gem, this 1822 church was originally intended as a court house. Don't miss the superb 1930s mural in the Children's Chapel.

Queen's Square
Governor Macquarie en-visaged this small square as Sydney's civic centre. In the 1890 it was a rallying point for pro-testers, among them Republican who would mount Queen Victoria statue to address the masses.

Sign up for DK's email newsletter on traveldk.com

Top 10 Convicts Made Good

1. Francis Greenway (1777–1837), forger to government architect
2. William "Billy" Blue (1734–1834), sugar thief to pioneer ferryman
3. Simeon Lord (1771–1840), fabric thief to merchant, magistrate
4. William Redfern (1774–1833), naval mutineer to surgeon
5. Mary Reiley (1777–1855), horse thief to entrepreneur
6. Henry Kable (1763–1846), burglar to merchant
7. George Howe (1769–1821), shoplifter to publisher
8. Edward Eagar (1787–1866), forger to lawyer
9. George Crossley (1749–1823), perjurer to lawyer
10. Samuel Terry (1776–1838), stocking thief to publican, landowner and moneylender

Inside the barracks

Replica convict hammocks stretch across the third floor of the barracks.

Francis Greenway: Convict Architect

Detail of Hyde Park Barracks wall

Inspired. Vain. Delusional. No single epithet adequately describes Francis Howard Greenway. In 1809 Greenway, a partner in an architectural firm, was found guilty of forging a contract, and was sentenced to 14 years in the colony. Soon after his arrival in 1814, Governor Macquarie realised that Greenway's architectural talent was equal to his own Enlightenment aspirations, and in 1816 he appointed Greenway as Colonial Architect and Assistant Engineer. Starting with the Macquarie Lighthouse on South Head, Greenway and Governor and Mrs Macquarie set about transforming Sydney's civic landscape. Unfortunately, not everyone shared their ambitions, and reports of extravagance filtered back to London. Commissioner JT Bigge arrived in Sydney in 1819 to investigate and halted most public works. His censure of the Macquaries' taste for ornamentation deprived Greenway of his patrons, who departed the colony in 1822. Despite his major contribution to the standard of Colonial architecture, Greenway struggled in private practice and died a poor man in 1837.

Hyde Park Barracks

The Historic Houses Trust run tours of Hyde Park Barracks and the Mint Museum; call 8239 2311 for details.

Art Gallery of New South Wales

Conceived in the 1870s and opened to the public in 1909, AGNSW contains some of the finest artworks in Australia. Situated on a grand drive in The Domain, it has always been a wonderful place to escape the heat and bustle of the city. More than a million visitors a year enjoy its permanent collection of Australian, Asian, Aboriginal, contemporary and European art. The Yiribana Gallery is of particular interest, presenting Aboriginal and Torres Strait Islander artists from different communities and backgrounds.

Entrance to AGNSW

🍴 Re-energise your tired eyes and feet with a snack at the AGNSW café.

🛍 The AGNSW shop stocks unique fine art objects including prints, cards and locally produced gifts as well as imaginative children's merchandise.

Sundays are Fundays for kids, with art shows on various topics. There are also frequent classes and workshops.

• Map N3
• Art Gallery Rd, The Domain
• 9225 1744
• www.artgallery.nsw. gov.au
• See works on paper that are not on display in the Study Room. It's best to make a booking 9225 1758

Top 10 Attractions

1. Exterior
2. Grand Courts
3. Yiribana Gallery
4. Asian Galleries
5. Australian Art Galleries
6. Temporary Exhibitions
7. Art After Hours
8. Archibald, Wynne & Sulman Prizes
9. Contemporary Galleries
10. Café & Restaurant

Exterior
Walter Liberty Vernon designed the striking colonnaded entrance and ornamented walls of this stucture in the Classical style *(below)*.

Grand Courts
These rooms contain the first works acquired by the AGNSW, for the largely British art *(below)* displayed here was initially the gallery's focus. The lovely rooms complement the many noteworthy works.

Yiribana Gallery
Dedicated to Aboriginal art and culture, the works here range from bark paintings and traditional designs on canvas to works by contemporary Aboriginal artists.

Asian Galleries
The Asian Galleries are spread over two floors. The upper gallery is housed within a white glass pavilion inspired by the floating lanterns found throughout Asia. The lower one includes a fully operational Japanese tea room.

9

Key

▢	Upper Level
▢	Ground Level
▢	Lower Level 1
▢	Lower Level 2
▢	Lower Level 3

5 Australian Art Galleries

Featuring major names in Australian art, these galleries display works by luminaries such as Sidney Nolan, Grace Cossington-Smith *(left)*, Roy de Maistre and Russell Drysdale. There are many works by local Sydney artists *(see p26)* and several great images of the city.

6 Temporary Exhibitions

Several spaces at AGNSW are dedicated to temporary exhibitions. While some display contemporary art, others are retrospectives spanning a movement or an artist's career. Entry can entail a minor fee.

7 Art After Hours

On Wednesday nights until 9pm, the gallery draws a keen evening crowd with its free film screenings, celebrity talks, music events and access to all exhibitions.

8 Archibald, Wynne & Sulman Prizes

An annual exhibition, the Archibald prize is awarded to artists for portrait painting, the Sulman for genre painting and the Wynne for landscape painting.

9 Contemporary Galleries

An entire floor of galleries dedicated to contemporary art. They feature a vibrant selection of international and Australian works by artists such as Anish Kapoor, Ugo Randinone and Sol LeWitt.

10 Café & Restaurant

The AGNSW café is a great spot to take a break. The award-winning restaurant serves an extensive menu featuring locally-sourced ingredients and a selection of wines. It also offers a well-priced high tea daily.

Looking Towards Asia

AGNSW's collection of Asian art began in 1879, when the Japanese Government made a large donation of ceramics and bronzes. However, it didn't become a distinct department until 1979, when Edmund Capon was appointed gallery director. Capon wisely noted that the art of Asia is the art of half of the world. With him at the helm, the AGNSW extended the collection to include Southeast Asian textiles, Buddhist arts, Japanese Screens, Indian sculptures and Ming, Qing and modern Chinese paintings.

Catch the train to Martin Place and walk through the grounds of Sydney Hospital and across the Domain.

Left **Brett Whiteley** Centre **John Olsen** Right **Detail from Grace Cossington-Smith's** *Self Portrait*

Top 10 Sydney Artists

1 Brett Whiteley (1939–92)
The bad boy of Australian art, Whiteley *(see p93)* was a prodigious talent who won the trifecta of Archibald, Wynne and Sulman prizes *(see p25)* twice in consecutive years. He died of a heroin overdose in 1992.

2 John Olsen (b. 1928)
Considered Australia's most esteemed living painter, Olsen was awarded the Order of Australia in 2001. Olsen has travelled widely in Australia and abroad, continuously mapping his travels with paintings.

3 Lloyd Rees (1895–1988)
Renowned for his landscape paintings, Rees also produced hundreds of drawings, many of which are in the collection of AGNSW. He began printmaking in his 80s, and continued to etch even while losing his sight.

4 Grace Cossington-Smith (1892–1984)
Sydney's first significant female artist, she was particularly interested in form and colour. She painted still lifes, landscapes and religious subjects.

5 Max Dupain (1911–92)
Dupain recorded much of Australia's architectural history through his art, both Colonial and Modern. However, it is for his wonderful iconoclastic 1937 photo, *The Sunbaker*, that he is most celebrated.

6 Margaret Olley (b. 1923)
Olley has always concentrated on painting still lifes and interiors. In 1948 William Dobell won the Archibald for his portrait of Olley, which is in the AGNSW's collection.

7 Margaret Preston (1875–1963)
Preston's art was highly influenced by Pacific Islander, Chinese and Japanese cultures. Recognising the value of Aboriginal art, she was a key figure in the Australian Modernist movement.

8 William Yang (b. 1943)
Initially a playwright, he moved into social photography and documented Sydney's blossoming gay community, bringing it from the underworld into the spotlight.

9 Susan Norrie (b. 1953)
One of Australia's most successful contemporary artists, Norrie works in multiple media. Her works are displayed in the collections of significant galleries such as the Guggenheim and the MCA *(see p44)*.

10 Imants Tillers (b. 1950)
A former architect, he designed the roof of the Federation Pavilion in Centennial Park *(see pp39 & 47)*. Interestingly, Tillers works on small canvas boards simply because they fit on his drawing board.

Share your travel recommendations on traveldk.com

Top 10 Images of Sydney

1. Watkin Tench, *A Direct North General View of Sydney Cove*, 1794
2. Eugene Von Guérard, *Sydney Heads*, 1865
3. Margaret Preston, *Circular Quay*, 1925
4. Grace Cossington-Smith, *The Curve of the Bridge*, 1928–9
5. Henri Mallard, *Untitled Photograph (Sydney Harbour Bridge workers)*, c. 1930
6. Max Dupain, *Sydney from Harbour Bridge Pylon*, 1982
7. Roland Wakelin, *Down The Hills To Berry's Bay*, 1958
8. Jeffrey Smart, *Australian Cahill Expressway*, 1962
9. Brett Whiteley, *The Balcony 2*, 1975
10. David Moore, *Sydney Harbour from 16,000 ft*, 1976

Images of Sydney

Since the first Europeans arrived in the late 18th century, artists have been documenting the changing landscape of Sydney. In early years, Sydney was often painted as a kind of fantasy, using the familiar green slopes of England instead of the new dry, strange land. Eventually Sydney's settlers stopped wishing for the pastures left behind, and subsequent generations rejoiced in the blue skies and sparkling harbour. The construction of the Harbour Bridge inspired a whole new group of artists, who photographed as well as painted it, signalling the emergence of Sydney as an international city. Brett Whiteley concocted luscious images of the harbour and its surrounds in the 1970s, and in the 1980s Ken Done made his fortune selling clothes printed with bright sketches of the Opera House. Now more than ever, Sydney artists are part of the global artistic community.

Eugene Von Guerard, *Sydney Heads*, 1865

Brett Whiteley, *The Balcony 2*, 1975
This powerful oil on canvas can be found at the AGNSW, where it has been exhibited since 1981. Brett Whiteley produced some of the most distinctive and vivid images of Sydney and its harbour ever painted.

Darling Harbour & Chinatown

Cockle Bay was once a working harbour district where some of Sydney's poorest lived in hovels surrounded by shipyards, cargo wharves and quarries. For the 1988 Bicentenary, a huge redevelopment project was launched to reclaim this 54-ha (133-acre) site, and the area was revitalised through the wonderful Aquarium, the Maritime and Powerhouse Museums, and the Cockle Bay and King St Wharf developments. Darling Harbour's convention, exhibition and entertainment centres will reopen in 2016 after renovation.

Endeavour replica

○ **Pop into Maxim's Cakes for something delicious; Goulburn and Sussex Streets.**

- Map L5
- Sea Life Sydney Aquarium: Aquarium Pier, Darling Harbour; 8251 7800; Open 9am–8pm daily; www.sydney aquarium.com.au; adult/child $35/$20 • Chinese Garden: Darling Harbour; 9240 8888; Open 9:30am–5:30pm daily, closed Good Fri & 25 Dec; www.chinesegarden. com.au; adult/child $6/$3 • Capitol Theatre: 13 Campbell St, Haymarket; 9320 5000; www. capitoltheatre.com.au • Paddy's Market: Hay & Thomas Sts, Haymarket; 1300 361 589; Open 9am–5pm Wed–Sun • Market City: Haymarket (above Paddy's Market); Stores open 10am–7pm daily except 10am–8pm Thu • Wild Life Sydney: Aquarium Pier, Darling Harbour; 9333 9288; Open Dec–Mar: 9am–8pm daily; Apr–Nov: 9am–6pm daily; adult/child $35/$20

Top 10 Attractions

1. Australian National Maritime Museum
2. Pyrmont Bridge
3. Cockle Bay & King St Wharves
4. Sea Life Sydney Aquarium
5. Chinese Garden
6. Chinatown
7. Capitol Theatre
8. Paddy's Market
9. Powerhouse Museum
10. Wild Life Sydney

Australian National Maritime Museum

At this exploration of Australia's relationship with the sea, visitors can climb aboard vessels, or view exhibits dealing with immigration, maritime archaeology, beach culture and more *(above & p42).*

Pyrmont Bridge

Opened in 1902, this 369-m (1,210-ft) bridge, with a quaint copper-roofed control cabin, is the oldest electrically-operated swingspan bridge in the world. It swings open to allow vessels up to 14 m (46ft) tall to enter or depart Cockle Bay.

Cockle Bay & King St Wharves

King St Wharf is a social mecca for the working crowd. Cockle Bay *(above)* comprises a three-storey hive of cafés, restaurants, bars and gift shops.

Sea Life Sydney Aquarium

Discover over 12,000 Australian aquatic animals, including sharks, rays and crocodiles. Walk through the main oceanarium to see hundreds of tropical reef fish, sharks and sawfish *(below).*

Chinese Garden

5 The garden *(left)* was China's gift to Sydney during Australia's 1988 bicentenary celebrations. Interpretation boards provide insights into Chinese garden design and philosophy, and the Tea House makes for a peaceful retreat from the harbour.

Wild Life Sydney

10 Next door to Sea Life Sydney Aquarium, visit over 100 Australian native animals in their natural habitats. There are various tours available which provide interactive experiences with the animals *(below)*.

Chinatown

6 This is the spirited epicentre of Sydney's very large Chinese community, where restaurants vie for attention with fabric shops, Asian grocers, jewellers, music stores and gift shops. It is best visited for a Friday night market. Chinese New Year celebrations here (Jan/Feb) are among the largest and most spectacular outside Asia.

Capitol Theatre

7 Built in the 1920s, this theatre has seen many comebacks. In 1990 Mediterranean-blue ceiling and twinkling stars were added to the inside of the theatre. The orchestra pit at Capitol is the largest in the country. It is now a well-known venue for popular musicals.

Paddy's Market

8 Associated with the Haymarket area for 150 years, Paddy's Market is the place to find a pair of koala oven mitts or an Opera House watch, as well as food *(below)*, souvenirs, flowers and cheap accessories. Market City has a large food court, clothing outlets and entertainment venues.

Powerhouse Museum

9 At Australia's most inventive museum, children are not the only ones to enjoy the interactive displays. A child-friendly café and playground is located on the lowest gallery level of the museum *(see pp30–31)*.

"Buffalo Bill" Cole's Wild West Show

In the early 1900s, the intersection opposite Paddy's Market was a regular venue for "Buffalo Bill" Cole's Wild West Show. The English-born owner of the circus, Edward Cole, and his American partner, "Texas Jack," recruited a cast of locals to dress as cowboys and Indians and enact a wagon train ambush on horseback. Cole, as Buffalo Bill, always rode to the rescue of the besieged pioneers. In later years Cole modified his performances and included Australia's most famous bushranger, Ned Kelly, in the show's line-up.

Enjoy a leisurely yum cha at one of Chinatown's many excellent restaurants (see p82).

TOP10 Powerhouse Museum

One of Sydney's most distinguished and popular cultural institutions, the Powerhouse Museum has an extraordinary array of treasures across decorative arts and design, science, technology, space, transport and social history. A superb series of temporary exhibitions complements the range of inspiring permanent galleries. Kids can lose themselves in the interactive play spaces in the Magic Garden. It's also worth setting aside time to explore the shop for unusual and exclusive gifts.

Powerhouse Museum

🍴 Get a foccacia, salad, pasta or an excellent coffee from Lush Bucket at 623 Harris Street. Alternatively, take a bag lunch to Darling Harbour playground. There are shaded seats outside the Chinese Garden.

🧒 Let the kids burn off energy on the climbing equipment at the innovative outdoor "Cog's" playground.

• Map L5
• 500 Harris St, Darling Harbour
• 9217 0111
• www. powerhousemuseum. com
• Open 10am–5pm daily
• Adult/child/family $12/$6/$30

Top 10 Exhibits

1. Experimentations
2. Cyberworlds
3. Boulton & Watt Engine
4. EcoLogic
5. Hargrave's Box Kites
6. Kings Cinema
7. Space
8. The Steam Revolution
9. The Magic Garden
10. Transport

Experimentations

This interactive exhibit explores scientific and technological breakthroughs that have altered our understanding of daily phenomena. Come find out how a battery works, why a freezer door sticks, and much more.

Cyberworlds

At this exhibit, meet Robot from the 1960s *Lost in Space* TV series, or chat with Charles Babbage, the inventor of 1832's mechanical computer *(above)*.

Boulton & Watt Engine

The power source behind the Industrial Revolution. The world's oldest surviving rotative steam engine, *(left)* built in 1785, stands 10-m (32-ft) tall and is most significant item in the museum's collection.

EcoLogic

Sustainable options for house are explored in this innovative display, which demonstrates the relationship between homes and the natural environment. It examines alternative building approaches and materials, such as recycled timbers and aerated concrete bricks.

➤ *Pick up a copy of* Ecologic: Creating a Sustainable Future *by Sandra McEwen, available at the Powerhouse Shop.*

Hargrave's Box Kites
Lawrence Hargrave *(see p97)* joined four box kites and lifted himself 4.8 m (16 ft) off the ground in 1894. The kites' stability provided the basis for future aircraft designs.

Kings Cinema
At this beautiful, miniature Art Deco cinema *(right)*, you might discover old newsreels or enjoy a classic silent film

Space
Find out what it is like to live in space, thanks to the museum's popular space exhibition. Hear commentary by astronaut Dr Andy Thomas, and experience the new Zero Gravity Space Lab.

The Steam Revolution
Trace the development of steam from the first experiments of the 1660s to today's steam turbine-generated electricity in this hands on exhibition.

The Magic Garden
In this fun and imaginative environment for 2–8 year olds, children learn about wholesome eating habits and can enjoy fun activities such as fishing in a digital pond and chasing butterflies.

Key

☐	Level 1
☐	Level 2
☐	Level 3
☐	Level 4

Transport
Beneath the Catalina flying boat, a collection of railway exhibits includes an old signal box, Locomotive 1243 *(left)* and the destination board used at Central Station from 1906–82.

The Sustainable House

Michael and Heather Mobbs created the "Sustainable House" in 1996, when deciding to renovate their inner-city terrace with minimum environmental impact. It had to generate electricity through solar power, supply water from rainwater tanks and treat its own sewage. In the process, the Mobbs explored everything from the least toxic floor sealants to raising the efficiency of their refrigerator. "EcoLogic" features an interactive 3D model that shows how energy and water are used in the Sustainable House.

TOP 10 Taronga Zoo

The zoo occupies a spectacular setting amid 28 ha (75 acres) of landscaped bushland overlooking the harbour. Just above the wharf is the Sky Safari, which carries visitors up the hill, over the enclosures and terraced slopes to the historic Edwardian Entrance Pavilion and Information Centre. The centre provides tour information and brochures describing the zoo's 380 resident species and 2,200 individual animals. Many enclosures recreate natural habitats, such as the Australian Walkabout, which enables visitors to actually experience the animals' original environments. Finally, magical views complement the enjoyable ferry ride returning to Circular Quay.

The Entrance Pavilion

🍴 The Taronga Food Market seats 600 and offers a variety of fare. The zoo's many picnic areas have fantastic views over Sydney Harbour.

🕐 Arrive early as many animals are more active in the morning.

• Map F1
• Bradley's Head Rd, Mosman; 9969 2777; Open 9am–5pm daily
• ZooPass adult/child $51.50/$25.50 (includes return ferry ticket from Circular Quay and zoo, admission)
• Tours: 9978 4782; VIP Aussie Gold Tour: 1.5 hrs; adult/child $88/$45; Wild Australian Experience: adult/child $124/$78
• Free Flight Bird Show: noon & 3pm; Chimpanzee Talk: 12:30pm; Giraffe Talk: 1:30pm; Gorilla Feeding: 11am & 2pm; Kids' Zoo: 10:30am & 1:30pm; Koala Talk: 3:30pm; Koala Encounters: 11am & 2:45pm; Penguin Talk: 2:40pm; Reptile Talk: 11:30am

Top 10 Exhibits

1. Wild Australia
2. Great Southern Ocean
3. Backyard to Bush
4. African Species
5. Wild Asia
6. Big Cats
7. Primates
8. Serpentaria
9. South American Species
10. Free Flight Bird Show

1 Wild Australia

Meet emus, koalas *(above)*, kangaroos and wallabies in the Australian Walkabout section. The Nocturnal House is home to bilbies, wombats, quolls, platypus and feathertail gliders. Don't miss Ken and his harem in the Koala Walkabout exhibit.

2 Great Southern Ocean

A 3-acre (1.2 ha) precinct houses Taronga's seals, sealions, pelicans and penguins. The exhibit recreates the animals' natural habitat with the glass-fronted enclosure revealing their movements.

3 Backyard to Bush

This innovative exhibit melds the suburban home and the natural environment. Children can engage with farmyard animals at a small farm, and a wombat *(left)* burrow enables a glimpse into the domestic life of these little mammals. There's a playground too.

→ *Take the Sky Safari up, get a map, and enjoy a leisurely walk down the terraces and back to the ferry wharf.*

4 African Species

Perched high above Sydney Harbour, the giraffes are one of the many African species at Taronga. The zoo is also home to meerkats, hippopotami, zebras and barbary sheep.

7 Primates

You don't need the map to find the Gorilla Forest, the Orangutan Rainforest *(below)*, or the Chimpanzee Park. just follow the delighted screams of youngsters. Wild Asia celebrated the birth of a Francois' Langur infant in 2010 to parents Hanoi and Saigon. Check out the primates' outlandish hairstyles as well as their gymnastics.

9 South American Species

It's hard to ignore the world's largest bird of prey, the Andean condor, the flamboyant Victoria-crowned pigeon, or the antics of the Central American squirrel monkey. The colourful macaws and sun conures are like feathered rainbows.

10 Free Flight Bird Show

This show features a variety of free flighted birds including Frodo, the barking owl, who joins the Andean Condor, Leslie, and a host of native and exotic species who fly and swoop above the heads of spectators.

Australian Shark Attack File

The zoo maintains the Australian Shark Attack File. The first recorded fatality was in 1791 on the north coast of NSW. The last fatal attack in Sydney Harbour was in 1963. Don't let this put you off the beaches; they are extremely safe from sharks. Curiously, one of Sydney's most famous crimes, the "shark arm murder," was initially blamed on a shark. A shark captured in 1935 regurgitated a tattooed human arm. The victim was soon identified as a criminal underworld type, James Smith, whose arm had apparently been severed by a knife, not a shark. To this day, no one whodunit.

5 Wild Asia

Housing the Zoo's much-loved seven Asian elephants, Wild Asia is an experience not to be missed. Follow the leafy trail to see spotted deer, langurs and binturongs. Don't miss seeing the Malaysian tapir swim with otters and coi carp.

8 Serpentaria

Some of the exhibits here are stunning. the Komodo dragon, the red eyed tree frog and the Fijian banded iguana for starters. If you enjoy a shiver running down your spine, don't miss Australia's deadly taipan or the South American boa constrictor

6 Big Cats

Taronga Zoo's big cats – the lions, tigers, snow leopards and fishing cats – are a sight to behold, especially when they enjoy their meals. Take a tour to find out more about these amazing creatures.

TOP 10 Bondi Beach

Bondi may just be the most famous stretch of sand in the world. This glorious 1-km (0.6-mile) long sweep of golden sand, with rugged Ben Buckler at its northern end and the Bondi Icebergs to the south, is Sydney's favourite

Statue of a lifesaver

playground, packed with swimmers, surfers and people-watchers. Just before the beach is the lively Campbell Parade, beyond which is a diverse suburb that embraces surf culture, artists, actors, media tycoons and the vibrant Jewish, Kiwi, Brazilian and Pacific Islander communities. There is some serious money and glamour in Bondi, but it's never snobbish and always great fun.

Sign indicating undertow

🍴 For cheap eats with a million-dollar view, get a table on the balcony of the North Bondi Returned Servicemens' League (RSL) at the northern end of the beach.

🛍 Visit Bikini Island at 38 Campbell Parade for a great range of women's swimwear.

• Map H5
• Let's Go Surfing: www. letsgosurfing.com.au
• Bondi Beach hire (box trailer on the promenade): deck chairs $5/3hrs or $10/day, beach umbrellas $15/day, surfboards $15/hr or $50/day, www. bondibeachhire.com.au
• Bondi Pavilion Community Cultural Centre: 8362 3400; www.waverley.nsw.gov. au Open 9:30am–5:30pm Mon–Fri, 10am–5pm Sat-Sun • Bondi Markets: Bondi Beach Public School; Campbells Parade; Open 10am–5pm Sun, www. bondimarkets.com.au

Top 10 Attractions

1. The Beach
2. Swimming
3. Surfing
4. Ben Buckler
5. Campbell Parade
6. Pavilion
7. Bondi Icebergs
8. Coastal Walk
9. Sculpture by the Sea
10. Surf Lifesavers

1 The Beach
It's hard to resist this gorgeous arc of golden sand *(right)*, even given how crowded it gets in peak season. Hire a deck chair if towels aren't your thing, and sit back and enjoy the scenery. One of Bondi's great attractions is its varied tribe of devotees.

2 Swimming
The sand shelves off gently at the northern end of the beach *(above)*, ideal for body surfing. Always swim between the flags. If the weather is on the wild side, leave the water to the surfers and enjoy the Coastal Walk instead.

3 Surfing
It would be a shame to visit this famous surfing beach without at least trying to catch a wave. The southern end of Bondi Beach is restricted to surfers; boards and wet suits are available for hire nearby. Get a lesson from Let's Go Surfing.

4 Ben Buckler
If you ever doubted the power of the ocean, check out the rock just below Bondi's northern headland, Ben Buckler. According to its brass plaque, this 240-tonne monster washed up during a storm in 1912. The nearby rock pool is great for children.

➡ *Let's Go Surfing (see p54) offers surfing lessons for beginners.*

5 Campbell Parade
Bondi's main tourist drag *(above)* is always buzzing. Backpackers and tourists rub shoulders with supermodels, surfies and actors. It's a great place for gelati, fish and chips, or a beer overlooking the water.

8 Coastal Walk
Start this spectacular 5-km (3-mile) walk behind the Bondi Icebergs. Follow the path around to Tamarama Beach, also known as "Glamarama" for its "beautiful people". Further down the path is Bronte Beach *(right)*, followed by tiny Clovelly Beach *(see pp48–9)*, Gordon's Bay and Coogee, a less crowded version of Bondi.

10 Surf Lifesavers
Those tanned and athletic men and women patrolling the beach in red and yellow caps *(below)* are members of either Bondi Beach's Surf Bathers' Life Saving Club or North Bondi SLSC. These are two of the oldest clubs in Australia.

6 Pavilion
This 1920s pavilion is home to a lively community cultural centre that hosts movies, theatre, workshops, free art exhibitions and special events. There are also showers and changing rooms inside.

7 Bondi Icebergs
So named because its members swim throughout winter, this clubhouse *(right)* is a Bondi institution. It's home to a fine restaurant *(see p58)* and the world's only surf-life saving museum. Don't miss its saltwater pool washed clean by ocean swells.

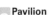

9 Sculpture by the Sea
Combine your coastal walk with this annual festival, at which more than 100 artists take full advantage of Bondi's wind-sculpted sandstone headlands as the setting for their works. They are exhibited from late October to November.

Black Sunday
On 6 February 1938, three large waves rolled into Bondi Beach in quick succession. As they receded, hundreds of swimmers were swept out to sea in the backwash. By good fortune, almost 80 members of the Bondi Surf Bathers' Life Saving Club were gathered on the beach in readiness for a competition. Suddenly they were faced with the real thing. Between them, they rescued more than 250 swimmers, which was a remarkable achievement. Unfortunately and despite their best efforts, five swimmers drowned. To this day the tragedy is remembered as Black Sunday.

Left **First Fleet arrives** Centre **The arrest of Governor Bligh** Right **Governor Macquarie**

🔟 Moments in History

1 Aborigines Reach Cadi
The original settlers of Sydney Harbour, the Aboriginal Eora people, arrived almost 50,000 years ago. They fished in the summer months, and during winter they sought food inland and north towards the Hawkesbury River. At the time of white settlement, 1,500 Eora were estimated to live around the Sydney Harbour area.

2 Captain Cook Lands
After observing the Transit of Venus in Tahiti for the Royal Society, Captain James Cook was instructed by the British Admiralty in 1769 to discover and claim the "Great South Continent". He arrived at Botany Bay on 28 April 1770.

3 First Fleet Arrives
Governor Phillip and the First Fleet of 11 ships, carrying 1,500 convicts, guards, military officials and their families, arrived at Botany Bay in 1788. Unable to find sufficient fresh water, Phillip sailed north and found one of the world's "finest harbours". The colony was established at a small cove named in honour of Phillip's neighbour, Viscount Sydney.

4 Rum Corps
The irascible and disliked Governor Bligh threatened to curtail the privileges enjoyed by officers of the NSW "Rum Corps", so named for their use of liquor as a form of currency. They "arrested" Bligh as retaliation in 1808, but their coup was short-lived as they were soon ordered back home to England.

5 Macquarie Takes Charge
Governor Lachlan Macquarie took charge of the colony in 1810 and restored order. During his 12-year governance, he managed to transform the outpost from a ramshackle penal colony into a town with regular roads and civic amenities. He also encouraged Emancipists, convicts who had served their time, to stay and contribute to the colony's growth, thus ensuring a thriving future for Sydney.

6 Dunbar Sinks
On a wild night in 1857, the migrant ship *Dunbar*, en route to Sydney from England, struck rocks near the Heads. Only one passenger survived, while 121 others drowned. It remains the state's worst ever maritime disaster and came as a bitter blow to the young colony.

Captain James Cook

7 Troops Set Sail
The first of Australia's World War I volunteers set sail from Sydney Harbour on 1 November 1914, destined for battlefields in Europe and the Middle

 Share your travel recommendations on traveldk.com

Mural depicting Green Bans

East. Almost 330,000 Australian troops served overseas and 60,000 died, which was the highest death rate per head of population of all nations involved in the war.

8 Builders' Labourers Impose Green Bans

Several areas, including The Rocks and Woolloomooloo, were saved from developers' wrecking balls in the 1970s. Fortunately for Sydney's future, the Builders' Labourers Federation imposed "Green Bans" on projects that clearly threatened environmentally or historically significant buildings and precincts.

9 Mardi Gras is Born

Over 1,000 gay rights activists took to Sydney's streets demanding equal rights in 1978. Several protestors were arrested, but they vowed to return the following year. The parade that followed in 1979 established an annual event that is now a major tourist attraction *(see p72)*.

10 Cathy Freeman Lights the Olympic Flame

With increasingly more citizens calling for reconciliation between black and white Australia, many rose to their feet when champion Aboriginal runner Cathy Freeman lit the Olympic flame to signal the start of the first Olympic Games of the new millennium in September 2000.

Top 10 Sydney Personalities

1 Pemulwy
This Eora warrior resisted white settlement until he was caught and beheaded in 1802.

2 John & Elizabeth Macarthur
The resourceful Macarthurs established Australia's agricultural industry in 1790.

3 William "Billy" Blue
He started a ferry service between Dawes Point and the North Shore *(see p115)*.

4 Wentworth, Blaxland & Lawson
Opening up Australia's interior, these European explorers crossed the Blue Mountains *(see p121)* in 1813.

5 Caroline Chisholm
She arrived from Madras in 1838 to establish much-needed services for poor immigrant women.

6 Sir Henry Parkes
A five-time premier of NSW, Parkes was a major proponent of Federation in the late 1890s *(see p39)*.

7 Tilley Devine & Kate Leigh
These madams of crime vied for control of Sydney's 1920s and 30s "razor gangs".

8 Lars Halvorsen
This boatbuilder arrived from Norway in 1921 to establish Sydney's most famous boatbuilding dynasty.

9 Jack Mundey
Secretary of the Builders' Labourers Federation, Mundey led the Green Bans *(see p85)* movement in the 1970s.

10 Ita Buttrose
Indomitable media doyen and former editor-in-chief of the Australian Womens Weekly during the 1970s and 1980s.

Left **Collins Beach** Centre **Mural at Federation Pavilion** Right **Old Government House façade**

🔟 Historic Sites & Buildings

1 Aboriginal Rock Art
Several locations around Sydney contain Aboriginal rock art, including Ku-ring-gai Chase National Park *(see p122)*, the Royal National Park *(see p123)*, and the Brisbane Water National Park *(see p127)*. One of the most accessible sites is the North Bondi Golf Course, where you'll find rock carvings just below the tower on Military Road.

2 Captain Cook's Landing Place
Captain James Cook and the crew of the *Endeavour* came ashore at what is now Botany Bay on 29 April 1770. On 6 May they sailed north, soon passing the entrance to a harbour which appeared to offer safe anchorage. Cook named this Port Jackson; the

Captain Cook's landing place

southern part of the great expanse of water was subsequently named Sydney Harbour. 🗺 *Map U5 • Discovery Centre: Captain Cook Drive, Kurnell • 9668 9111 • Open 11am–3pm Mon–Fri, 10am–4pm Sat–Sun • Botany Bay National Park: open 7am–7:30pm daily • Adm*

3 Tank Stream
The freshwater Tank Stream determined the site of white settlement in 1788. Other than two artworks near Circular Quay *(see p18)*, its only visible remains are in a small display including several items found during excavations, located beneath the old GPO. 🗺 *Map M3 • 1 Martin Place • Viewing Room: lower level • Open 8:15am–5:30pm Mon–Fri, 9am–1pm Sat*

4 Collins Beach
Landing at Collins Beach *(see p118)* in 1790, Governor Phillip and his officers met a group of Aborigines including Bennelong *(see p9)*. An Eora man, never having seen white men before, speared Phillip through the shoulder. Assuming the man had misunderstood his intentions, Philip made no reprisal – that time. 🗺 *Map U3*

5 Fort Denison
This small island was once named "Pinchgut" due to the meagre rations doled out to its recidivist convicts. The body of a criminal, Francis Morgan, who was executed in 1796, was left to rot out on the gallows for

three years as a warning to new convicts. ☯ *Map M2* • *NPWS Information Line: 1300 361 967* • *Sydney Harbour Tours: Cadman's Cottage, 110 George St, The Rocks* • *9247 5033* • *Open 9:30am–4:30pm Mon–Fri, 10am–4:30pm Sat–Sun*

Old Government House
Governor Phillip's cottage and country retreat *(see p125)*, constructed in 1790, was rebuilt by Governor Hunter in 1799. Governor and Mrs Macquarie later made numerous alterations. The oldest public building in Australia, it is now a National Trust museum. ☯ *Map S3* • *Parramatta Park, Parramatta* • *9635 8149* • *Open 10am–4pm Tue–Sun* • *Adm* • *www.oldgovernmenthouse.com.au*

"Granny" Smith Memorial Park
A small park in Eastwood on Sydney's North Shore commemorates Maria "Granny" Smith who, in 1868, discovered in her orchard a mutated variety of apples sprung from the cuttings of French crab apples. Then a curiosity, it soon became the world's best-known variety, particularly valued for its virtues as a cooking apple. ☯ *Map S3* • *Threlfall Street, Eastwood*

Federation Pavilion
Prior to Federation on 1 January 1901, Australia was not a united nation but actually six unaligned and competing colonies, comprising New South Wales, Victoria, Tasmania, Queensland, South Australia and West Australia. This 1988 pavilion in Centennial Park *(see p50)* marks the site of the historic original pavilion, which was right at the centre of celebrations in 1901. ☯ *Map F5*

Manly Beach
Newspaper editor William Gocher challenged the laws in 1902 by enjoying a midday swim at Manly *(see p118)*. His crime? It was illegal to swim in public between 6am and 8pm. Thanks to Gocher's bold action, daylight bathing was legalised within a year, provided that one always wore a conservative neck-to-knee swimsuit. ☯ *Map U3*

Sydney Olympic Park
Most events of the 2000 Olympic Games, including the opening and closing ceremonies, took place at Sydney Olympic Park *(see pp52–53)*, 14 km (8.5 miles) west of the city. The park also contains the Tennis Centre, the Aquatic Centre and the Sydney Showgrounds. The Visitor Gateway provides maps and runs tours. ☯ *Map S4* • *Homebush Bay* • *www.sydneyolympicpark.com.au* • *Visitor Gateway (next to Olympic Park railway station): 1 Showground Rd* • *9714 7888* • *Open 9am–5pm daily*

Left **May Gibbs' studio at Nutcote** Right **Henry Lawson**

TOP 10 Writers

1 Patrick White (1912–90)

Australia's Nobel prize-winning author for the *Eye of the Storm* (1973) hailed from a family of wealthy Australian pastoralists. He spent much of his early life in Europe but settled near Centennial Park *(see p50)* in 1964. Although he wrote poetry and plays, he is best remembered for his novels, which often explore individuals' efforts to divine meaning from the circumstances of their lives.

2 Kylie Tennant (1912–88)

Best known for her 1943 novel *Ride on Stranger*, Kylie Tennant often presented life from the perspective of the dispossessed. Despite her later success as an author, reviewer and lecturer, Tennant also experienced life on the other side of the tracks, including a short stint in jail in the 1930s.

Kylie Tennant

3 Frank Moorhouse (b. 1938)

His early stories focused on middle-class, small-town Australia, demonstrating his affinity with the "new journalism" of Americans such as Tom Wolfe. *Grand Days* and *Dark Palace* trace the aspirations and disappointments of the League of Nations through the eyes of an Australian woman.

4 Peter Corris (b. 1942)

Sydney's Raymond Chandler, Peter Corris writes hard-boiled crime fiction set in and around Sydney. His main protagonist, Cliff Hardy, is a private detective forever sorting through the trash of the powerful and wealthy.

5 Kenneth Slessor (1901–71)

Poet Kenneth Slessor will always be remembered for his 1939 elegy "Five Bells", written for a friend who drowned. Another poem, "Beach Burial" (1944), written while serving as a war correspondent near El Alamein, describes the burial of sailors washed up on shore after battles in the Mediterranean.

6 May Gibbs (1876–1969)

May Gibbs wrote and illustrated children's stories that were distinguished for their inventiveness and their use of Australian flora and fauna. Nutcote *(see p116)*, her home for more than 40 years, is now a museum dedicated to her work.

7 Miles Franklin (1879–1954)
Franklin struggled for years following the success of her 1901 novel, *My Brilliant Career*, but found renewed interest in 1928 when she published *Up the Country*. She was an early feminist and worked with women's groups in the USA and as a nurse in Europe during World War I. Upon her death, her estate established Australia's most prestigious literary award, named in her honour.

8 Henry Lawson (1867–1922)
Lawson's writing is often humorous and inspired by romantic notions of the Australian "character". In stories such as 1892's *The Drover's Wife* he exalted the "mateship" of rural Australians surviving the harsh and isolated environment. He often led an itinerant life and struggled with alcoholism. He was the first Australian writer granted a state funeral.

9 Ruth Park (b. 1923)
Park's two most famous novels, *The Harp in the South*, (1948) and its sequel *Poor Man's Orange* (1949), explored life in 1930s Surry Hills, which was then one of Sydney's poorest slums. She also wrote *Playing Beatie Bow*, a children's novel which is set in The Rocks in 1873.

10 Thomas Keneally (b. 1935)
Keneally is a prolific and prize-winning author who has had several of his historical novels translated into film. His subjects have ranged from Aboriginal resistance, in *The Chant of Jimmy Blacksmith* (1972), to the Holocaust, in 1982's *Schindler's Ark*.

Top 10 Novels set in Sydney

1 A Timeless Land (1941)
This novel by Eleanor Dark includes several historical Sydney characters.

2 Come in Spinner (1951)
By Dymphna Cusack and Florence James. A group of Sydney women are thrown into turmoil during WWII.

3 They're a Weird Mob (1957)
Memoirs of John O'Grady, an "Italian immigrant journalist" turned builders' labourer.

4 Riders in the Chariot (1961)
A satire by Patrick White.

5 Careful He Might Hear You (1963)
By Sumner Locke Elliot. A 1930s orphan resists his aunt's efforts to adopt him.

6 The Glass Canoe (1976)
David Ireland's darkly comic novel is set in the masculine world of a suburban pub.

7 Puberty Blues (1979)
A coming-of-age 1970s beach culture story by Kathy Lette and Gabrielle Carey.

8 Oscar and Lucinda (1988)
This Booker Prize-winning novel by Peter Carey traces a romance between a gambling minister and an heiress.

9 Looking for Alibrandi (1992)
Melina Marchetta's coming-of-age novel features a young girl struggling to find her identity.

10 Monkey's Mask (1994)
Dorothy Porter's verse novel features a lesbian private detective and several poetic red herrings.

Left **Exhibit at the Australian Museum** Centre **Maritime Museum** Right **Susannah Place shop**

Museums

1 Museum of Sydney
The MOS *(see p77)* is located on the site of the first interaction between Sydney's Cadigal people and the British First Fleet. See what the city looked like 100 years ago and discover the history of its indigenous people. ⊗ *Map N2 • Phillip & Bridge Sts • 9251 5988 • Open 9:30am–5pm daily • Dis access • Adm*

2 Australian Museum
Established in 1827, Australia's first museum is the place to explore the country's natural and cultural history through its huge collection of artifacts. Experience indigenous culture with dance performance every Sunday, and enjoy interactive features for kids and inspired temporary exhibitions. ⊗ *Map N4 • 6 College St • 9320 6000 • Open 9:30am–5pm daily • Dis access • Adm*

3 Powerhouse Museum
This museum of science, design and technology is interesting and great fun, offering many interactive displays *(see pp30–31)*.

Powerhouse Museum

4 Hyde Park Barracks Museum
In Francis Greenway's historic building, this museum *(see p22)* uses objects, soundscapes and testimonies to recreate the lives of convicts in early Sydney. Learn about their crimes, their difficult voyage from England and their building of the colony. Then have a look at the dormitory hammocks. ⊗ *Map N3 • Queens Sq, Macquarie St • 8239 2311 • Open 9:30am–5pm daily • Adm*

5 National Maritime Museum
Darling Harbour is the ideal spot for this museum *(see p28)* dedicated to life at sea. From the water-craft of indigenous Australians to the history of the Royal Australian Navy, the museum has it all covered. It is possible to tour some of the historic boats moored nearby including the replica of Cook's *Endeavour.* ⊗ *Map L3 • 2 Murray St, Darling Harbour • 9298 3777 • Open 9:30am–5pm daily • Dis access*

***Endeavour*, Maritime Museum**

6 Sydney Jewish Museum
This museum traces the history of Jewish life in Sydney, from a tiny group who arrived on the First Fleet in the 18th century to today's thriving community of over 30,000. There is also a Holocaust memorial and section, tours of which can be arranged *(see p85).*

The Historic Houses Trust manages many museums. If you plan to visit lots of them, a Ticket Through Time offers great value.

Montage at the Justice & Police Museum

9 Nicholson Museum

In Sydney University's *(see p103)* Gothic sandstone Quadrangle, the Nicholson Museum is beautifully built and has an impressive collection of antiquities, including a large range of Egyptian and Eastern Mediterranean artifacts. § *Map C5 • Southern Entrance, Main Quadrangle, University of Sydney • 9351 2812 • Open 10am–4:30pm Mon–Fri, noon–4pm first Sat of the month • www.sydney.edu.au/museums*

7 Justice & Police Museum

Sydney's convict past was the start of a colourful history of crime and prosecution. Find out about the thugs of the past, the heroic cops who caught them and Sydney's current underworld. The museum has a vast collection of police and judicial evidence. § *Map N2 • Phillip & Albert Sts, Circular Quay • 9252 1144 • Open 10:30am–5pm daily • Adm*

8 Susannah Place Museum

Built in 1844, Susannah Place Museum is as much a historic site as it is a museum; the row of quaint terrace houses evokes life in early Sydney The houses have the city's oldest original outdoor laundries and brick lavatories. One of the houses has been recreated as a corner shop that sells goods from that historical era. § *Map M2 • 58–64 Gloucester St, The Rocks • 9241 1893 • Open 2–6pm Mon–Fri, 10am–5pm Sat–Sun (and during NSW school holidays) • By guided tour only, every half hour • Adm*

10 Macleay Museum

Also at the University of Sydney *(see p103)*, Macleay Museum was built in 1887 to house the vast entomological collection of the Macleay family. Since then, the collection has been added to by various ethnographers, naturalists and anthropologists. The pieces exhibited, mostly collected in the 1870s, include the oldest Aboriginal bark paintings in existence. The collection now includes over 1,000 antique scientific instruments. § *Map C5 • Gosper Lane, University of Sydney • 9036 5253 • Open 10am–4.30pm Mon–Fri, noon–4pm first Sat of the month • www.sydney.edu.au/museums*

A Ticket Through Time allows unlimited entry for three months to 13 HHT properties and museums.

43

Left **AGNSW** Centre **Brett Whiteley Studio** Right **Australian Centre for Photography**

Art Galleries

1 Art Gallery of NSW
It's easy to spend a whole day in Sydney's most extensive art gallery *(see pp24–7)*.

2 Museum of Contemporary Art
This 1950s mock Art Deco edifice housed the Maritime Services Board until it became a gallery in 1991, dedicated to exhibiting the work of contemporary Australian and international artists. ® *Map M2*
• *Circular Quay West* • *9245 2400*
• *Open 10am–5pm Fri–Wed, 10am–9pm Thu* • *Closed 25 Dec* • *www.mca.com.au*
• *Dis access*

3 Object
Also known as the Australian Centre for Craft and Design, this gallery exhibits works by textile designers, jewellers, furniture designers, ceramicists and glass-blowers, demonstrating crafts as real art forms. Its store sells a great range of limited edition design-pieces. ® *Map N6* • *Gallery 417: Bourke St, Surry Hills* • *9361 4511*
• *Open 11am–5pm Tue–Fri, 10am–5pm Sat & Sun* • *www.object.com.au* • *Dis access*

4 Artspace
A non-commercial gallery, Artspace presents contemporary works including not only tradi-tional artforms such as painting, but also the experimental through new media, installations and performance. ® *Map P3* • *43–51 Cowper Wharf Rd, Woolloomooloo*
• *9356 0555* • *Open 11am–5pm Tue–Sun*
• *www.artspace.org.au* • *Dis access*

5 Brett Whiteley Studio
When Brett Whiteley died in 1992, his wife turned his studio into a memorial *(see pp26 & 93)*. Now an adjunct of the AGNSW, his bedroom and workspace have been left intact. Get to know the artist through his unfin-ished paintings or the gallery space that exhibits his work.
® *Map N6* • *2 Raper St, Surry Hills*
• *9225 1881* • *Open 10am–4pm Sat–Sun*
• *www.brettwhiteley.org*

6 SH Ervin Gallery
Enjoy a unique Australian art experience at one of Sydney's premier galleries. Set in heritage surrounds, the programme features changing exhibitions, weekly talks and guest speakers. ® *Map M1*
• *Watson Rd, Observatory Hill, The Rocks*
• *9258 0173* • *Open 11am–5pm Tue–Sun*
• *www.nsw.nationaltrust.org.au* • *Adm*

Interior wall of the Brett Whiteley Studio

The MCA offers free guided tours at 11am Mon–Fri, noon Sat–Sun

7 Australian Centre for Photography

Founded in 1973, Australia's longest established contemporary gallery presents the best in local and international photography and new media. A photo wall features works by emerging artists, while the main space contains temporary exhibitions. ◈ Map Q6 • 257 Oxford St, Paddington • 9332 0555 • Open 10am–5pm daily • www.acp.org.au

8 Kate Owen Gallery and Studio

Spread over three floors, Kate Owen displays and sells Aboriginal art by established as well as emerging artists. A friendly and knowledgable staff is on hand in the gallery to answer questions. The third floor is the only commercial gallery space in Sydney. ◈ Map B3 • 680 Darling St, Rozelle • 9555 5283 • Open 10am–6pm daily • www.kateowengallery.com.au

9 2 Danks Street

Home to ten commercial galleries, this converted warehouse is a forerunner of the arty precinct southeast of the CBD. German Conny Dietzschold shows exciting international art, Utopia exhibits Aboriginal art and Gow Langsford presents a range of international art. ◈ Map P5 • 2 Danks St, Waterloo • 9690 0215 • Open 11am–6pm Tue–Sat • Dis access • www.2danksstreet.com.au

10 State Library Galleries

Exhibitions are presented in five galleries. The Library hosts photography, posters, monographs, ephemera, and historical material (see p22) such as postage stamps, coins, architectural plans and sound recordings. ◈ Map N3 • Macquarie St • 9273 1414 • Open 9am–8pm Mon–Thu, 9am–5pm Fri, 10am–5pm Sat & Sun • Dis access • www.sl.nsw.gov.au

Top 10 Paddington Private Galleries

1 Sherman Galleries
Exhibits top contemporary Australian artists. ◈ Map Q6 • 16–20 Goodhope St • 9331 1112

2 Roslyn Oxley9
Renowned contemporary Australian artists. ◈ Map R6 • 8 Soudan Lane (off Hampden St) • 9331 1919

3 Tim Olsen Gallery
Works by John Olsen and other contemporary Australian artists. ◈ Map F5 • 63 Jersey Rd • 9327 3922

4 Australian Galleries
Contemporary Australian works by artists such as Jeffery Smart. ◈ Map R6 • 15 Roylston St • 9360 5177 • Works On Paper: 24 Glenmore Rd • 9380 8744

5 Savill Galleries
Specializes in paintings by important Australian artists. ◈ Map R6 • 156 Hargrave St • 9327 8311

6 Blender Gallery
Specialises in photography. ◈ Map R6 • 16 Elizabeth St • 9380 7080

7 Stills Gallery
A wide range of Australian photography. ◈ Map Q5 • 36 Gosbell St • 9331 7775

8 Kaliman Gallery
Contemporary Australian art ◈ Map R6 • 56 Sutherland St, Paddington • 9357 2273

9 Eva Breuer Art Dealer
A conservative collection of Australian art from every period. ◈ Map F5 • 83 Moncur St, Woollahra • 9362 0297

10 Maunsell Wickes
Mid-career and young emerging artists cover a range of art practices. ◈ Map E4 • 19 Glenmore Rd, Paddington • 9331 4676 • www.maunsellwickes.com

The monthly magazine Art in Australia lists countrywide exhibitions and is available at most galleries.

Left **Sydney Opera House against the city skyline** Right **Walsh Bay**

Architectural Highlights

1 Sydney Opera House
If you only manage to explore one building in Sydney, make it this World Heritage-listed one. Not simply beautiful from afar, a close look at the shells' interior reveals the complexity of the gravity-defying construction. Modifications are underway to improve facilities and realise Jørn Utzon's original vision for the interiors. ⊗ *See pp8–11*

2 Sydney Theatre & Walsh Bay
The Walsh Bay wharves were the first World Heritage-listed urban site in Australia, encompassing an elegant precinct made up of theatres, restaurants, a hotel and apartments. Shipping timbers and dock machinery have been incorporated into the new buildings. ⊗ *Map M1 • Pier 4, 22 Hickson Rd, Walsh Bay*

3 Aurora Place
The ethereal white glass skin and sails atop Renzo Piano's office block and apartment buildings, built in 2000, echo the Opera House's shells and the spinnakers of yachts on the harbour. They also regulate the temperature, making the skyscraper one of the most energy-efficient buildings in the CBD. ⊗ *Map N3 • 88 Phillip St*

4 Governor Phillip Tower
Part of a large development on a historic site, the base of this elegant high-rise carefully slopes over several 19th-century terrace houses. The neighbouring Museum of Sydney *(see p42)* preserves the footings of the first Government House. In *Mission Impossible 2*, Tom Cruise abseiled through the roof's steel blades. ⊗ *Map M3 • 1 Farrer Place*

5 Altair
Designed by Sydney's arbiters of style, Engelen Moore, Altair has won two World Architecture Awards. It is recognised for its environmental performance and sleek lines. Mechanical louvres on the building's façade open to catch the breeze. ⊗ *Map Q5 • 3 Kings Cross Rd, Rushcutters Bay*

6 Australia Square
Built in the 1960s, this structure was a revisioning of Sydney's downtown, combining office, retail and public space. The building is still revered as a marvel of concrete construction. Architect Harry Seidler chamfered the building's corners to reduce its shadow, giving the tower its iconic round form. ⊗ *Map 3 • 264–27 George St • Adrn*

Governor Phillip Tower

Sydney Architecture Walks runs excellent tours of architecture and public art. Visit www.sydneyarchitecture.org

7 Republic 2

Over-scaled openings animate the grand façade of this cool white apartment complex, designed by the architectural style gurus Burley Katon Halliday. The large apartments are situated around a sunny, stone-paved courtyard, complete with sculpture and a great breakfast café. ⊗ Map P5 • 46–50 Burton St, Darlinghurst

8 Rose Seidler House

Sydney's most significant architect, whose work spans over 50 years, Harry Seidler was almost single-handedly responsible for bringing Bauhaus and European Modernism to Australia. This modest but lovely house, commissioned by Seidler's mother in 1950, assimilates the best Modernist features. Also check out its interesting collection of original furniture and appliances. ⊗ Map T2 • 71 Clissold Rd, Wahroonga • Open 10am–5pm Sun • 9989 8020 • Adm

9 Allianz Stadium

The roof of this stadium (see p53) is a low-slung "Mexican hat" which allows tantalising glimpses of sports crowds from nearby Fox Studios. Designed by local architect Phillip Cox, it was built to coincide with Sydney's Bicentenary in 1988. ⊗ Map E5 • Driver Ave, Moore Park

10 Homebush Train Station

Not often is a station so architecturally interesting: this one is a rare beast. Supporting a delicate membrane roof, 18 vaulted arches hover over the rail platform and provide an impressive gateway to the extensive Homebush sporting complex (see pp52–53). ⊗ Map S4 • Olympic Park, Homebush

Top 10 Public Art

1 Edge of the Trees

Janet Laurence and Fiona Foley. Symbolises reconciliation with Aborigines (see p77). ⊗ Museum of Sydney

2 Almost Once

Brett Whiteley's sculpture of two matchsticks representing life and death. ⊗ AGNSW

3 Federation Pavilion

Alexander Tzannes and Imants Tillers. Built for the Bicentenary celebrations. ⊗ Centennial Park

4 Veil of Trees

Janet Laurence and Jisuk Han. Ethereal images on glass reflect the changing light. ⊗ The Domain

5 Magnolia & Palm

Bronwyn Oliver. Giant seeds recall botanical studies by Australia's explorers. ⊗ Botanic Gardens

6 Dual Nature

Nigel Helyer. Whimsical structures play with the tides. ⊗ Woolloomooloo Bay

7 Wuganmagulya

Brenda L Croft. Describes the significance of the Botanic Gardens to the Aborigines. ⊗ Botanic Gardens

8 Memory is Creation Without End

Kimio Tsuchiya. Sandstone blocks from demolished buildings are strewn on the grass ⊗ Tarpeian Way, South Domain

9 Tankstream

Lynne Roberts-Goodwin. Marks the colony's original water supply (see p18). ⊗ Pitt Street Mall to Alfred St

10 Tied To Tide

Jennifer Turpin and Michaelie Crawford. A dynamic sculpture that responds to water levels. ⊗ Pyrmont Bay Park, Pirrama Rd, Pyrmont

Sydney Heritage Walk is a self-guided tour. Maps can be obtained at www.cityofsydney.nsw.gov.au

47

The Eastern Suburb's crescent-shaped Bondi Beach

🔟 Beaches

1 Bondi
Australia's most famous beach is a perfect crescent of sand with good surfing spots at either end, and usually calm enough for a swim in the middle. Being so close to the city, it won't take too long to get your toes wet (see pp34–5).

2 Manly
On the peninsula's ocean side, this popular long beach (see p118) is the homeground of many of Australia's ironmen and women, and the site of surf lifesaving championships. The esplanade is good for jogging and rollerblading, and goes all the way round to lovely, sheltered Shelly Beach.

3 Palm
An hour's drive north of Sydney, the area around this beach is a magnet for the city's glitterati. "Palmie" is a lovely beach fringed by pine trees, and was made famous by the soap opera Home and Away. For a cruisy afternoon, catch the Pittwater ferry for a loop around the bay (see p122).

Pelicans at Palm Beach

4 Cronulla
This beach in the southern suburbs was immortalised in Puberty Blues. Still a grommet (young surfer wannabes) training ground, it hasn't lost any of its teen appeal. Grab a chiko roll and get into the spirit. ◈ Map T6

5 Maroubra
The Eastern Suburbs' most serious surf beach has big waves and a wide stretch of sand. When you're done with the water, walk round the coast to see a series of rockpools brimming with sealife. Maroubra offers good facilities such as a shaded playground, changing rooms and a kiosk. ◈ Map U5

6 Clontarf
This harbour beach is wonderful for small children. There's plenty of shade, a playground, a shallow tidal pool, and a great view of yachts moving to and from the marina opposite. After your swim, satisfy your hunger across the bay at The Spit with a satisfying plate of fish and chips. ◈ Map U3

7 Balmoral
Another excellent children's beach, Balmoral has a large enclosure of shark nets bordered by a wooden boardwalk which kids love to jump off. Grassy picnic areas abound, the water is warm and calm, and there are many places to buy the kids an ice cream. ◈ Map U3

For Security and Health tips, see p137.

Bronte's swimming baths

Bronte
8 The picnic area at this small beach is dotted with little huts that provide picnic tables and shelter from the wind. On the weekends it's packed with groups of 20-somethings and families enjoying barbecues and beer. Bronte also boasts a great ocean pool and a fabulous row of cafés. ⊗ Map G6

Clovelly
9 If you walk between the cliffs that separate Bronte and Clovelly, you'll pass through Waverley Cemetery, where Aussie poet Henry Lawson (see p41) rests. Due to its backwater, Clovelly's waters are very calm, making it wonderful for children, laps and snorkelling. ⊗ Map U4

Nielsen Park
0 On summer weekends, this sheltered harbour beach is packed with picnicking families. The adjacent park (see p51) has good spots for cricket or frisbee. Small children can safely play in the water, but keep in mind that the harbour floor dips away suddenly. ⊗ Map G2

Top 10 Swimming Pools

1 Andrew "Boy" Charlton
Sydney's style set love the picturesque setting (see p20). Outdoor, saltwater. ⊗ The Domain • 9358 6686

2 Sydney Olympic Park Aquatic Centre
Facilities include a water park for kids (see p52). Indoor. ⊗ Olympic Boulevard, Sydney Olympic Park • 9752 3666

3 Cook & Phillip Park
In the heart of the CBD; also has a gym. Indoor. ⊗ 4 College St • 9326 0444

4 North Sydney Olympic
Swim looking up at the Harbour Bridge. Indoor and outdoor. ⊗ 4 Alfred St South, Milsons Point • 9955 2309

5 Bondi Icebergs
The home of winter swimming since 1929 (see p35). Outdoor. ⊗ 1 Notts Ave, Bondi Beach • 9130 4804

6 Dawn Fraser Baths
See the tidal pool where the world record breaker got her start. Outdoor, saltwater. ⊗ Fitzroy Ave, Balmain • 9555 1903

7 Wylie's Baths
Popular ocean rock pool. ⊗ Neptune St, Coogee

8 McIver's Baths
Coogee's women-only pool, a favourite of the lesbian community. Ocean rock pool. ⊗ Neptune St, Coogee

9 Fairy Bower
Tiny, with incredible views over the Pacific. Ocean rock pool. ⊗ Bower St, Manly

10 Forty Baskets Beach
Relatively inaccessible but worth it for the peace and views of Manly. Tidal harbour pool. ⊗ Balgowlah Hts

Left **Basking in the sun at Centennial Park**

Parks & Gardens

1 Bradleys Head

Walking trails take you around the tip of one of Sydney Harbour National Park's highlights, where you can often spot noisy flocks of rainbow lorikeets. At the end of the headland is the tripod mast of the original HMAS *Sydney (see p13)* and a small Doric column marking one nautical mile from Fort Denison *(see p38)*. ◈ *Map F2*

2 Centennial Park

Sydney's Central Park is a gorgeous 220-ha (543-acre) expanse of playing fields, horse-riding facilities *(see pp54 & 57)*, ornamental lakes and ponds, cultivated gardens, sports grounds, cycle and jogging paths and light bushland with beautiful paperbark trees. It is the largest open space in the central area and a popular destination for barbecues and picnics. ◈ *Map E5*

3 Garigal National Park

This rainforest zone on the North Shore may offer you the best chance to spy the elusive lyrebird in its natural habitat. You will also find tree ferns and cabbage tree palms *(Livistonia Australis)*, which were used by white settlers for everything from hats to building materials. ◈ *Map T3*

Giant chess board at Hyde Park

4 Hyde Park

Standing at the edge of the city centre, this formal park provides a respite from the city's bustle. It features a magnificent avenue of figs, the Art Deco Archibald Fountain at its northern end and the Anzac Memorial *(see p78)*. A site for public executions in 1802, only one year later it was used for Sydney's first cricket match. Australia's first horse race was run here in 1810. ◈ *Map N4*

5 Lane Cove National Park

The park follows Lane Cove River, which flows into Sydney Harbour. Here you'll find echidnas, sugar gliders, mangroves, dusky moorhens, sheltered gullies and open eucalypt forests with stately Sydney red gums *(Angophora costata)* growing out of the sandstone. At dusk their smooth pink bark is almost luminous. ◈ *Map S3*

Red gum tree at Lane Cove

Left **Greycliffe House at Nielson Park** Right **North Head's Shelly Beach**

Arthur McElhone Reserve

6 Tucked below Kings Cross, this tiny manicured park is located in Elizabeth Bay (see p86). It has a stone bridge over a trickling pond filled with Koi, and magnificent views of the yachts moored in Rushcutters Bay and the ritzy Eastern Suburbs enclave of Darling Point. ⊗ Map Q3

Nielsen Park

7 Overlooking Shark Bay, this park (see p49) has been a Sydney favourite since 1912. At its north end is Shark Beach and the historic Greycliffe House (see 98). To the west is Steel Point, site of a former defensive battery, and the start of the 1.5-km (1-mile) Hermitage Foreshore Walk back to Rose Bay.

North Head

8 The more rugged of the two Heads, this section of the Sydney Harbour National Park features windswept heathlands, shaded gullies, secluded Collins Beach and the old Quarantine Station (see p118). Pretty Cabbage Tree Bay and Shelly Beach (see p118) are to the north. ⊗ Map U3

Observatory Park

9 Given its location beside the southern approach to the Sydney Harbour Bridge, this small park below the Observatory (see p19) is surprisingly peaceful. It offers great views of the working harbour. Near the bandstand is a memorial to the Australians who served in the South African War (1899–1902). ⊗ Map D3

South Head

10 In January 1788, Governor Phillip spent his first night in Sydney Harbour, inside South Head (see p98). The headland features the red and-white striped Hornby Lighthouse, so-painted to distinguish it from the Macquarie Lighthouse. It's a prime vantage spot for viewing the Sydney to Hobart yacht race (see p73)

Left **Track events at the Sydney 2000 Olympics** Right **Sydney Cricket Ground**

Sporting Venues & Olympic Sites

1 ANZ Stadium

Sydney's largest stadium was designed as the centerpiece of the 2000 Sydney Olympics. Millions tuned in to watch this venue's opening and closing ceremonies and athletics events. The stadium seats over 80,000 and hosts Australian Rules football, Rugby League and Union, and soccer. ◉ Map S4 • Sydney Olympic Park • 8765 2000 • www.anzstadium.com.au

2 Sydney Olympic Park Aquatic Centre

Australia prides itself on its competitive swimmers, and the Aquatic Centre is a testament to this national obsession. The centre includes a water park and the main competition pool, which accommodates short and long course swimming, water polo, synchronized swimming and underwater hockey. A sauna, steam room, river rapid ride, spray jets, bubble beach, five spas, spurting volcanoes and water slides will keep the whole family happy. ◉ Map S4 • Sydney Olympic Park • 9752 3666 • www.aquaticcentre.com.au

Sydney Olympic Park Aquatic Centre

3 Sydney Olympic Park Tennis Centre

Built on an old horse stud-farm, this complex was designed in consultation with Australian tennis pro John Newcombe and the creators of Wimbledon's Court 1. It features a centrepiece circular centre court with shade cover, two show courts, seven match courts and six practice courts, all surfaced with Rebound Ace. Special loops aid those with hearing impairments. ◉ Map S4 • Sydney Olympic Park • 9764 1999 • www.tennis.com.au/soptennis

4 Sydney Olympic Park Hockey Centre

The unique grandstand roof of this centre is suspended from a single mast, giving the 4,000 spectators an uninterrupted view of the entire pitch. The world-class venue is home to NSW state hockey, and also plays host to gridiron, touch football, Oz tag and lacrosse. ◉ Map S4 • Sydney Olympic Park • 9763 0111 • www.hockeycentre.com.au

5 Royal Randwick Racecourse

First established in 1833 as "Sandy Course", it became known as Royal Randwick in 1992. The racecourse is a lush green surface surrounded by charming old stands. Autumn and Spring Racing Carnivals attract large crowds to watch Australia's top horses in action. ◉ Map E6 • Alison Rd, Randwick • 9663 8400 • www.ajc.org.au

The SCG Tour Experience runs tours of the SCG and Allianz Stadium at 11am & 2pm Mon–Fri & 11am Sat; call 1300 724 737.

6 Showgrounds Exhibition Building

From Royal Easter Shows to international baseball games and rock concerts, this site has hosted them all. The Showground features a main arena, a Clydesdale pavilion inspired by the architecture of 18th- and 19th-century English churches, an open-air woodchop stadium and numerous pavilions. ◎ Map S4
• Sydney Olympic Park • 9704 1111
• www.sydneyshowground.com.au

7 Allphones Arena

Seating 21,000 people, the Superdome is the largest indoor entertainment and sporting arena in Australia. One of the major venues for the 2000 Sydney Olympics, the venue hosted the basketball finals, artistic gymnastics, trampoline and wheelchair basketball. ◎ Map S4
• Sydney Olympic Park • 8765 4321
• www.acerarena.com.au

8 Sydney Cricket Ground

This area was granted to the British Army in 1851 (see p92). In 1870 Rugby Union was first played here. Today, the hallowed turf hosts cricket in the summer, Australian Rules Football in the winter, and various sports and concerts in between. ◎ Map E5
• Moore Park Rd, Paddington • 9360 6601
• www.sydneycricketground.com.au

9 Allianz Stadium

Home of the Sydney Roosters RLC, the NSW Waratahs and the Sydney FC, Sydney Football Stadium, the former Aussie Stadium, is adjacent to the Sydney Cricket Ground. ◎ Map E5 • Moore Park Rd, Paddington • 9360 6601

10 Monster Skatepark

The only skating facility in Australia to include an indoor street course, outdoor ramp, mini-ramps and a foam pit for trying out air tricks. Sessions cater for skateboarders, scooters and BMX riders of all skill levels. The park hosts regional, national and international action sports events. Helmets compulsory, hire available. ◎ Map S4 • Grand Parade, Sydney Olympic Park • 9763 7359
• www.monster.com.au

The Novotel's top-floor viewing room gives a breathtaking view of the Olympic site and its surrounds.

Left **Boating at the Royal National Park** Right **Horseriding at Centennial Park**

Outdoor Activities

Swimming & Surfing

Sydney has dozens of beaches and most are safe for swimming. The harbour beaches are generally calm, good for a relaxing paddle and for children. The ocean beaches *(see pp48–9)* are likely to have a rougher swell, perfect for surfing, body-boarding and body-surfing; you can take lessons at Let's Go Surfing. At ocean beaches, make sure to swim between the flags, in the lifeguard-patrolled area. ◈ *Let's Go Surfing: Map H5 • 128 Ramsgate Ave, North Bondi • 9365 1800 • www.letsgosurfing.com.au*

Kayaking

Get up close to Middle Harbour's mansions by kayaking around the foreshore. While the more energetic prefer to join the fast-paced traffic of the harbour, others can slowly drift along simply admiring the view. ◈ *Sydney Harbour Kayaks: Map U3 • The Spit Bridge, Mosman • 9960 4389 • www.sydneyharbourkayaks.com.au*

Cycling

There are dedicated cycle tracks in Centennial Park and in streets throughout Sydney. For a real cycling adventure, take a tour of the foreshore and ride across the Harbour Bridge, or mountain bike down the lovely Blue Mountains *(see p121)* with Life's An Adventure. ◈ *Bike Hire: Woolys Wheels • Map P6 • 82 Oxford St, Paddington • 9331 2671 • Cycle maps: www.rta.nsw.gov.au • Life's An Adventure: 9913 8939, www.lifesanadventure.com.au*

Horseriding

Centennial Park has a show-jumping area and an equestrian track that runs the 3.6 km (2.2 miles) around the park. Escorted park rides and lessons in dressage and jumping are available from several stables. ◈ *Centennial Stables/Eastside Riding Academy: Map E5 • Cook & Lang Rds, Centennial Park • 9360 5650/9360 7521 • Moore Park Stables: Map E5 • 9360 8747*

Golf

Many of the city's golf courses are private, but there are also some good public ones. Moore Park's is a championship 18-hole, par-70 course close to the CBD. There is also a three-tiered driving range, floodlit at night. ◈ *Moore Park: Map E5 • Anzac Parade & Cleveland St • 9663 1064 • Open dawn–10pm • www.mooreparkgolf.com.au*

Cycling at Centennial Park

 Protect yourself from UV rays and dehydration by applying sunscreen, wearing a hat and sunglasses and carrying water.

Bushwalking

Bushwalking

The bush is just a short train ride away from the bustling city of Sydney. There are 24 national parks in and around Sydney *(see pp50–51)*, and all offer excellent bushwalks of varying experience levels. Take a guided tour with the NPWS and learn all about native animals and bush foods. ◈ *NPWS: 1300 361 967, 1300 131 555* • *www.nationalparks.nsw.gov.au*

Waterskiing

The idyllic environs of the Hawkesbury River *(see 121)* make it one of the most popular locations for watersports. Try waterskiing, wakeboarding, kneeboarding or barefooting with a lesson at Sydney Waterski and Wakeboard; they cater to all levels of experience. Pickups from train stations or the CBD can be easily arranged. ◈ *Sydney Waterski and Wakeboard: 0418 633 106* • *www.sydneywaterski.com.au*

Ballooning

Dawn balloon flights over the Sydney region are a great experience, tranquil yet exhilarating, with lovely views of the sprawling city and the hazy Blue Mountains. Weather permitting, Balloon Aloft offers daily flights from Camden, followed by a barbecue and champagne breakfast. Ballooning might not be appropriate for those scared of heights. ◈ *Balloon Aloft. 4990 9242* • *www.balloonaloft.com*

Sailing

Charter a skippered yacht and relax as you sail around the harbour, or navigate yourself and up to seven friends in a 6.1-m (20-ft) cruiser. Hiring a 20-footer includes a fishing license and costs $395 for 4 hours. ◈ *Sydney Harbour Escapes: Map G3* • *Rose Bay Marina, New South Head Rd, Rose Bay* • *9328 4718* • *www.sydneyharbourescapes.com.au*

Barefoot Bowls & Beer

It may be every Aussie grandma's pastime, but it has also undergone a surge in popularity, thanks mainly to the patronage of certain Sydney celebrities and a bunch of trendy kids. Try the original and the best, Sunday arvo bowls at Paddington Bowling Club. ◈ *Paddington Bowling Club: 9363 1150* • *www.paddobowls.com.au*

Sailing on Sydney Harbour

The City to Surf is a 14-km (8.7-mile) fun run weaving through Sydney, from William Street to Bondi Beach every August.

The famous laughing clown face welcomes visitors to Luna Park

Activities for Children

Opening poster for Luna Park, 1935

Luna Park

Luna Park has been a harbourside icon and favourite with Sydney children since the 1930s. Modelled on New York's Coney Island, this amusement park is located on the North Shore (see p115), beside the Harbour Bridge. Enter through the 9-m (29.5-ft) clown face to enjoy classics such as the dodgems and the ferris wheel, and other attractions such as the UFO. ⊛ Map D2 • 9922 6644 • www.lunaparksydney.com

Kids' Deck

The National Maritime Museum (see p42) runs Kids' Deck, a programme of creative activities for children aged 5 to 12. With events often linked to current exhibitions, kids might build their own ships or dress up. There are also regular activity sessions during school holidays and Mini Mariners sessions with story-times for pre-schoolers on Tuesdays. ⊛ Kids' Deck: every Sun 11am–3pm • Adm

Gallery Kids

The Art Gallery of New South Wales (see p24–5) has an extensive program of events for children of all ages. School holidays are peak times with special performances and workshops. There are kids' art classes once a month and Fundays on most Sundays, at 2:30pm, at which children might find themselves giggling at a mime artist or discovering Aboriginal art and culture.

Imax Theatre

The eight-storey-high screen and 15,000 watt digital surround sound system will have kids pinned to their seats, or jumping out of them, as the case may be. This Darling Harbour icon with the distinctive black-and-yellow chequerboard façade presents 2D and IMAX 3D films. State-of-the-art electronic headsets with infrared sensors have replaced the quaint 1950s cardboard glasses that parents might recall from their youth. ⊛ Map L4 • 9281 3300 • www.imax.com.au

Circus Oz

Circus Oz mixes social commentary with satire, rock and roll, acrobatics and comedy to deliver performances that live up to their credo: Community, Diversity, Humanity, Hilarity.

Horseriding at Centennial Park

They are a travelling troupe but usually perform at Sydney's Moore Park in January and February. Check out their website for performance dates. ◈ *Map E5* • www.circusoz.com

6 Centennial Park

This parkland *(see p50)* has two main attractions for kids: a designated cycle path near Alison Road, and the Equestrian Centre on Lang and Robertson Roads *(see p54)*. The Centre runs tours for children and conducts hand held pony rides. Centennial Park Cycles rents bikes and helmets for younger riders.

7 Kids at the House

This excellent program at the Sydney Opera House *(see pp8–11)* introduces children to the world of performance art. The Babies and Family proms acquaint kids aged two to nine with musical forms, often through interactive performances. Older children can enjoy Australian and international theatre at venues such as The Studio.

8 Storytime Readings

Children under five who fancy some downtime can attend preschool Storytime sessions at the Balmain Library. ◈ *Map C3*
Darling St, Balmain • *9367 9211*
Sessions: 11am Thu

9 Fishing on the Harbour

One of the best spots to drop a line is at the Ives Steps Wharf, just under the Sydney Harbour Bridge west of Dawes Point Park *(see p13)*. This is a popular haunt for chatty older anglers who are happy to share their knowledge with children. ◈ *Map D2*
• *Ives Steps Wharf*

10 Discovering Nature and Culture

The Australian Museum *(see p42)* is the place for youngsters that are curious about the world around them. The museum offers unique tours, workshops and activities for children of all ages. Kids might take part in a mini dinosaur dig, get up close to spiders or explore the museum by torchlight after dark. Visit http://australianmuseum. net.au for further information on child-centred activities at the museum.

Sydney's Child is a free monthly magazine with tips for parents, available at bookstores and the Town Hall Information Centre.

57

Left **Interior of Tetsuya's** Center **Quay interior** Right **Bondi Icebergs**

🔟 Restaurants

1 Tetsuya's

The emphasis of this serene space is on the food and wine. The dégustation *(see p141)* menus fuse Japanese flavours with French technique. Vegetarian dégustations are available on request. ✆ *Map M4 • 529 Kent St • 9267 2900 • Lunch Sat, dinner Tue–Sat • www.tetsuyas.com • $$$$$*

2 est.

This stylish spot is ideal for a luxurious meal. The Mod Oz menu features fresh and exotic ingredients with an emphasis on seafood and game. Don't miss the fabulous passion-fruit soufflé. ✆ *Map M2 • Level 1, Establishment Hotel, 252 George St • 9240 3000 • Lunch Mon–Fri, dinner Mon–Sat • Dis access • www.merivale.com/establishment • $$$$*

An entrée

3 Guillaume at Bennelong

You can't beat dining at the Opera House *(see p9)*. Celebrity chef Guillaume Brahimi prepares Australian food with French skill. A less expensive option is to order tapas-style dishes from the cocktail bar on the upper level of

Guillaume at Bennelong

the restaurant. ✆ *9241 1999 • Lunch Thu–Fri, dinner Tue–Sat • www. guillaumeatbennelong.com.au • $$$$*

4 Marque

Extraordinary, contemporary French food overseen by Mark Best, multiple winner of the Sydney Chef of the Year award, is served in a bold dining room featuring black, glossy walls. An indulgent wine list complements the innovative menu. Producing consistently great food, Marque remains at the top of its game. The Friday lunch special is great value. ✆ *Map N6 • 4–5/355 Crown St, Surry Hills • 9332 2225 • Lunch Fri, dinner Mon–Sat • Dis access • www.marquerestaurant. com.au • $$$$$*

5 Quay

Go for the views and for international flavours. The elegant dishes explore unique food combinations and tastes from France, Italy, Spain, Japan and China combine perfectly. ✆ *Map M1 • Overseas Passenger Terminal, Circular Quay • 9251 5600 • Lunch Tue–Fri, dinner daily • Dis access • www.quay.com.au • $$$$$*

6 Icebergs Dining Room

This swish dining room is above the famous swimming pool *(see p49)*. Glamorous decor and modern Italian Mediterranean food ✆ *Map H5 • 1 Notts Ave, Bondi Beach • 9365 9000 • Open Tue–Sun • www.idrb.com • $$$$*

Definitely make reservations at Sydney's fine diners, particularly Tetsuya's, which can be booked months in advance.

Aria

7 Having deservedly gained its second hat (an award from the *Sydney Morning Herald Good Food Guide*), Aria continues with its elegant and inspired take on contemporary Australian cuisine, all prepared using the freshest produce. The views over the harbour and Opera House are spectacular. A more reasonably priced, pre-theatre menu is available. ⬡ *Map N2* • *1 Macquarie St, East Circular Quay* • *9252 2555* • *Dis access* • *www.ariarestaurant. com.au* • *$$$$*

Aussie Wine

Sepia

8 While the cuisine is inspired by Japan, the decor at Sepia is pure urban sophisticated. Head chef Martin Benn has created a contemporary menu that uses the best local produce. ⬡ *Map L4* • *201 Sussex St* • *9283 1990* • *Lunch Fri & Sat, dinner Tue–Sun* • *www.sepiarestaurant.com.au* • *$$$$*

Pier

9 Every table enjoys stunning harbour views at this exceptional restaurant, which sources the very best seafood species. Service is also flawless. ⬡ *Map G4* • *594 New South Head Road, Rose Bay* • *9327 6561* • *Lunch daily, dinner Mon–Sat* • *www.pierrestaurant.com.au* • *$$$*

Sean's Panaroma

10 Intimate and friendly, Sean's serves a lovely range of dishes such as lthe famous white chocolate, fig and rosemary nougat. ⬡ *Map H5* • *270 Campbell Parade, Bondi Beach.*• *9365 4924* • *Lunch Fri–Sun, dinner Wed–Sat* • *Optional BYO* • *Bookings essential* • *www.seanspanaroma.com.au* • *$$$*

Top 10 Seafood Highlights

1 Sydney Fish Market
The epicentre of all that's fishy in Sydney *(see p105)*.

2 Rockpool
Star chef Neil Perry's seafood restaurant. ⬡ *Map M2* • *107 George St, The Rocks* • *9252 1888*

3 Flying Fish
Glam meets clams, with Mod Oz and Sri Lankan flavours. ⬡ *Map K3* • *Jones Bay Wharf, 19–21 Pirrama Rd, Pyrmont* • *9518 6677*

4 Boathouse on Blackwattle Bay
Relaxed waterfront setting. Sydney rock oysters are a speciality. ⬡ *Map C4* • *End of Ferry Rd, Glebe* • *9518 9011*

5 Coast
Very popular Darling Harbor spot. ⬡ *Map L4* • *The Roof Terrace, Cockle Bay Wharf* • *9267 6700*

6 Manta Seafood
Great seafood in a beautiful marina setting. ⬡ *Map P3* • *Wharf 9, 6 Cowper Wharf Rd, Woolloomooloo* • *9332 3822*

7 Fishface
Tiny but fab, serving the freshest fish. ⬡ *Map P5* • *132 Darlinghurst Rd* • *9332 4803*

8 A Fish Called Coogee
Get a feast from this seafood emporium. ⬡ *Map U5* • *229 Coogee Bay Rd, Coogee* • *9664 7700*

9 Mohr Fish
Popular fish and chips at a tiny but classy spot. ⬡ *Map D5* • *202 Devonshire St, Surry Hills* • *9318 1326* • *BYO*

10 Garfish
The best fishy place on the north side. ⬡ *Map D2* • *2/21 Broughton St, Kirribilli* • *9922 4322* • *Optional BYO*

For more restaurants and a key to price categories see pp82, 89, 101, 107, 112, 119, 129.

Left **Museum of Sydney** Centre **Bill & Toni's** Right **Café Mint**

Casual Dining

1 Museum of Sydney Café
The food at a museum's café isn't normally a reason to visit, but this café is a treasure, serving breakfast, lunch and dinner to an appreciative crowd. Opening onto the paved forecourt, it offers excellent café standards such as sandwiches, salads and cakes, as well as bistro-style dishes such as steaks and tea-smoked trout. ◎ Map N2 • Bridge & Phillip Sts • 9241 3636 • Open 7am–9pm Mon–Fri, 8:30am–4pm Sat–Sun • Dis access • $$$

2 Longrain
Thai food lends itself well to sharing at Longrain. The menu includes dishes such as duck and potato curry with ginger and cucumber relish. Snack at the bar or sip offerings from the wine list. ◎ Map N5 • 85 Commonwealth St, Surry Hills • 9280 2888 • Lunch Fri, dinner Mon–Sun • Lunch bookings only • Dis access • www.longrain.com.au • $$$

3 Pizza Mario
At this relocated restaurant, wood-fired, sparingly topped, thin and crusty pizzas are as close to the real thing as you will find in the inner city. The calzones are terrific, as is the fried calamari. ◎ Map E4 • Shop 9, 417 Bourke St, Surry Hills • 9332 3633 • Dinner daily from 6pm • No booking • www.pizzamario.com.au • $$

4 Bill & Toni's
This Sydney stalwart is loved for its strong coffee, free old-fashioned cordial and checked tablecloths. Upstairs, you'll find delicious home-style Italian food. Head downstairs for gelato. ◎ Map N5 • 74 Stanley St, East Sydney • 9360 4702 • Upstairs open noon–2:30pm & 6–10:30pm daily, downstairs open 7am–midnight daily • BYO • $

5 Billy Kwong
If the long queues aren't a dead give away, the delicious smells that greet you will make it clear that this place is special. Run by Kylie Kwong, Sydney's celebrity chef, Billy Kwong specializes in traditional Chinese family food souped up with a modern edge. ◎ Map N6 • Shop 5, 355 Crown St, Surry Hills • 9332 3300 • Open 6–10pm Mon–Thu, 6–11pm Fri–Sat, 6–9:30pm Sun • Optional BYO • No bookings • $$$

6 Bills Surry Hills
Really the best for breakfast but also great at other times, this restaurant is the showpiece of celebrity chef Bill Granger. At breakfast tuck into their speciality: delectable ricotta hotcakes with honeycomb butter and a sunrise juice. ◎ Map N6 • 359 Crown St, Surry Hills • 9360 4762 • Open 7am–10pm daily • Dinner bookings Mon–Fri only • Dis access • www.bills.com.au • $$

Bills Surry Hills

If you're craving fast food, try a Bondi burger from Oporto, a Portuguese chicken chain that has outlets all over Sydney.

Café Zoe

7 A light and airy room and pleasant service make this a good option. Eggs come with a choice of sides, the lunch menu contains great salads. Be sure to try an unusual fresh juice combo. ✆ Map N6 • 688 Bourke St, Surry Hills • 8399 0940 • Open 7am–4pm Mon–Fri, 8am–4pm Sat • $

Café Mint

8 The North African food at this small café is loaded with aromatic flavours such as cinnamon, mint and cumin. Try the varied *meze* plates with *dukkah*-coated Turkish bread. The big servings are great value. ✆ Map N6 • 579 Crown St, Surry Hills • 9319 0848 • Open 6–10pm Tue–Sat, 8am–3pm Fri & Sat, 9am–3pm Sun • www.cafemint.com.au • $$

Café Sopra

9 There are often queues at this bustling Italian eatery but it's worth the wait to sample the tempting options. ✆ Map C6 • 7 Danks St, Waterloo • 9699 3174 • Open 10am–3pm Sun–Fri, 8am–3pm Sat • $

The Bathers' Pavilion Café

10 Beachside at Balmoral (see p48), this café is in the restored bathers' changerooms. The varied menu has great choices, and the ambience is wonderful. ✆ Map U3 • 4 The Esplanade, Balmoral Beach • 9969 5050 • Open 7am–midnight daily • Dis access • No bookings • www.batherspavillion.com.au • $$$

The Bathers' Pavilion Café

Top 10 Breakfasts

1 Three Blue Ducks
Close to the beach, enjoy hot coffee with a cool crowd. ✆ Map G6 • 111–143 Macpherson St, Bronte • 9389 0010

2 Danks Street Depot
Try the creamed eggs at this fabulous café located in a gallery complex (see p45). ✆ 9698 2201

3 Lush on Bondi
Enjoy toasted wraps and uninterrupted views. ✆ Map H5 • Queen Elizabeth Drive, Bondi Beach • 9300 8555

4 Brown Sugar
Groovy locals cosy in for big breakfasts and good coffee. ✆ Map H4 • 106 Curlewis St, Bondi Beach • 9130 1566

5 Ripples at Milson's Point
Café prices in a five-star setting. ✆ Map D2 • Olympic Drive • 9929 7722

6 Blue Water Café
Soak up the view over breakfast. ✆ Map U3 • 28 South Steyne, Manly • 9976 2051

7 Corelli's Café
A bohemian vibe and large servings. ✆ Map M3 • 325 King St, Newtown • 9550 4080

8 Bourke Street Bakery
Gourmet tarts, sourdough breads and pasties, in or out. ✆ Map N6 • 633 Bourke St, Surry Hills • 9699 1011

9 Flat White
Try the sweet or savoury toast with fresh fluffy ricotta at this smart café. ✆ Map F5 • Jersey Rd & Holdsworth St, Woollahra • 9328 9922

10 Le Petit Crème
French café au laits and croque monsieurs. ✆ Map P5 • Shop 2, 116–18 Darlinghurst Rd, Darlinghurst • 9361 4738

For a quick, healthy snack, try one of the many sushi bars located throughout the city.

Right **Leichhardt's Bar Italia** Centre **Dixon street entrance to Chinatown** Left **Lebanese baklava**

🔟 World Flavours

1 Italian
Leichhardt's thriving strip boasts a wonderful range of Italian food. The main section of Norton Street, running from its corner on Parramatta Road, is packed with cafés, bars and restaurants. Try the gelato in the cheap and cheerful surroundings of Bar Italia.
⊗ Map A4 • Bar Italia: 169–171 Norton St • 9560 9981

2 Spanish
In a corner of the CBD you'll find the Torres Deli, selling chorizo and jamon, as well as several tapas joints. The Spanish Club serves yummy but lethal sangria. La Campana has Latin dance lessons on Wednesdays and Thursdays. ⊗ Map M5 • Torres Deli: 75 Liverpool St • 9264 6862 • The Spanish Club: 88 Liverpool St • 9267 8440 La Campana: 53–55 Liverpool St • 9267 3787

3 Japanese
A large Japanese community resides in the lower North Shore, and many good restaurants line Neutral Bay's Military Road. Sushi Studio (see p119) is the pick of them, but all offer authentic food, super-fresh sushi and good prices. Enjoy authentic Japanese BBQ – Yakiniku– at the Koh-Ya restaurant, around the corner.
⊗ Map D1 • Koh-Ya: Shop 1, 9–17 Young St, Neutral Bay • 9904 5036

Fresh sushi

4 Cantonese
Excellent Cantonese food can be found all over Sydney, but head to Chinatown (see p82) for the widest selection. The market on Dixon Street makes it particularly lively on Friday nights. Browsing the arcades off the Dixon Street Mall often leads to interesting discoveries such as herbal remedies, dried fish snacks and jade carvings.
⊗ Map M5

5 Turkish
Catch a train into Auburn and it's a short stroll to the heart of the Turkish community. Try kebabs and pide, Turkish pizza, at Sofra. Finish up with a thick Turkish coffee and dondurma, traditional ice cream made from salep (orchid tubers) at Mado.
⊗ Map S4 • Al Sofra: 35–39 Auburn Rd • 9649 9167 • Mado: 63 Auburn Rd • 9643 5299

6 Portuguese
Portuguese custard tarts, natas, are found all over Sydney, but you haven't really tasted them until you've tried Honeymoon Patisserie. Silvas offers traditional charcoal chicken and Gloria's Café serves up great country dishes. ⊗ Map A5 • Honeymoon Patisserie: 96 New Canterbury Rd, Petersham • 9564 2389 • Silvas: 82–86 New Canterbury Rd • 9572 9911 • Gloria's Café: 82 Audley St • 9568 3966

Thai restaurants are on almost every Sydney corner. The food is fresh and tasty but be careful if you can't handle spices.

7 Lebanese

The central Lebanese mosque is at Lakemba but the best food can be found at the suburb of Punchbowl. Head to The Boulevarde for hummus, falafel and baklava. Jasmin1 is a good place for a very quick, cheap and tasty meal. Nearby Summerland is a bit more swish and has bellydancers most nights. ◈ Map S5 • Jasmin1: 224 The Boulevarde • 9740 7866 • Summerland: 457 Chappel Rd, Bankstown • 9708 5107

8 Kosher

Any kind of food could be kosher, but two main styles, Israeli and traditional Jewish food, are readily available in the Bondi area. Savion is the stalwart, offering Israeli street food such as chicken shwarmas. Try Katzy's for chicken soup with matza balls, and don't miss the bagels and cakes at Glicks. ◈ Map C5 • Savion: 38 Wairoa Ave • 9130 6357 • Katzy's: 113 Hall St • 9130 6755 • Glicks: 173 Bondi Rd • 9386 9949

9 Greek

While there are many Greek businesses in Marrickville and it's fun to browse the many shops on Marrickville Road, the best Greek restaurants are spread further out. For wonderful modern food, visit Perama. Steki Taverna is more traditional, plate-smashing included. ◈ Map A5 • Perama: 88 Audley St, Petersham • 9569 7534 • Steki Taverna: 2 O'Connell St, Newtown • 9516 2191

10 Indian

Many of Sydney's Indian community choose to eat at the authentic restaurants in Surry Hills, several of which are packed into a small section of Cleveland Street between Crown and Bourke Streets. Have a South Indian flavoured thali or masala dosa at the vegetarian restaurant Maya, and then sample some of the traditional sweets. The neighbouring shops sell Indian ingredients, spices, incense, and Bollywood movies. ◈ Map D5 • Maya: 470 Cleveland St • 9699 8663

Indian Sweets

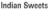

About 31% of Sydneysiders were born overseas and over 900,000 people speak a language other than English at home.

63

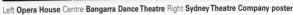

Left **Opera House** Centre **Bangarra Dance Theatre** Right **Sydney Theatre Company poster**

Performing Arts Companies

Opera Australia
Experience the energy and passion of the national opera company when the young singers and international stars of Opera Australia perform throughout the year at the Sydney Opera House *(see pp8–11)*. ✆ 9318 8200
• www.opera-australia.org.au

Sydney Symphony
Also a resident of the Opera House, the Sydney Symphony performs in the spectacular concert hall. The orchestra performances range from jazz and film soundtracks to classical orchestral masterpieces with the world's most illustrious conductors and soloists. ✆ 8215 4600 • www.sydneysymphony.com

Sydney Theatre Company
Performing regularly at the Sydney Theatre at Walsh Bay *(see p46)*, Sydney's premier theatre company are also in residence at the Sydney Opera House as well as performing at their home theatre at the Wharf under the Sydney Harbour Bridge. The STC presents an exciting mix of classics and new Australian drama. ✆ Map M1
• 9250 1777 • www.sydneytheatre.com.au

Sydney Dance Company
With acclaimed dancers and guest choreographers, Sydney Dance Company has paved the way for the development of Australia's fun-loving dance scene. The studio also runs daily dance classes for jazz, hip-hop and ballet, after which you can feast in the Sydney Dance Café, which has views of the Sydney Harbour Bridge. ✆ 9221 4811
• www.sydneydancecompany.com

Bangarra Dance Theatre
This unique company blends traditional Aboriginal and Torres Strait Islander history and culture with international contemporary dance. Powerful, startling and inherently spiritual, Bangarra speaks with an ancient yet completely modern voice.
✆ 9251 5333 • www.bangarra.com.au

Australian Chamber Orchestra
Daring programming and stylistic versatility set this chamber orchestra apart – and the fact that the violinists play standing up. The players have a sense of cohesion usually only found in smaller ensembles. ✆ 8274 3800
• www.aco.com.au

Australian Chamber Orchestra

Bell Shakespeare

Witness Shakespeare like you've never seen. Since its foundation in 1990 by John Bell and Anna Volska, Sydney's theatrical blue-bloods, this company has presented the works of the Bard and modern classics in an accessible style. 🕾 8298 9000 • www.bellshakespeare.com.au

Company B Belvoir

Housed in the historic Belvoir St Theatre, Company B deserves its great reputation for producing sharp contemporary theatre. Its edgy shows are always popular, particularly with the young, hip crowd, so get in early for tickets. Landmark productions have included *Cloudstreet, Toy Symphony, The Alchemist, The Small Poppies, Exit the King* and *Stuff Happens.* 🕾 Map M6 • 9699 3444 • www.belvoir.com.au

Ensemble Theatre

Australia's longest continuously running professional theatre is located in a converted boatshed on Careening Cove. The company performs a mix of local and international plays with an emphasis on ensemble values. Reliable and definitely rewarding. 🕾 Map D2 • 9929 0644 • www.ensemble.com.au

Australian Theatre for Young People

Australia's flagship youth theatre company presents radical versions of classics, plays by young writers, physical theatre and works written by leading Australian writers, such as Louis Nowra and Debra Oswald. Many up-and-coming stars get their first taste of the limelight here. Nicole Kidman is one of its celebrity patrons. 🕾 9251 3900 • www.atyp.com.au

Top 10 Sydney Celebrities

1 Nicole Kidman
The famous Australian actress lives in her Walsh Bay penthouse for at least part of the year.

2 Russell Crowe
From a penthouse atop the Woolloomooloo Finger Bay Wharf, the star of *Master and Commander* continues to enjoy water views.

3 Dame Joan Sutherland
The late Opera diva Dame Joan Sutherland lived in Potts Point for much of her long and prestigious career.

4 Toni Collette
A daring lead performance in *Muriel's Wedding* launched Collette on the world stage; she lives in Tamarama.

5 Ben Lee
Former Noise Addict, now solo strummer, Lee beds down at Bondi when he isn't hanging out in New York.

6 Megan Gale
A supermodel in Italy, Gale often returns to Sydney to hit the runways.

7 Judy Davis
One of Australia's most respected actors, Davis has taken some of film's top honours; she lives in Balmain.

8 David Wenham
The critically-acclaimed actor is at home in Sydney's Eastern Suburbs.

9 Hugo Weaving
Despite roles in *The Matrix* and *The Lord of the Rings*, the modest Weaving still calls Sydney home.

10 Bryan Brown
The iconic Aussie actor is often seen on Sydney's northern beaches.

The Australian Chamber Orchestra performs regularly at the City Recital Hall

Nightlife & Live Music

Metro Theatre
Tiered levels rising to the bar at the back of the main room mean you can see the stage from anywhere in the room. That, plus great acoustics, makes this one of Sydney's best live music venues. ⊗ *Map M4 • 624 George St • 9550 3666 • www.metrotheatre.com.au*

City Recital Hall
The first specifically-designed concert venue built in Sydney since the Opera House, the 1973 City Recital Hall is an uplifting space, ideal for acoustic music. The quality of sound has already attracted Australia's leading companies, including the Australian Chamber Orchestra, Musica Viva and the Sydney Philharmonic Choir. ⊗ *Map M3 • Angel Place • 8256 2222 • www.cityrecitalhall.com*

Home
There's no place like Home. Since its opening night performance by Paul Oakenfold, Sydney's only true superclub has been packed solid. The massive club features a multi-levelled main room, a chill-out zone, the infamous padded "Box" and an outdoor terrace.

Also attached is Homebar, a casual café and mellow bar. The hottest Sydney DJs have residencies here, and top international acts are regularly featured. ⊗ *Map L4 • Cockle Bay Wharf, Darling Park • 9266 0600 • www.homesydney.com*

The Basement
A landmark of the Australian jazz, blues and roots scene since the early 1970s, the walls of The Basement are covered in autographed photos of the stars who have graced its stage. The venue boasts live music every night of the week, and both dinner-and-showpackages or standing-tickets are available to buy. ⊗ *Map M2 • 29 Reiby Place, Circular Quay • 9251 2797 • www.thebasement.com.au*

The Cat & Fiddle Hotel
Sydney's hardest-working live venue hosts more than 30 bands and solo artists every week, so there's music to suit every taste. This musician-friendly bar has a strong local following, particularly for their Sunday afternoon sessions ⊗ *Map K1 • 456 Darling St, Balmain • 9810 7931 • www.thecatandfiddle.com.au*

Sign for The Cat & Fiddle Hotel

Pick up a copy of free weekly music newspaper The Drum Media *for gig listings, or* 3D World *for club and dance listings.*

Rock band Fur Patrol at the Annandale Hotel

The Vanguard

This Newtown venue specializes in jazz, blues and roots music. Bands play Tuesday to Sunday, and you're likely to hear anything from Latin jazz to country soul on their eclectic bill. The non-smoking venue also features a cocktail bar and offers dinner-and-show packages. ◈ Map B5 • 42 King St, Newtown • 9557 7992 • www.thevanguard.com.au

Enmore Theatre

In the heart of Newtown's entertainment district, this refurbished old theatre hosts a wide range of local and inter-national music acts such as Florence and the Machine, Paul Weller and Richard Ashcroft, as well as comedy performances. ◈ Map B5 • 130 Enmore Rd, Newtown • 9550 3666 • www.enmoretheatre.com.au

Annandale Hotel

This legendary Sydney live venue is a must-visit for anyone interested in the local music scene. The pub hosts live music most nights of the week, featuring everyone from local stalwarts to smaller international acts. If you get peckish, step out back for healthy Thai-Asian inspired food at Annandale's Wok & Roll, a laid back local eat-in and take-away spot. ◈ Map B5 Parramatta Rd & Nelson St, Annandale 9550 1078 • www.annandalehotel.com

Ivy

A world class massive urban water-hole with a range of restaurants, bars and cocktail lounges spread over three floors, including a rooftop pool. A wonderful night out for live music. ◈ Map M2 • 330 George St • 9254 8100 • www.merivale.com.au

Selinas at Coogee Bay Hotel

Selinas marks the revival of a once-mighty live venue. This spot caters to devotees of Oz Rock and those who don't mind their ears ringing the next day. It's located in the backpacker haven of The Coogee Bay Hotel, which accommodates six bars. ◈ Map U4 • Coogee Bay Rd & Arden St • 9665 0000 • www. coogeebayhotel.com.au

The Drum Media and 3D World newspapers are available at most record shops and venues.

Left **Jetty Bar at the Manly Wharf Hotel** Right **Opera Bar**

TOP 10 **Pubs & Bars**

1 Opera Bar
Views don't come much better than the Opera Bar's *(see p9)* panorama of the harbour, Harbour Bridge and city skyline. Soak up the sun on the terrace during the day, or sip cocktails in the evening. A good bar menu means you can make a night of it, adding to the perfect Sydney experience. ◈ *Lower Concourse, Sydney Opera House • 9247 1666 • Open 11:30am–late daily • www.operabar.com.au*

2 Cruise
Cruise offers great views of the Opera House. Modern and stylish, the glowing feature wall of this bar periodically changes in colour and mood. A chic crowd makes up for the slightly haphazard service. ◈ *Map M2 • Level 1, Overseas Passenger Terminal, West Circular Quay • 9251 1188 • Open 11am–late daily • www.cruisebar.com.au*

3 Establishment
Resurrected from the burnt-out shell of an 1892 emporium, this hotel boasts a 42-m (138-ft) marble bar and designer fit-out. Fridays are usually packed with the after-work crowd. There are seating areas where you can escape the hordes. Upstairs, the exotic Hemmesphere bar specialises in mojitos. ◈ *Map M2 • 252 George St • 9240 3000 • Open 11am–late Mon–Fri, 6pm–late Sat • www.merivale.com.au*

4 Arthouse Hotel
This city hangout boasts fou cocktail bars and a restaurant over three levels. The main bar, The Verge, was once a chapel and features 19th-century stencilling and skylights. The Dome lounge and Attic bar provide more intimate surrounds, and the cocktai bars merge into the Arthouse Club nightclub four nights a wee featuring local and international DJs. There is also a programme o performances and special events, and permanent art installations. ◈ *Map M4 • 275 Pitt St • 9284 1200 • Open 11am–late Mon–Fri, 5pm–late Sa • www.thearthousehotel.com.au*

5 The Loft
This hip bar brings style to Darling Harbour. Spectacular views and good service make it a winner. Tapas-style snacks are available till 10pm. ◈ *Map L3 • King Street Wharf, 3 Lime St • 9299 4770 • Open 4pm–1am Mon–Thu, noon–3am Fri–Sat, noon–1am Sun • www.theloftsydney.com*

6 The Tilbury
This once-grungy dive has been revamped as a stylish bar and Italian restaurant. A DJ plays at the bar Friday and Saturday, and Sunday afternoons feature live jazz at the restaurant. ◈ *Map P3 • 12–18 Nicholson St, Woolloomooloo • 9368 1955 • Open 7am–midnight Mon–Fri, 9am–midnight Sat, 10am–10pm Sun • www. tilburyhotel.com.au*

Toohey's Bitter

The dress code in Sydney bars is fairly relaxed, but usually thongs, sandals, shorts and singlets are out.

7 Manly Wharf Hotel

If the large public bar with its communal tables and lively atmos- phere is too hectic for you, head outdoors to the Jetty Bar to watch the sun set over the harbour, or hide away in the cocktail lounge. Fireplaces provide cosy winter warmth. ◎ Map U3 • Manly Wharf East Esplanade, Manly • 9977 1266 • Open 11:30am–midnight Mon–Fri, 11am–midnight Sat, 11am–10pm Sun • www.manlywharfhotel.com.au

8 Darlo Bar

A hip local hangout with a relaxed 1950s and 60s decor. Close to the Victoria and Oxford Street restaurants, it's a good place to meet for a drink. Grab a drop from the bottle shop before leaving. ◎ Map P5 • 306 Liverpool St, Darlinghurst • 9331 3672 • Open 10am–midnight Mon–Sat, noon–midnight Sun • www.darlobar.com.au

9 Flying Squirrel

"Good eats and funky eats" is the slogan at this tiny space featuring a menu of small, mainly Spanish and Asian-inspired dishes, along with a good cocktail and wine list. ◎ Map G5 • 249 Bondi Rd, Bondi • 9130 1033 • Open 7am–noon, 5pm–midnight Tue–Fri, 7am–midnight Sat, 7am–10pm Sun • www.flyingsquirreltapasparlour.com.au

10 Bondi Icebergs

A great local tradition and a true Iceburg experience, is to watch a Bondi sunset over a beer in the low-key Icebergs club (see p35). If you're feeling flam and your wallet can take the strain, don't miss the stylish bar attached to the Icebergs Dining Room (see p58). ◎ 1 Notts Ave, Bondi • 9130 3120 • Open 9am–11pm Mon–Fri, 9am–11pm Sat & Sun • www.icebergs.com.au

Top 10 Late-Night Haunts

1 Wildfire

The kitchen here is open until 1am on Fridays and Saturdays. ◎ Map M1 • Overseas Passenger Terminal (ground floor), Circular Quay West • 8273 1222

2 BBQ King

Chinese food and famous Peking Duck 'til 2am. ◎ Map M5 • 18 Goulburn St • 9267 2586

3 The Victoria Room

Melbourne meets the Med. ◎ Map E4 • 235 Victoria St, Darlinghurst • 9357 4488

4 Bar Cleveland

Trendy but unpretentious, open 'til the small hours. ◎ Map D5 • Bourke & Cleveland Sts, Surry Hills • 9698 1908

5 Hugo's Lounge

Great cocktails and $5 pizzas. ◎ Map P4 • Level 1, 33 Bayswater Rd, Kings Cross • 9357 4411

6 Civic Hotel

This Art Deco pub runs 'til 6am Friday and Saturday. ◎ Map M4 • 388 Pitt St • 8080 7000

7 Town Hall Hotel

This legendary hangout doesn't even fire up until midnight. ◎ Map D5 • 326 King St, Newtown • 9557 1206

8 Maisys

Tasty snacks and light meals at this 24-hour café. ◎ Map D1 • 164 Military Rd, Neutral Bay • 9908 4030

9 Café Hernandez

Open 24 hours for coffee and Spanish treats. ◎ Map P5 • 60 Kings Cross Rd, Potts Point • 9331 2343

10 Iguana Bar

Open 'til guests stop rolling in; three bars, dance floor and pool table. ◎ Map P4 • 13–15 Kellet St, Potts Point • 9357 2609

In Australia, pubs and bars are commonly known as "hotels".

Left **The Bookshop Darlinghurst** Right **Public bar at the Imperial Hotel**

Gay & Lesbian Friendly Places

1 Oxford Street Shops

Called the Golden Mile, the stretch of Oxford Street *(see p92)* between Taylor Square and Hyde Park has long been home to gay and lesbian bars, clubs and shops. Each February the Mardi Gras parade *(see p72)* passes this route. Check out Aussie Boys for Sydney Speedos and the Grumpy Baker for a snack and coffee.

Bank Hotel façade

2 The Colombian

The best of the Oxford Street bars is a mock Central American jungle. Giant windows open to the street, allowing the Colombian to serve up people-watching with the beer. The crowd is a mixed bunch of gay, lesbian and straight. After sundown the vibe turns from relaxed afternoon drinks to a party. ✪ *Map N5 • Corner of Oxford & Crown Sts, Surry Hills • 9360 2151 • Open late daily*

3 Green Park Hotel

A good spot for those who'd rather avoid a mainstream gay bar, this pub attracts a trendy Darlinghurst crowd. On Sundays it's packed with those recovering from their weekends with a beer and game of pool. ✪ *Map P5 • 360 Victoria St, Darlinghurst • 9380 5311 • Open 10am–2am Mon–Sat, noon–midnight Sun • www.greenparkhotel.com.au*

4 The Bank Hotel

One of the more upmarket haunts on King Street, this pub is spread over four floors, each with a different theme. There are multiple bars and a wide range of beers to choose from. A popular spot for after-work drinks, the cocktail bar and Thai restaurant are packed and boisterous most of the time. ✪ *Map B5 • 324 King St Newtown • 8568 1900 • Open noon–late daily • www.bankhotel.com.au*

5 Trademark Hotel

This elegant venue draws a mixed crowd. There is plenty to do at Trademark – enjoy a post-work late night supper and drinks in the Piano Room or spice up your evening with dancing and some live jazz music in the Lounge Bar. ✪ *Map E4 • 1 Bayswater Rd, Kings Cross • 9360 8778 • www.pianoroom.com.au/trademark*

6 Imperial Hotel

Some of the classic drag show venues have closed down but this stalwart is still going strong. The hotel was featured in the cult film *Priscilla, Queen of the Desert*. There are shows at the Imperial most nights, so call ahead to find out events and times. ✪ *Map C6 • 35 Erskineville Rd, Erskineville • 9519 9899 • www.theimperialhotel.com.au*

Sydney's Top 10

Pick up the weekly Sydney Star Observer *and monthly magazine* Lesbians On The Loose *to find out what's happening in Sydney.*

7 The Bookshop Darlinghurst

All kinds of queer fiction are packed into this great shop, which covers everything from photography tomes to contemporary lesbian fiction and life-style books. ◈ Map N5 • 207 Oxford St, Darlinghurst • 9331 1103 • Open 10am–10pm Mon–Wed, 10am–11pm Thu, 10am–midnight Fri–Sat, 11am–11pm Sun • www.thebookshop.com.au

8 Toolshed

An extremely popular adult store and an institution among the gay and lesbian community for over three decades. Toolshed offers the ultimate in novelty adult shopping at its quirky best. ◈ Map N5 • Level 1, 81 Oxford St, Darlinghurst • 9332 2792 • Open 9:30–1am Mon–Sat, 9:30am–midnight Sun

9 Café Lounge

A mix of a cocktail bar, restaurant, live music venue and performance space, Café Lounge is patronised by art school kids and grungy types. Arty ambience with comfy sofas, good coffee, and vegetarian options such as tofu and juices. ◈ Map N5 • 277 Gouldburn St, Surry Hills • Open 4pm–10:30pm Tue–Thu, 11:30am–midnight Fri, 9am–midnight Sat, 9am–9pm Sun • 9356 8888 • www.cafelounge.com.au

10 Daly Male

Daly Male offers a wide range of gorgeous gifts and wardrobe essentials including menswear, underwear, swimwear and gymwear. Tickets to upcoming events and parties are also available here. ◈ Map N5 • 90 Oxford St, Darlinghurst • 9361 0331 • Open 10am–6pm Mon–Wed, Fri & Sat, 10am–8pm Thu, 11am–5pm Sun

Top 10 Mardi Gras Events

1 Festival
A month-long arts and cultural festival with dance parties, performing arts, community and sports events.

2 Parade
Thousands attend the notorious Mardi Gras parade, the finale of the festival.

3 Party
Held after the parade, this is one of the largest and most spectacular gay dance parties.

4 Fair Day
Features stalls, music, food and "Kid's Zone", an area that offers a range of activities for children and their families.

5 Mardi Gras Film Festival
A great collection of global queer cinema is screened over two weeks. ◈ www.queerscreen.com.au

6 History Walks
"The Sisters of Perpetual Indulgence" present hilarious walking tours of Toronga Zoo and other sites across Sydney.

7 Shop Yourself Stupid
The largest shopping day in the gay and lesbian calendar offers an array of attractions and specials.

8 Hats Off
A gala night of music, entertainment and celebrities to raise money for HIV/AIDS charities. ◈ 9360 5557 • www.acon.org.au

9 Bike & Tattoo Show
The "Dykes on Bikes" present entertainment, games, bikes and tattoos for your viewing pleasure.

10 Team Sydney
Various sporting events, competitions and games. ◈ www.teamsydney.org.au

Information about the annual Mardi Gras Festival and surrounding events can be found at www.mardigras.org.au

Left **Gay & Lesbian Mardi Gras** Right **Sydney to Hobart Yacht Race**

Festivals & Events

1 Sydney Festival
Time your visit to coincide with this month-long international extravaganza of music, theatre, visual arts, dance and more. Past performers have included Michael Nyman, the London Sinfonietta, the Kronos Quartet, the Russian National Orchestra, the Steppenwolf Theatre Company, Vietnamese Water Puppets and Les Ballets Africains. ◈ Jan • www.sydneyfestival.org.au

2 Big Day Out
This rock-and-roll road show began in the early 1990s. Today, international acts mix it up with alternative and popular local outfits. Acts have included Muse, Lily Allen, Ladyhawke, Neil Young, The Prodigy, and The Ting Tings. ◈ Jan/Feb
• Sydney Showgrounds
• www.bigdayout.com

3 Australia Day
Celebrating the arrival of Sydney's First Fleet, this national holiday sees Sydney ferries and Tall Ships competing in the big race from the Harbour Bridge to Manly and back. There are free concerts and performances held across the city. Do keep in mind that to many indigenous people, this date is known as "Invasion Day". ◈ 26 Jan • www. australiaday.com.au

4 Gay & Lesbian Mardi Gras
This carnival is more than just a street parade down Oxford Street (see p92), for more than a quarter-million people line the route. The parade naturally ends with a party, but there is also an energetic programme of associated events that celebrates the strength and diversity of gay Sydney (see pp70–71). ◈ Feb & Mar • www.mardigras.org.au

5 Sydney Writers' Festival
The roll-call at this week-long event includes more than 200 international and local speakers, with the odd Nobel Laureate thrown in for good measure. There are panel discussions, master classes, book launches and readings aplenty. The festival caters to all ages and tastes, from sci-fi to romance. ◈ May • www.swf.org.au

6 NAIDOC Week
The Australia-wide National Aborigines and Islanders Day Observance Committee Week celebrates the survival, diversity and strength of Torres Strait Islander and Aboriginal cultures. Themes change annually, but regular events include a prestigious art award and prizes in a variety of categories ranging from sports to community leadership. ◈ Early Jul
• www.naidoc.org.au

Tall Ship on Australia Day

7 Rugby League Grand Final
Although Australian Rules football is catching on in Sydney, the locals still go nuts when the big fellas from Sydney's professional league battle it out at Allianz Stadium. If you can't book a ticket, catch the action on the big screen at your local pub. Oct

8 Festival of the Winds
Ever since Hargrave took to the sky with four box kites (see p31), Sydneysiders have loved their kites. And there's no better venue for a day of mass kiting than Bondi Beach (see pp34–5), site of Australia's largest kite-flying festival. Highlights include live music, dance shows, food stalls and workshops. Sep • www.waverley.nsw.gov.au/info/pavillion/fotw

9 Manly International Jazz Festival
Australia's largest community-based celebration of jazz in all its forms, from trad to bebop, has been running for 30 years. Manly (see p118) gives itself over to jazz for the Labour Day long weekend. In addition to travelling bands, there are performances held at outdoor venues such as the ocean beachfront, and indoor venues such as St Matthews church on The Corso. Oct • www.manly.nsw.gov.au/manly–jazz-festival

10 Sydney to Hobart Yacht Race
Organized by the Cruising Yacht Club of Australia, this blue-water classic has been Australia's best known yacht race for over half a century. Crowds line the harbour to wave off the crews as they pass through The Heads (see p51) and head down the coast to Tasmania, almost 628 nautical miles south. 26 Dec, Boxing Day • rolexsydneyhobart.com

Top 10 Film Festivals

1 Sydney Film Festival
Watch films all day, everyday, for 2 weeks. Jun • www.sff.org.au

2 Mardi Gras Film Festival
Screens worldwide gay cinema and camp classics (see p71). Feb or March • www.queerscreen.com.au

3 Tropfest
The biggest short film festival in the world screens outdoors at the Domain. Feb • www.tropfest.com

4 Italian Film Festival
Classic and contemporary cinema. Oct • www.italianfilmfestival.com.au

5 Festival of German Cinema
A mix of dramas, docos, shorts and cult movies. Apr • www.goethe.de/australia

6 Japanese Film Festival
The Japan Foundation, Sydney – Cultural Section organizes international guests and retrospectives. Nov • www.jpf.org.au

7 Alliance Française French Film Festival
Presents the latest, most stylish and provocative in French cinema. Mar • www.frenchfilmfestival.org

8 Spanish Film Festival
Often very cheeky, always great fun. May • www.spanishfilmfestival.com

9 Australian Festival of Jewish Cinema
Diverse Jewish films from around the globe. Nov

10 Flickerfest
Australia's only competitive international short film festival. Jan • www.flickerfest.com.au

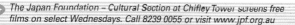

The Japan Foundation – Cultural Section at Chifley Tower screens free films on select Wednesdays. Call 8239 0055 or visit www.jpf.org.au

73

AROUND
TOWN

City Centre
76–83

Kings Cross &
Darlinghurst
84–89

Paddington &
Surry Hills
90–95

Eastern Suburbs
96–101

Newtown & Glebe
102–107

Balmain & Leichhardt
108–113

The North Shore
114–119

Beyond Sydney
120–129

SYDNEY'S TOP 10

Left **State Theatre interior** Centre **Statues on Anzac Memorial** Right **Sydney Tower Deck**

City Centre

SYDNEYSIDERS WORK HARD AND PLAY HARD. *And there's no better place to see them in action than the city centre, which is a manic tide of shoppers, opinionated taxi drivers, daredevil cyclists and bicycle couriers, and office workers talking furiously into their mobile phones as they power-walk to their next appointment. The city centre is surrounded by Circular Quay, The Rocks, the Botanic Gardens, the Domain, Central Station, Darling Harbour and Chinatown. Within this precinct you'll find historic sites and buildings sandwiched between chi-chi boutiques, $2 shops, groovy bars and restaurants, elegant Victorian shopping arcades and a host of entertainment venues. While it's easy to get caught up in the flow, don't forget to stop every once in a while to enjoy the architecture or the numerous street performers.*

View of the harbour from Sydney Tower

Sights

1. Museum of Sydney
2. Martin Place
3. St Mary's Cathedral
4. Sydney Tower
5. Strand Arcade
6. State Theatre
7. Anzac Memorial
8. Queen Victoria Building
9. Town Hall
10. St Andrew's Cathedral

Previous pages: **Bondi Beach**

Left **Entrance to the Museum of Sydney** Right **Martin Place**

Museum of Sydney

1 This stunning museum (see p42) occupies the site of Australia's first Government House, a prefabricated structure that was shipped over with the First Fleet in 1788. That structure was demolished in 1846, but some of its original footings are still visible through glass panels set into the floor. The museum places the history of white settlement against the Aboriginal custodianship of the land. The museum's plaza features *Edge of the Trees* (see p47), an installation and soundscape which explores Aboriginal history and culture.

Martin Place

2 Martin Place runs from the General Post Office on George Street uphill to Macquarie Street. The 1891 GPO was designed by James Barnet (see p85) and built over the Tank Stream (see p18). Check out the amusing characters above the Pitt Street colonnade (see walk, p79) and the grand 1912 Commonwealth Bank Head Office. The bank's equally impressive 1928 sibling resides just up the hill. Opposite the GPO is the striking 1925 Neo-Classical National Australia Bank, and the Cenotaph commemorating Australia's war heroes. ◉ *Map N3*

St Mary's Cathedral

3 One of the world's largest Gothic Revival churches, the original 1833 structure of this cathedral was destroyed by a fire in 1865. Its replacement was designed by William Wardell and work began on it the same year. The twin spires, which featured in Wardell's original plans, were completed in 2000. The design of the magnificent terrazzo floor in the crypt is based on the Story of Creation and the *Book of Kells*. A historical exhibition is open year round. ◉ *Map N4 • 9220 0400 • Worship only; Mass several times daily*

Sydney Tower

4 This 305-m (1,000-ft) icon offers 360 degree views over the Sydney region. The turret has revolving restaurants, a coffee shop and an observation deck. Above this is a 162,000-litre (35,500-gallon) water tank that acts as a stabilizer on windy days. The tower offers two attractions – Skywalk, an adrenaline-filled 45-minute guided walk around the roof with incredible views of the city and the 4D Cinema Experience, a virtual reality ride across Australia with 180-degree cinema screens, holographic imagery and real-motion seating ◉ *Map M4 • Podium Level, 100 Market St • 9333 9222 • Observation Deck and 4D Cinema: Oct–Apr: 10am–8pm daily, May–Sep: 10am–7pm daily • Skywalk: 9am–10pm daily • Adm • www.sydneytowereye.com.au*

Cenotaph at Martin Place

Strand Arcade
Although Melbournians will disagree, this may be Australia's most impressive Victorian-era glass-roofed shopping arcade. Designed by John Spencer and opened in 1892, this quiet and elegant arcade *(see p80)* is home to boutiques, jewellers, tailors, coffee shops and groovy homeware stores such as Funkis and Dinosaur Designs *(see p81)*. Pressed-metal stairs and quaint lifts service the three levels and there is a seating area at the western end of the upper levels where you can enjoy a cup of tea overlooking the shoppers below. ⑤ *Map M3 • 412–414 George St • 9232 4199 • www.strandarcade.com.au*

Strand Arcade

Baroque foyer of the State Theatre

State Theatre
Originally a cinema with over-the-top Gothic, Baroque and Art Deco elements, this 1929 National Trust-classified "Palace of Dreams" was designed by Henry White, who also worked on the Capitol Theatre *(see p29)*. Sweeping staircases embrace its lavish Grand Assembly foyer, and the massive 20,000-piece Koh-i-Nor chandelier dominates the 2,000-seat auditorium. Since 1974, this theatre has been the premier venue for the Sydney Film Festival *(see p73)*. During the year it presents live acts and musical performances, which have included Bette Midler and kd lang. ⑤ *Map M4 • 49 Market St • 9373 6655 • www.statetheatre.com.au • Guided tours, call to book • Adm*

Anzac Memorial
Mirrored in Hyde Park's Pool of Reflection is this 1934 Art Deco monument built to

Anzac Memorial

commemorate Australia's WWI dead *(see p36)*. It now records the sacrifices made by thousands of Australians in subsequent conflicts. The Hall of Memory is on the upper level, overlooking Raynor Hoff's moving statue, and the Hall of Silence is on the ground floor. A small museum on the ground floor features photographs and artifacts. ⑤ *Map N5 • Hyde Park • 9228 5393 • www.anzacmemorial. nsw.gov.au • Open 9am–5pm daily*

Façade of the Queen Victoria Building

8 Queen Victoria Building

The five-storey Romanesque QVB *(see p80)* staggers visitors with its beautiful tiled floors, elegant staircases, stained glass, barrel-vaulted glass ceiling and copper domed roof. Built on the site of the old Sydney markets, this landmark was designed by George McRae and opened to applause in 1898. Today, the QVB houses local and international fashion brands. 🕘 *Map M4*

9 Town Hall

John Henry Wilson originally designed Sydney's civic head-quarters in 1868. The front steps of this Victorian building, with its 1884 clock tower, elegant 1877 vestibule and grand 1889 Cent-nnial Hall, have been a favourite meeting place for Sydneysiders since the original *porte cochère* facing George Street was removed in 1934. 🕘 *Map M4 • 9265 9189 Open 8am 6pm Mon–Fri*

0 St Andrew's Cathedral

Australia's oldest Gothic revival cathedral was designed in 1868 by Edmund Blaket, who also designed St Stephen's *(see p103)*. It contains many memorials to Sydney pioneers, such as the 19th-century merchant-prince Thomas Mort, a major figure in the history of Sydney's harbour.
Map M4 • Sydney Square • 9265 1661 Open 10am–4pm Mon–Sat, 8am–8pm Sun Tours • www.sydneycathedral.com

A Walk from Circular Quay to the QVB

Morning

From **Circular Quay** *(see p18)* follow Loftus Street to **Macquarie Park**, exhibiting the anchor from the First Fleet HMS *Sirius*. Across the road is the 1876 **Lands Department Building**, seat of early European land ownership. Its façade features statues of explorers, including Ludwig Leichhardt and Major Thomas Mitchell. Head to **Martin Place** via George Street and check out the **GPO**'s Pitt Street colonnade with characters representing trades, professions and industries, then sneak a peek through the windows of Martin Place's grand banks. Turn right into **Macquarie Street** *(see p22)*, taking care not to bump into one of the city's "wigs", for this is Sydney's legal district. At **Hyde Park** *(see p50)*, note the lovely Art Deco **Archibald Fountain** and wander down the glorious avenue of fig trees to Park Street. Turn right and take a seat outside the classy **Bambini Trust Café** at 185 Elizabeth Street. Sample an antipasto while you peruse the Specials menu and the passers by.

Afternoon

Head to Market Street and turn left: **Sydney Tower** is one block down on your right and the **Pitt Street Mall** *(see p80)* two blocks down. Turn into the mall and left into the **Strand Arcade** and it's time for a caffeine fix at **Elixir Espresso**. Exit at George Street and turn left. On the next corner is the **QVB** where you can spend the rest of the afternoon happily window-shopping.

For more city centre shopping centres and shops, **see pp80–81**.

Left **Queen Victoria Building** Centre **Entrance to Strand Arcade** Right **Darling Harbour**

🔟 City Shopping Centres

1 Castlereagh Street
Some of Sydney's most glamorous shopping, where you'll find international labels such as Omega, Georg Jensen and Chanel.
⬕ Map M3 • Between Park St & Martin Place

2 Westfield Sydney
Sydney's most expensive retail real estate space, offering six levels of chain stores and food outlets. It includes the Myer and David Jones department stores and designer boutiques. ⬕ Map M3 • Pitt St between King & Market Sts

MLC Centre

3 Strand Arcade
The best of the Pitt Street arcades (see p78) houses gems such as Strand Hatter's, the source of authentic Akubras.

4 Queen Victoria Building
Over five levels, this heritage building houses the best of fashion, food, art, jewellery and antiques (see p79). ⬕ 455 George St • 9264 9209 • www.qvb.com.au

5 The Galeries
Shop for fashion, dine in the food-court or browse at Books Kinokuniya, the largest bookshop chain in the southern hemisphere.
⬕ Map M4 • 500 George St • 9265 6888 • www.thegaleries.com

6 Darling Harbour
Right next to the Aquarium, Maritime and Powerhouse Museums. Stop by for a quick lunch or to buy Aussie souvenirs (see pp28–9).

7 Paddy's Markets
People swarm to the fresh food section of this Chinatown hub. From clothes to souvenirs, you'll find almost anything here (see p29). ⬕ Map L5 • Open Wed–Sun • www.paddysmarkets. com.au

8 Market City
Situated above Paddy's Markets, this centre contains a mix of quirky Korean clothes ("small" is the most common size), electronics, discount outlets and Asian food. ⬕ Map L5

9 MLC Centre
Ideal for large budgets and corporate types. If that's you, head straight to Hunt Leather and the ready-to-wear women's designer store, Belinda (see p100). ⬕ Map M3 • 19–29 Martin Place • 9224 8333 • www.mlccentre.com.au

10 Argyle Stores
In a historic, converted warehouse, this eclectic array includes unique gift shops and fashion houses. ⬕ Map M2 • 18–2 Argyle St, The Rocks

A trademark brand of felt hats, Akubras are distinctively Australian in their wide-brimmed style, durability and comfort.

Interior of Dinosaur Designs

Top 10 One Of A Kind Shops

1 David Jones
Shopping at Sydney's oldest department store is a glamorous experience. DJ's stocks almost everything; pop in for a browse and a snack. ◎ Map M4 • Elizabeth & Market Sts • 9266 5544

2 Art Gallery of NSW
This place is a treasure trove of fine art objects as well as being a great resource if you're looking for imaginative presents for both adults and children. ◎ Map N3 • Art Gallery Rd, The Domain • 9225 1744

3 Done Art & Design
Loud prints of Sydney icons such as the Opera House and cockatoos adorn bright T-shirts and swimwear, which have been hot souvenir items since the 1980s. ◎ Map M1 • 123–25 George St 9251 6099

4 Mooks
Browse through Australian streetwear that's developing a following overseas. Great clothes for boys and girls, including G-Star jeans and Camper shoes.
◎ Map M4 • Ground Floor, Galeries Victoria • 9283 8388

5 Red Eye Records
Sydney's best range of rock music and rare records in an old-style music store. They also sell tickets to local gigs. ◎ Map M3 • 143 York St • 9267 7440

6 Sydney Opera House Store
This is a good place to come for souvenirs that aren't too kitsch, and some great ones that are.
◎ Map N1 • Foyer, Sydney Opera House • 9250 7858

7 Flame Opals
Buy some of Australia's unique opals at this store in The Rocks. ◎ Map M2 • 119 George St • 9247 3446

8 Dinosaur Designs
The team behind this original jewellery and homewares are some of Australia's most celebrated designers. They craft their pieces from jewel-coloured resin. ◎ Map M3 • Strand Arcade • 9223 2953

9 The ABC Shop
This shop has an exciting range of merchandise including DVDs, books and clothing from the national broadcaster's most popular programs. ◎ Map M4 • Shop 48, QVB, 455 George St • 9286 3726

10 Haigh's
Australia's oldest chocolate manufacturer and retailer makes delectable treats using traditional artisan methods. ◎ Map M3 • Shop 1, Ground Floor, Strand Arcade • 9221 6999

World-renowned Aussie wine makes an excellent souvenir or gift, and is available at all bottleshops.

Left **Live seafood tanks at Golden Century** Right **Sign for East Ocean**

Chinatown Eateries

1 Golden Century
The menu is huge, the staff are friendly and the live seafood, which includes coral trout and parrot fish, is amazing. ❧ Map M5 • 393–399 Sussex St • 9212 3901 • www. goldencentury.com.au • No dis access • $$ • Optional BYO

Selection of yum cha

2 The Chinese Noodle
Head to this hole-in-the-wall for home-made Chinese dumplings and noodles. ❧ Map M6 • Thomas St Level, Prince Centre, 8 Quay St, Haymarket • 9281 9051 • $ • Optional BYO

3 Red Chilli
Located in the Harbour Plaza, Red Chilli offers innovative Sichuan cuisine. Try the Chilli Steamboat with noodles, vegetables and meat. ❧ Map M5 • 25–29 Dixon St, Haymarket • 9211 8130 • $$

4 The Emperor's Garden
Their consistent and enticing menu includes classics such as Peking duck and grilled scallops. ❧ Map M5 • 96–100 Hay St, Haymarket • 9211 2135 • $ • Optional BYO

5 Emperor's Garden BBQ & Noodles
A meaty experience starts at the adjoining shop's window, full of hanging ducks and piglets, and ends with tasty duck and pork. ❧ Map M6 • 213–215 Thomas St, Haymarket • 9281 9899 • $$ • Optional BYO

6 Chat Thai
For a Thai restaurant to succeed in the heart of Chinatown, it must be doing something right. Open for breakfast and still serving supper in the small hours. ❧ Map M5 • 20 Campbell St, Haymarket • 9211 1808 • $

7 East Ocean
The food receives as much attention as the cool decor; try the braised sea cucumber or fresh abalone. ❧ Map M5 • Haymarket East Ocean Arcade • 421–29 Sussex St • No dis access • 9212 4198 • $$

8 Marigold
Choose from the indulgent banquet menus or stop in at lunchtime for the famous yum cha. ❧ Map M5 • Levels 4 & 5, 683–689 George St • 9261 8988 • www.marigold.com.au • $

9 Passion Flower
With a fabulous range of original flavours such as lychee, taro and sticky rice, this dessert café makes a great pit stop. ❧ Map M5 • Shop G12, Capitol Square, 730–742 George St • 9281 8322 • $

10 Mother Chu's Vegetarian Kitchen
Warm Buddhist hospitality, canteen decor and delicious vegetarian food. Try the hot pot dishes. ❧ Map M5 • 367 Pitt St • 9283 2828 • Closed Sun • $

Though most of these restaurants are fully licensed, some have an optional policy of BYO, or "bring your own" alcohol.

Price Categories

For a two course meal for one with a drink (or equivalent meal), plus taxes and extra charges.

$	under $35
$$	$35–$60
$$$	$60–$120
$$$$	$120–$200
$$$$$	over $200

View from Café Sydney

TOP 10 Pubs & Restaurants

1 The Living Room
Spectacular views and a luxurious yet relaxed setting make this an idyllic place for a casual meal. ◈ *Map M1 • Park Hyatt Sydney, 7 Hickson Rd, The Rocks • 9256 1661 • $$$*

2 Chinta Ria The Temple of Love
Happiness is welcomed into this lively restaurant by the giant Buddha that takes center stage. The delicious Malaysian food may be an aphrodisiac. ◈ *Map M4 • The Roof Terrace, Level 2, Cockle Bay Wharf, 201 Sussex St • 9264 3211 • $$*

3 Zaaffran
This Indian restaurant offers excellent versions of all the favourites and good value set menus. ◈ *Map L4 • Level 2, 345 Harbourside Shopping Centre, Darling Harbour • 9211 8900 • $$*

4 Café Sydney
The perfect place for a romantic dinner with its moody lighting, a Mod Oz/Asian menu and gorgeous harbour views. Check out the lounge bar and jazz on Sundays. ◈ *Map N2 • Level 5, Customs House, 31 Alfred St, Circular Quay • 9251 8683 • $$$*

5 Café Sopra
Housed in the basement of a heritage building, Café Sopra offers fresh and seasonal Italian food. Try buffalo or smoked mozzarella at the Mozzarella Bar. ◈ *Map M2 • 11 Bridge St • 8298 2701 • Open noon–3pm, 6–10pm Mon–Fri; Bar: noon–10pm Mon–Fri • $$*

6 Slip Inn
This place has five bars over three levels including an outdoor courtyard, with Chinese Laundry nightclub on Fridays and Saturdays. ◈ *Map L3 • 111 Sussex St • 8295 9999 • Open Mon–Sat • $$*

7 Cruise Bar & Restaurant
This swanky bar is perfectly placed for Opera House views and offers an extensive cocktail list. ◈ *Map M1 • Level 1–3, Overseas Passenger Terminal, West Circular Quay • 9251 1188 • $$$*

8 Bar Europa
In a city of glitzy views, this underground bar makes a pleasant change. Try the delicious cocktails and good bar food. ◈ *Map M3 • Basement, 82 Elizabeth St • 9232 3377 • Open Tue–Sat • $*

9 Bungalow 8
It doesn't do cocktails, but punters flock to this giant waterside pub until bouncers are turning the hordes away. Get there early and be prepared for the very mainstream crowd. ◈ *Map L3 • The Promenade, King St Wharf • 9299 4660 • $$*

10 Eleni's at Civic
This bistro, in a charming 1930s-style Art Deco pub, serves generous portions of Greek comfort food. Eleni's moussaka is her signature dish, with a rustic Greek salad designed for sharing. ◈ *Map M5 • Civic Hotel, cnr Pitt & Goulburn sts • 8080 7030 • $*

Unless otherwise stated, all restaurants are open daily, accept credit cards, serve vegetarian meals, and provide disabled access.

Left **Detail of Del Rio's Façade** Right **Elizabeth Bay**

Kings Cross & Darlinghurst

THE REPUTATION OF "THE CROSS" *as a hotbed of sex and decadence may be well earned, but behind this red-light district's resident junkies and prostitutes is an interesting suburb with a rich bohemian history. Cool cafés and great Art Deco apartment buildings make up its backstreets. To the north, you'll find Potts Point with its fine Colonial villas and Victorian terrace houses, and to the east the solid middle-class enclaves of Rushcutter's Bay and Elizabeth Bay, named after Mrs Macquarie (see p20). Darlinghurst is far more hip than its northern neighbour, with a heady parade of groovers and wannabes competing with the suburb's less well-heeled residents. To the northwest is East Sydney, with its "Little Italy" centred around Stanley Street, and to the north Woolloomooloo or "the Loo", a former docklands precinct with an energetic mix of public housing estates and smart apartments.*

Left **Café on Victoria Street** Right **Neon sign marking the entrance to Kings Cross**

🔟 Sights

1. Darlinghurst Court House & Old Darlinghurst Gaol
2. Sydney Jewish Museum
3. Victoria Street
4. Darlinghurst Road
5. El Alamein Fountain
6. Elizabeth Bay
7. The McElhone Stairs
8. Tusculum & Rockwall Villas
9. Elizabeth Bay House
10. Rushcutters Bay Park

Share your travel recommendations on traveldk.com

Old Darlinghurst Gaol

1 Darlinghurst Court House & Old Darlinghurst Gaol

Mortimer Lewis designed the central section of this Greek Revival court house in 1844, and James Barnet *(see p99)* designed the side wings in 1880. The 1841 Old Darlinghurst Gaol behind the court house was also designed by Mortimer Lewis and added to by James Barnet. In its early years, public hangings were conducted inside the gaol. In 1914 it became an internment facility for WWI "enemy aliens". It now houses the National Art School. ◎ Map P5 • Forbes St, Darlinghurst • Court House: • 9368 2947 • Open Feb–Dec: 10am–4pm Mon–Fri

2 Sydney Jewish Museum

Following WWII almost 30,000 Holocaust survivors migrated to Australia, many of them settling in Sydney. This museum *(see p42)* explores Australian Jewish history through recordings of survivors, audio-visual displays and photographs. The ground floor deals with Jewish life following white settlement, and the upper levels focus on the Holocaust, whose survivors act as guides. ◎ Map P5 • 148 Darlinghurst Rd, Darlinghurst • 9360 7999 • Open 10am–4pm Sun–Thur, 10am–2pm Fri • Adm • www.sydneyjewishmuseum.com.au

3 Victoria Street

This leafy stretch of Victorian terrace houses in Potts Point was a major flashpoint during the 1970s Green Bans *(see p37)*. Pressure to demolish the terraces to make way for high-rise developments was resisted by residents and Juanita Nielsen, the local community newspaper publisher. On 4 July 1975, Nielsen attended a meeting at the Carousel Club in nearby Kings Cross; she was never seen again. Nobody in Sydney has any doubt as to the motive of her killer or killers. ◎ Map P3

4 Darlinghurst Road

Darlinghurst Road runs from the court house to the El Alamein Fountain. "The Wall", a sandstone wall running beside the gaol, is a nocturnal beat for male prosti-tutes. The pleasant Green Park is thought to be named after a former hangman at the gaol, Alexander "The Strangler" Green. Beyond the park is a colourful strip of terrace houses, hotels and cafés that ends at William Street. In the 1920s and 30s the area beyond William Street had some bohemian charm, but since WWII it has been Australia's most notorious red-light district. ◎ Map P4

> **Mr Eternity**
>
> During the Depression, a near-illiterate, reformed alcoholic took to writing "Eternity" in perfect copperplate script on pavements across the city. Arthur Stace thought he'd received instructions from God while at the Baptist Church in Darlinghurst, and he wrote the word "Eternity" half a million times before his death in 1967. An aluminium plaque in tribute to Stace can be found near the Sydney Square waterfall.

5 El Alamein Fountain

This dandelion-shaped fountain in the Fitzroy Gardens is especially pleasant when illuminated at night. Though many consider it overrated, it is still probably Sydney's most popularly known public artwork. Designed by Robert Woodward in 1961, it commemorates the participation of Australian soldiers in the Battle of El Alamein in Egypt during WWII, which precipitated Germany's defeat in North Africa. ◎ *Map Q4 • Fitzroy Gardens: Macleay St, Elizabeth Bay • Open 24 hrs daily*

El Alamein Fountain at dusk

6 Elizabeth Bay

A world away from the seediness of nearby Kings Cross, Elizabeth Bay's narrow, winding streets are packed with apartment buildings, including Art Deco gems such as Del Rio on Billyard Avenue, near Elizabeth Bay House. It is also home to several harbourside mansions, including Boomerang (see p15), and nearby Berthong, which Russell Crowe owned before moving up to the industrial chic of the Woolloomooloo Finger Wharf. The tiny Arthur McElhone Reserve (see p51), is overlooked by 100 apartment balconies, but the unpretentious Beare Park can be found just down the hill, on the harbour's edge. ◎ *Map Q3*

7 The McElhone Stairs

These stone stairs link Woolloomooloo Bay with Potts Point and The Cross. Near the bottom of the stairs on Cowper Wharf Road is Harry's Café de Wheels, a pie cart that's been a Sydney late-night institution for over 50 years. Its walls are festooned with photos of famous patrons, mostly politicians and pop stars, tucking into meat pies. Nearby is the Woolloomooloo Finger Wharf (see p15), which houses upmarket bars and restaurants. ◎ *Map P3*

8 Tusculum & Rockwall Villas

"Villa conditions" were actually established in the 1830s to ensure that the hillside overlooking Woolloomooloo Bay attracted the "right sort". All new houses had to face Government House (see p21), cost a fortune, and be approved by the governor of the day. John Verge designed both Tusculum and Rockwall. The Australian Institute of Architects now occupies the former, which has a great bookshop specialising in architectural titles. Rock-wall is a private residence originally built for engineer John Busby, whose bore delivered Sydney's first permanent fresh water supply. ◎ *Map Q4 • Tusculum: 3 Manning St, Potts Point • Bookshop: Open 9am–5:30pm Mon–Fri, 10am–4pm Sat • Rockwall: Macleay St, Potts Point*

Tusculum Villa window

9 Elizabeth Bay House

Alexander Macleay, Colonial Secretary of NSW from 1825 to 1837, had architect John Verge design this residence for his large family in 1839. Macleay was also a distinguished botanist

The dining room at Elizabeth Bay House

and the first president of the Australian Museum. This Greek Revival residence is said to contain the finest example of a Colonial interior anywhere in Australia. Macleay's family subdivided the original 23 ha (56 acres) of land following his death. In 1941 the house was further divided into 15 apartments. The NSW government purchased the property in the 1960s and the Historic Houses Trust undertook major restoration. It finally reopened as a museum in 1977. ◈ Map Q3 • 7 Onslow Ave, Elizabeth Bay • 9356 3022 • Open 9:30am–4pm Fri–Sun • Adm

Rushcutters Bay Park

Rushcutters Bay, now the mooring of choice for some of Sydney's finest yachts and the home of the Cruising Yacht Club, was the site of one of the settlers' first run-ins with the local Eora people, on 30 May 1788. The Eora speared two convicts, who were collecting rushes for roof thatching after having stolen a fishing canoe. Today, this pleasant park contains tennis courts, a quaint picket-fenced cricket ground and stadium, lovely Moreton Bay fig trees and a pleasant kiosk and café. The park is much loved by both locals and their poodles. ◈ Map Q4

Afternoon Meander Through Kings Cross

🕐 Begin at the El Alamein Fountain Walk down Macleay Street and you'll pass the **Rex Hotel**, site of Sydney's first gay bar in the 1940s, the **Bottoms Up**. Turn into Greenknowe Avenue and walk down the hill and left into leafy Ithaca Road, where you'll catch glimpses of the harbour. **Beare Park** is tucked between the high-rise apartments. From the wharf there's a good view of **Boomerang**, the Spanish Mission mansion. Walk up Billyard Avenue to **Elizabeth Bay House**, passing the **Del Rio**, another Californian Spanish Mission building. Steps on Onslow Avenue will bring you back up the hill to Macleay Street.

☕ Turning right, stroll down to the **Brass** (see p89). Have a coffee or choose from the wide range of cocktails.

Refreshed, walk down Challis Avenue into **Embarkation Park** for great views of the Naval Base at **Woolloomooloo**. Continue up Victoria Street, past the terrace houses to Hughes Street. Turn left into the Tusculum Street, and then Manning Street. Next door to **Tusculum Villa**, the **Werrington** and the **Wychbury** are some of the best Art Deco buildings in the Cross.

On your way back up Macleay Street, pop into Orwell Street to see the old **Metro Theatre**, where a nightclub roared in the 1930s. Finish up your afternoon tour with a drink at the lively and elegant **Trademark Hotel** (see p70).

Bar at ARQ Sydney

TOP 10 Gay Bars

1 ARQ Sydney
The giant dance floor here is overlooked by a mezzanine where you can people-watch. Pounding commercial house music ensures it's packed by midnight. ✪ *Map N5 • 16 Flinders St, Taylor Square • 9380 8700 • www.arqsydney.com.au • Dis access*

2 Midnight Shift Hotel
Although this stalwart of the Sydney scene is known as a meat market, it can be fun. It's usually the last stop on a club crawl. Women are not really welcome. ✪ *Map N5 • 85 Oxford St, Darlinghurst • 9358 3848 • www.themidnightshift.com*

3 Colombian
Grab a cocktail and enjoy people-watching from a window seat or hit the dance floor at weekends. ✪ *Map N5 • 117 Oxford St, Darlinghurst • 9360 2151 • www.colombian.com.au*

4 Oxford Arts Factory
The After Dark Bar here is a meeting place for Sydney's art crowd. It's a versatile venue hosting everything from bands to computer game launches. ✪ *Map N5 • 38–46 Oxford St, Darlinghurst • 9332 3711 • www.oxfordfactory.com*

5 Stonewall
Three levels include a bar, dance floor and lounge bar. There is entertainment seven nights a week with the Male Box on Wednesday being very popular. ✪ *Map Nb • 175 Oxford St, Darlinghurst • 9360 1963 • www.stonewallhotel.com*

6 Phoenix Bar
This dance bar features underground and alternative music. Doors open at 5am on weekends for popular "Recovery" parties. ✪ *Map N5 • Exchange Hotel basement, 34 Oxford St, Darlinghurst • 9331 2956 • www.exchangehotel.biz*

7 Slide Bar
Billed as the most surprising venue in Sydney, this bar can produce anything from Parisian cabaret to international DJs. ✪ *Map N5 • 41 Oxford St, Darlinghurst • 8915 1899 • www.slide.com.au*

8 Brighton Up Bar
Enjoy the dance nights with special guest DJs at this laid-back bar located on the second level of an unspoilt, traditional pub. ✪ *Map N5 • Level 2, 77 Oxford St, Darlinghurst • 9361 3379*

9 Oxford Hotel
Its central location, Underground Nightclub downstairs and two cocktail lounge bars upstairs, make this a great place to meet friends. ✪ *Map N5 • 134 Oxford St, Darlinghurst • 8324 5200 • www.theoxfordhotel.com.au • Dis access*

10 Headquarters
This is a men-only cruise club with a video lounge, a gym and regular skin and themed parties. ✪ *Map N5 • 273 Crown St, Darlinghurst • 9331 6217 • www.headquarters.com.au*

Male Box is a pick-up game in which men wear numbers and send "mail" (messages) to each other via a big screen.

Price Categories

For a two course meal
for one with a drink
(or equivalent meal),
plus taxes and extra
charges.

$	under $35
$$	$35–$60
$$$	$60–$120
$$$$	$120–$200
$$$$$	over $200

The interior of The Fish Shop

TOP 10 Places to Eat

1 Brass
Van-Gogh-yellow walls and creative food make one of the most famous buildings in the Cross stand out. A café by the day and a hip bar and bistro when the sun sets. ⊗ Map Q3 • 57 Macleay St, Potts Point • 9357 3400 • $$

2 The Fish Shop
A comfortable bistro offers freshly-cooked seafood and an effortlessly stylish crowd. ⊗ Map Q3 • 22 Challis Ave, Potts Point • 9326 9000 • Dinner daily • $

3 Spring Espresso
Get coffee and snacks with Sydney's most glamorous people, where it's all about being seen. ⊗ Map Q3 • 66 Macleay St, Potts Point • 9331 0190 • No dis access • $

4 Fratelli Paradiso
Another haunt of the style set, this time with a distinct Melbourne twist. Servings of the Italian food are small, so make sure to order some home-made pastries. ⊗ Map Q3 • 12–16 Challis Ave, Potts Point • 9357 1744 • $$

5 Jimmy Liks
A buzzing joint with Asian-inspired cocktails that set off the fresh and delicious flavours of the curries and stir-fries. ⊗ Map P4 • 188 Victoria St, Potts Point • 8354 1400 • Dinner daily • $$

6 Hugo's Bar Pizza
The creative Italian food here includes pizza that has been named the best in the world at the New York pizza challenge. ⊗ Map P4 • 33 Bayswater Rd, Kings Cross • 9332 1227 • Dinner daily • $$

7 Buon Ricordo
Owner and chef Armando Percuoco's award-winning Italian restaurant is extremely popular with local foodies. ⊗ Map P5 • 108 Boundary St, Darlinghurst • 9360 6729 • No dis access • $$$

8 Fu-Manchu
A tiny, excellent Chinese noodle bar with good vegetarian options. ⊗ Map P4 • 229 Darlinghurst Rd, Darlinghurst • 9360 9424 • Dinner daily • No dis access • $$

9 Tomislav
A casual appearance belies the expert approach to modern food at this understated restaurant. A small dining area opens out to an over sized balcony with iconic Sydney views. ⊗ Map P5 • 13 Kirketon Rd, Darlinghurst • 9356 4535 • Dinner Tue-Sat • $$

10 Phamish
Fun, cheap and bustling, this Vietnamese café serves fresh and tasty food. ⊗ Map N5 • 248 Palmer St • 9357 2688 • Dinner Tue–Sun • No dis access • $

When you have finished eating at Hugo's Bar Pizza, head upstairs to Hugo's lounge for drinks and a dancefloor.

Left **Five Ways in Paddington** Centre **Victoria Barracks** Right **Sydney Cricket Ground**

Paddington & Surry Hills

ACK IN THE 1960S, *Paddington's neglected Victorian charms were rediscovered by "trendies" who zealously set about restoring the area's* terraces. Most of Paddington's working-class residents took fright and fled to suburbs far away. Now mostly white-collar families occupy the renovated terraces, and this hilly district, bordered by Centennial Park, Moore Park, Darlinghurst and the Eastern Suburbs, is one of Sydney's smartest addresses.

Its main strip, Oxford Street, is a window-shopper's heaven and its backstreets a delight for anyone who loves Victorian architecture. Surry Hills' charms took a little longer to be appreciated, but now this suburb rivals Darlinghurst and Newtown as one of the grooviest districts in Sydney. But it wasn't always so. During the Great Depression, Surry Hills was one of Sydney's most notorious slums and the haunt of razor gang queen Kate Leigh (see p37). This dark period in its history was perfectly captured by the writer Ruth Park (see p41).

Victorian "Iron Lace" detailing

🔟 Sights

1. Victorian Terrace Houses
2. Paddington Markets
3. Paddington Town Hall
4. Juniper Hall
5. Victoria Barracks
6. Oxford & Crown Sts
7. Sydney Cricket Ground
8. Sydney Football Stadium
9. The Entertainment Quarter
10. Whiteley Studio

 Sign up for DK's email newsletter on traveldk.com

Victorian Terrace Houses

Many of Paddington's lovely terrace houses, with their narrow frontages, iron-work verandas and pocket-handkerchief gardens, were erected following the construction of the Victoria Barracks *(see p92)* in the 1840s. The area went into decline during 1931's Great Depression, but an influx of migrants revitalised the area after WWII. Many of those migrants moved out following the suburb's gentrification in the 1960s and '70s. Some of the most interesting examples of the Victorian terrace style are found in Glenmore and Jersey Roads, and Cascade, Liverpool, Windsor and Paddington Streets.

Victorian terrace houses in Paddington

Paddington Markets

These just might be Sydney's best loved weekend markets. They're held every Saturday in the shaded grounds of Paddington Village's St John's Uniting Church. Ever since 1973, this alfresco bazaar has been a great place to shop for jewellery, crafts, fashion, pottery, soaps, second-hand clothing and the like. It's always had a New Age bent, so you're also likely to find someone who can massage those travel-weary shoulders, read your tarot cards or fine tune your chakras. *Map Q6 • www.paddingtonmarkets.com.au*

Paddington Town Hall

This Classical Revival Town Hall on Oxford Street was designed by J Kemp, a local architect who won an international competition to design a civic centre that matched the suburb's increasing status. The main building was completed in 1891, and the clock tower that now dominates was added several years later. The town hall is no longer used by the council but is seen as the centre for community activities. The hall houses the suburb's library, offices, and a radio station. It is also a regular venue for private functions and corporate events. *Map Q6*

Juniper Hall

Robert Cooper (1776–1857) was one of Sydney's more successful emancipists and a self-confessed smuggler. Originally sent down for receiving stolen goods, Cooper made a small fortune as Sydney's first distiller, specialising in gin flavoured with juniper berries: hence the name of this residence. Situated diagonally opposite the Town Hall, Juniper Hall was built in 1824 to house his 28 children from three marriages. The house was threatened with demolition for several years, but finally spared in the 1980s and restored by the National Trust. *Map Q6*

Paddington Markets

Victoria Barracks

5 Occupying 12 ha (30 acres), these barracks were built between 1841 and 1848. They are immediately recognisable from Oxford Street by their high sandstone walls; many regard this complex of late Georgian buildings as one of the finest military barracks in the world. The architect was Major George Barney, who also designed Fort Denison *(see p38)*. Until 1870 the barracks were home to British troops; today they are an Australian Army facility. The Army Museum is housed in the former military prison and contains several interesting exhibits tracing the military heritage of New South Wales. ◉ *Map P6 • Oxford St • Open 10am–1pm Thu, 10am–3pm Sun; tours 10am Thu • Army Museum: 9339 3330 • Open 10am–12:30pm Thu, 10am–4pm Sun*

Oxford & Crown Streets

6 Despite past upheavals, Oxford Street has reclaimed its reputation as Sydney's most fashion-conscious shopping strip with distinctive boutiques. Although it runs all the way from Hyde Park to Bondi Junction, the prime shopping drag is on the north side of the road between Barcom Avenue and Queen Street *(see p97)*, which runs down to Woollahra. Surry Hills' Crown Street is less conspicuous and polished than its northern rival, but it's gaining a reputation as a good spot to source homewares, designer and retro furniture and fashion items. It has some great cafés, ethnic restaurants and grocers, pubs and factory outlets. ◉ *Map N5*

Sydney Cricket Ground

Sydney Cricket Ground

7 Stationed at Victoria Barracks in 1851, the British Army were told to take their bats and balls and entertain themselves on the empty land south of the barracks. Ever since, this site *(see p53)* has been the spiritual home for millions of cricket-mad Sydneysiders. In January 1928, fans saw Sir Donald Bradman's first-class cricket debut here. The venue has also hosted concerts by the Rolling Stones, Madonna and Green Day, as well as Australian Rules Football matches. Tours allow visitors into the dressing rooms and on to the hallowed turf.

Allianz Stadium

8 Designed by Phillip Cox, this stadium *(see pp47 & 53)* was completed in 1988 to coincide with Australia's Bicentenary. The ground was ostensibly designed for Sydney's preferred football code, Rugby League, but it has occasionally permitted upstarts from the southern code, Australian Rules, to take to the field. Soccer was played here during the 2000 Sydney Olympics and has now become a regular event. The Stadium has also held several concert performances, which have included

Entrance to Victoria Barracks

shows by U2, Robbie Williams and Barbra Streisand. ◈ *Tour Experience tours of Sydney Football Stadium, SCG and Cricket Museum: 1300 724 737 • 10am, noon & 2pm Mon–Fri, 10am Sat • Adm*

9 The Entertainment Quarter
This massive entertainment complex houses a variety of restaurants including Chinese, traditional Italian, the Bavarian Bier Café and modern Australian dining. Entertainment options include two movie complexes, bowling, pool, karaoke, a Comedy Store and three pubs. Late night shopping is open every night in an open-air area. There are two kids' playgrounds and two child entertainment venues. The Entertainment Quarter is also home to two of the best markets in Sydney, The EQ Farmers' Market and Sydney's Bent Street Bazaar merchandise market.
◈ *Map E5 • Lang Rd, Moore Park • Farmers' Market: 10am–3:30pm Wed & Sat • Bent Street Bazaar Market: 10am–4pm Sun • Most shops open 10am–10pm daily www.eqmoorepark.com.au*

10 Whiteley Studio
Tucked down a Surry Hills backstreet, the former studio of artist Brett Whiteley *(see pp26 & 34)* is now a public museum and art gallery. Whiteley painted some of Sydney's most iconic works. He loved the harbour and the nude, and both feature in his paintings. In 1985 he converted this former factory into a studio but, just seven years later, he was found dead from a heroin overdose in a motel room in the south coast township of Thirroul. The gallery has regular exhibitions and displays the artist's studio much as it was before he died.

A Morning Stroll Through Paddington

From the **Darlinghurst Court House** *(see p85)* follow Oxford Street as far as the imposing sandstone walls of **Victoria Barracks**. Turn left into Glenmore Road, which has a cluster of small but classy boutiques. Gipps Street leads to Liverpool Street, which is a winding road of elegant double-storey terraces reminiscent of some of London's wealthier Victorian districts, and the **Australian Galleries'** collection of works on paper *(see p45)*, is down Walker Lane. Rejoin Glenmore Road and follow this winding and busy thoroughfare to **Five Ways**, a quaint little intersection with several good cafés, including **Gusto**.

After coffee and a snack, head up Broughton Street to the narrow laneway and steps on your left. At the bottom of the lane turn right and walk down to steep Cascade Street. Turn right and walk uphill past Windsor Street's incredibly narrow terraces to Paddington Street. Follow this elegant fig tree-lined avenue up to Jersey Road, passing **Tim Olsen Gallery** *(see p45)* and several of Sydney's premier addresses en route. Turn right into Jersey Road, then into narrow Caledonia Street, which leads back to McGarvie Street where several eccentric balconies overhang the narrow pavement. Turn into Underwood Street and you'll find the **London Tavern**, happy to serve you a well-earned drink. The pub has a superb bistro attached and is located near William Street, which also has several boutiques.

Around Town – Paddington & Surry Hills

93

Left **Display at Mecca Cosmetica** Right **Interior of Zimmermann**

TOP 10 Fashion & Homewares

1 Orson & Blake
This one-stop shop for the hippest of hip combines a boutique, bookshop, furniture showroom, café and gallery.
Map D5 • 483 Riley St, Surry Hills • 8399 2525 • www.orsonandblake.com.au

2 Planet
There's plenty that's portable here, such as wonderful textiles and ceramics. Each piece comes with information about its creator, and can be giftwrapped. Map N6 • 114 Commonwealth St, Surry Hills • 9211 5959 • www.planetfurniture.com.au

3 Capital L
All the hottest names in Aussie design are crammed into this tiny shop. Map P6 • 100 Oxford St, Paddington • 9361 0111 • www.capital-l.com.

4 Mecca Cosmetica
Mecca stocks cult cosmetic brands such as Kiehl's and Stila, and is happy to advise on their application. Map P6 • 126 Oxford St, Paddington • 9361 4488 • www.meccacosmetica.com.au

5 Scanlan & Theodore
A darling of the Sydney fashion scene for over 20 years, Scanlan & Theodore offers simple yet elegant designs made from luxurious fabrics.
Map P6 • 122 Oxford St, Paddington • 9380 9388 • www.scanlantheodore.com.au

6 Andrew McDonald
On a street of designer names, this little shop may not stand out. But it hand-crafts gorgeous shoes for men and women. Map Q6 • 58 William St, Paddington • 9358 6793 • www.andrewmcdonald.com.au

7 Zimmermann
Check out the fantastic range of women's swimwear and gorgeous clothing. Map P6 • Shop 2, 2–16 Glenmore Rd, Paddington • 9357 4700 • www.zimmermannwear.com

8 Easton Pearson
This much-lauded designer duo specialises in unusual textiles and embellishments. Favoured by a slightly older clientele who can afford the hefty price tags. Map R6 • 30 Glenmore Rd, Paddington • 9331 4433 • www.eastonpearson.com

9 Cloth
Bold, original designs are hand-screened onto natural fibres. Buy lengths of fabric or soft furnishings. Map D5 • 35 Buckingham St, Surry Hills • 9699 2266 • www.clothfabric.com

Cushions at Cloth

10 Akira
Nothing compares to Akira's one-of-a-kind designs; his delicate and ephemeral garments are virtually art pieces and coveted by all. Map F5 • 12A Queen St, Woollahra • 9361 5221 • www.akira.com.a

If you need a break during shopping, stop for a bite at Sloane, 312 Oxford Street.

Price Categories

For a two course meal for one with a drink (or equivalent meal), plus taxes and extra charges.	
$	under $35
$$	$35–$60
$$$	$60–$120
$$$$	$120–$200
$$$$$	over $200

The entrance to Red Lantern

TOP 10 Hot Spots

1 Red Lantern
A relaxed atmosphere and red interior add to the fun, but also go for the fresh and spicy southern Vietnamese food and good vegetarian options. Booking is essential. ◎ Map D5 • 545 Crown St, Surry Hills • 9698 4355 • Tue–Sun dinner, Tue–Fri lunch • $$

2 Il Baretto
It's always packed and you can't reserve, but they'll send you to a nearby pub and collect you when a table's ready. Cheap, authentic and delicious pasta. ◎ Map D5 • 496 Bourke St, Surry Hills • 9361 6163 • Open Mon–Sat • BYO • No credit cards • $

3 Mahjong Room
Shanghai-style Chinese food, served on carved wooden mah-jong tables, offers that important comfort factor. ◎ Map J5 • 312 Crown St, Darlinghurst • 9361 7985 • Mon–Sat dinner • BYO • $$

4 Uchi Lounge
The warm but minimal design of this small bar provides excellent environs for the fusion French-Japanese food. ◎ Map N5 • 15 Brisbane St, Surry Hills • 9261 3524 • Mon–Sat dinner, Thu–Fri lunch • $$

5 Asslette
Local foodies lamenting the loss of Bécause were delighted when Assiette arrived with its fine modern European cuisine. ◎ Map D3 • 48 Albion St, Surry Hills • 9212 7979 • Tue–Sat dinner, Fri lunch • $$$

6 The Forresters
An unpretentious bar offering cold beer, wines and a large menu of Italian dishes. ◎ Map D4 • Cnr Foveaux & Riley St, Surry Hills • 9219 3035

7 Clock Hotel
This place surges into life after work with locals revelling in happy hour throughout its four bars. ◎ Map D5 • 470 Crown St, Surry Hills • 9331 5333 • $$

8 Light Brigade Hotel
Bypass the spruced-up sports bar and head upstairs to a fantastic modern Italian restaurant for a feast. ◎ Map E6 • 2a Oxford St, Woollahra • 9357 0888 • $

9 Lo-Fi
Sip a cocktail and watch Taylor Square from the balcony of this bar, which maintains the perfect balance of glitz and hip. ◎ Map N5 • Kinselas, 383 Bourke St, Taylor Square, Darlinghurst • 9331 3100

10 Muum Maam
Serving Thai food, Muum Maam is a street-style tuk shop by day and a casual eatery by night. ◎ Map D4 • Shop 1/50 Holt St, Surry Hills • 9318 0881 • Lunch: 11:30am–3pm Mon–Fri; Dinner: 6pm–10pm Mon–Sat • $$

> Unless otherwise stated, all restaurants are open daily, accept credit cards, serve vegetarian meals and provide disabled access.

Left **Detail on the Macquarie Lighthouse** Right **Beachside at Watsons Bay**

Eastern Suburbs

I F YOU'VE GOT THE MONEY *this is a fantastic place to buy real estate,
especially on the harbour. In Colonial times, some of Sydney's wealthiest
citizens built country estates on these north-facing slopes overlooking the
water. These were later subdivided, but the Eastern Suburbs remain leafy,
manicured and ever-so-well spoken. With exclusive private schools, million-
dollar marinas, golf clubs and more salons and day spas than you can count,
the Eastern Suburbs are absolutely "gorgeous". There are several idyllic
harbourside beaches and swimming pools, and numerous harbourside and
parkland walking options. If you're lucky, you might even spot the rare and
endangered "blue-rinse", a hairstyle once favoured by Eastern Suburbs
dowagers that could almost qualify as a heritage-listed feature. If spending
money is your thing, rest assured: where there's
money, there's shopping. And the Eastern Suburbs
have some prime retail strips, especially in
Woollahra and Double Bay.*

The Gap

🔟 Sights

1. Queen Street
2. Double Bay
3. Rose Bay
4. Nielsen Park
5. Greycliffe House
6. Vaucluse House
7. Watsons Bay
8. Camp Cove &
   South Head
9. The Gap
10. Macquarie Lighthouse

Share your travel recommendations on traveldk.com

Queen Street

Queen Street

You won't find any rustic treasures in the antiques shops that line this leafy street downhill from Paddington's Oxford Street. Items here are super expensive, such as Louis XIV clocks, original Colonial prints, 18th-century Persian rugs, and estate jewellery. Even if your wallet is drained, it's still a fun place to window-shop and there are some excellent cafés nearby. ◉ Map F5

Double Bay

The immense wealth of "Double Pay" is almost a joke; people call it the plastic surgery capital of Australia. To the west is exclusive Darling Point, where you'll find Major Mitchell's (see p79) former harbourside residence on Carthona Avenue. To the east is Point Piper, which was home to Sir Lawrence Hargrave (see p31) from 1902 to 1915. In between is Steyne Park and the delightful Redleaf Pool, just below the lovely Blackburn Gardens on New South Head Road. William Street, Bay Street and New South Head Road border the main shopping precinct, where you'll find all the best international retail stores. ◉ Map F4

Rose Bay

The largest cove in Sydney Harbour is embraced by Point Piper to the west and Vaucluse to the east. Northeast of Point Piper is Shark Island (see p15). To the east is Hermit Point, reputedly the haunt of a reclusive former convict. In 1942 a Japanese submarine lobbed shells into Rose Bay, presumably aiming for the former flying-boat base; it's still the base for Sydney Harbour's seaplanes (see p17). If you've followed New South Head Road over from Double Bay, you'll enjoy the walk along the waterfront from Rose Bay Park to Lyne Park. ◉ Map G4

Nielsen Park

Part of Sydney Harbour National Park, Nielsen Park (see p51) makes its way from winding Vaucluse Road down to Shark Bay, so named for the sharks caught here in the days before shark nets. In the centre of the park is the Mt Trefle Walk, and near the beach are changing pavilions, a great kiosk, Greycliffe House (see p98) and a memorial to the Harbour Foreshore Vigilance Committee (see p15). The Hermitage Foreshore Walk starts west of Shark Beach, and offers some of the best views of Sydney as it meanders along the shoreline back to Rose Bay via Hermit Point. Don't forget your swimsuit.

Snakes Alive

The lush grounds of Vaucluse House (see p98) owe a debt of gratitude to Sir Henry Browne Hayes. This Irish baronet, exiled for kidnapping a Quaker heiress, was so petrified of snakes that he imported tons of turf blessed by St Patrick in an effort to rid his 205-ha (508-acre) estate of the scaly vermin.

Left **Greycliffe House in Nielsen Park** Right **Watsons Bay**

Greycliffe House

After WC Wentworth's *(see p37 & below)* daughter was married, her husband commissioned the architect John Hilly to construct this Gothic residence. However, the couple left for England before its 1851 completion. It later became a home for mothers and babies, before the NSW government purchased the property in 1911. The ground floor is now open to the public, while the NPWS *(see p14)* occupies the rest of the building. ✆ *Map G2 • Nielsen Park • 9337 5511*

Vaucluse House

William Charles Wentworth purchased this property which was built in 1803, in 1827. Wentworth was a major figure in the early colony – a barrister, explorer and statesman, he railed against the privileges enjoyed by the English-born colonists and lobbied for self-government. The Wentworths lived in this Gothic house until 1861. It has been a public museum since 1910. ✆ *Map H2 • Wentworth Rd, Vaucluse • 9388 7922 • Open 9:30am–4pm Fri–Sun (daily Jan) • Adm*

Vaucluse House

Watsons Bay

Named after Robert Watson, the quartermaster on the HMS *Sirius (see p79)*, this bay has been the base for Sydney Harbour's pilot boats since the 1800s. Uphill from Robertson Park are the Greycliffe Memorial Gates, which commemorate the 41 people who lost their lives when the ferry *Greycliffe* went down in 1927. ✆ *Map H1*

Camp Cove & South Head

Just north of Watsons Bay is Camp Cove, where Governor Phillip spent the night after decamping from Botany Bay *(see pp36 & 38)* and entered Port Jackson for the first time. A track leads from the kiosk at the northern end of this protected beach over to tiny male-nudist Lady Bay Beach, which is overlooked by the HMAS *Watson* Naval Base. At the end of the track is South Head's Hornby Lighthouse and several old gun emplacements *(see p51)*. This windswept headland offers spectacular views out to sea, across to Manly and the North Harbour. ✆ *Map H1*

The Gap

9 Perhaps Sydney's most infamous headland, this bluff, overlooking the ocean and the wave-lashed rocks far below, has seen more than its fair share of suicides. South of The Gap is the rusting anchor of the *Dunbar* *(see p36)* and further south again is Jacob's Ladder: the sole survivor of the 1857 *Dunbar* tragedy was hauled to safety up this cleft in the rocks. Further south again is the signal station that has been monitoring shipping in and out of Sydney Harbour since 1848. ◎ *Map H1*

Macquarie Lighthouse

Macquarie Lighthouse

10 Australia's longest continuously operating lighthouse stands on the windswept clifftops of Vaucluse. The original lighthouse, built between 1816 and 1818, was designed by noted convict architect Francis Greenway *(see p23)*. It was the first of many projects Greenway completed for Governor Macquarie, earning him a conditional pardon. Within 60 years of its construction the eroded tower was held together with iron bands and in 1883 a new lighthouse was built by architect James Barnet *(seep85)* to closely resemble the original. The tower is open to the public every two months. *Map H2 • www.harbourtrust.gov.au*

An Eastern Suburbs Stroll

Morning

Catch the Bondi Explorer or a 325 bus from **Circular Quay** *(see p18)* and get off at **Nielsen Park**. It's a short walk downhill to **Greycliffe House** and **Shark Beach**. When you're ready, walk back to Vaucluse Road, which becomes Wentworth Road. The entrance to **Vaucluse House** is further down on the right. Continue along Wentworth and take the first right into Chapel Road. WC Wentworth's gloomy mausoleum is just up the hill on your left. Steps lead from behind the mausoleum to Fitzwilliam Street. Turn right and walk downhill to the lane on your left, which takes you across the Parsley Bay suspension footbridge. Take the steps on your left leading up to **The Crescent** and follow this around until you reach Palmerston Street, which leads to **Watsons Bay Pilot Station**. Follow Marine Parade north to the ferry wharf where you can get fish and chips.

Afternoon

After lunch, walk to Short Street at the end of the beach, turn immediately left into Cove Street, and then left again into Pacific Street. This leads up to **Green Point** overlooking **Camp Cove**. After enjoying a swim here, or at the nudist **Lady Bay Beach** further on, follow the path along the clifftops to **South Head**. Retrace your steps and catch the ferry from **Watsons Bay** back to Circular Quay, or the bus from Hopetoun Avenue.

Left **Jan Logan's interior** Centre **Jewellery at Jan Logan** Right **Axel Mano**

TOP 10 Luxury Shopping

1 Axel Mano
If you're planning some time in the sun, come here to find that very special hat. ⊗ *Map F5 • 46a Ocean St, Woollahra • 9362 3756*

2 Jan Logan
Logan is considered the doyenne of Australian jewellery, offering exquisite creations crafted from precious and semi-precious stones. ⊗ *Map F4 • 36 Cross St, Double Bay • 9363 2529*

3 Joh Bailey
Get a haircut, style and expert colour from Sydney's hairdresser to the stars. ⊗ *Map F4 • 7 Knox St, Double Bay • 9363 4111*

4 Becker Minty
An eclectic and ever-changing collection of books, furniture, ceramics, glassware, lighting and other home accessories as well as clothing and jewellery for men and women. ⊗ *Map E5 • Shop 4, Queens St, Woollahra • 9328 5185*

5 Sylvia Rhodes
Beautiful lingerie and swimwear from the world's best labels, professionally fitted by helpful staff. ⊗ *Map F4 • Shop 7, Bay Village, 28–34 Cross St, Double Bay • 9362 0173*

6 Belinda
This women's designer store stocks gorgeous labels such as Marni. A Belinda shoe emporium is around the corner. ⊗ *Map F4 • 8 Transvaal Ave, Double Bay • 9328 6288*

7 Napoleon Perdis
A lifestyle store offering creations from leading accessory designers, one-off vintage pieces and the Napoleon Perdis cosmetic line. ⊗ *Map E5 • 99 Queen St, Woollahra • 9328 3111*

8 Lesley McKay's Bookshop
A great bookshop with helpful and knowledgable staff, and couches for settling in with your finds. ⊗ *Map F4 • 118 Queen St, Woollahra • 9328 2733*

9 Westfield Bondi Junction
A luxury mall with dozens of designer boutiques such as Morrissey, Marcs and Leona Edmiston. ⊗ *Map F5 • 500 Oxford St, Bondi Junction • 9947 8000*

10 Collette Dinnigan
This multi award winning designer creates beautifully crafted women's clothing. Fans of her prized designs include Nicole Kidman, Cate Blanchett and Jerry Hall. ⊗ *Map Q6 • 104 Queen St, Woollahra • 9360 6691*

There are several branches of Belinda scattered around Sydney; for the store at the MLC Centre see p80.

Interior and views at Catalina

Relaxed Dining

1 Nina's Ploy Thai
A popular year-round eatery serving traditional Thai cuisine. In summer, the outdoor tables fill quickly with Bondi locals. ✆ Map H5 • 132d, Wairoa Ave, Bondi • 9365 1118 • $

2 Le Bukhara
Indian cuisine with a Mauritian touch and friendly service distinguishes this neighbourhood restaurant. ✆ Map F4 • 55 Bay St, Double Bay • 9363 5510 • No dis access • $$$

3 Vamps Bistro
Traditional French cuisine in the heart of Paddington means this long-established restaurant is full of locals every night. ✆ Map F4 • 227 Glenmore Rd, Paddington • 9931 2032 • Tue–Sat dinner, Sat, Sun lunch • $$$

4 Pompei
Pompei is renowned for its authentic thin-crust pizza and myriad gelato flavours. ✆ Map G5 • 126 Roscoe St, Bondi Beach • 9365 1233 • $$

Packed day at Barzura

5 Seasalt
Smart food and a great location make this beachside café very appealing. ✆ Map U4 • 1 Donnellan Circuit, Clovelly • 9664 5344 • $$

6 Barzura
At this large eatery, relaxed all-day meals, outdoor tables and beach views make for a great time. ✆ Map U5 • 62 Carr St, Coogee • 9665 5546 • No dis access • $$

7 Ceviche
Enjoy contemporary Australian cuisine made with the freshest seasonal produce. Book a table on the outdoor deck for great views. ✆ Map U5 • 56 Carr St, Coogee • 9315 8811 • Open noon–10pm Tue–Fri, 8:30am–10pm Sat & Sun • $$$

8 Blue Orange
An intimate restaurant, with a mix of European, Asian and African cuisine. ✆ Map H5 • 49 Hall St, Bondi Beach • 9300 9885 • $$$

9 Catalina
Contemporary Australian cuisine with Italian and Spanish influences. The interior is elegant and the views superb. ✆ Map G4 • 1 Sutherland Ave, Rose Bay • 9371 0555 • Mon–Sat dinner, lunch daily • $$$

10 North Bondi Italian Food
Italian classics served in a busy, buzzy atmosphere. Great for a lazy lunch or an atmospheric dinner. ✆ Map H5 • 118–120 Ramsgate Ave, North Bondi • 9300 4400 • Dinner daily, lunch Fri–Sun • $$$

Unless otherwise stated, all restaurants are open daily, accept credit cards, serve vegetarian meals and provide disabled access.

Left **King Street** Centre **Crabs at the Sydney Fish Market** Right **Entrance of Gleebooks**

Newtown & Glebe

SOME TIME AGO, *Newtown didn't even register a blip on the tourist radar. But a trendy crowd has given this suburb the raffish charm that several other suburbs have lost since falling victim to Sydney's relentless inner-city gentrification. It's still a bit rough around the edges, which makes it a great place to shop for funky clothes, books and retro furnishings, and it has some groovy cafés. Glebe, on the other hand, is almost the grand dame of gentrified inner-city suburbs. In 1789, Governor Phillip granted the chaplain of the First Fleet, Reverend Richard Johnson, 162 ha (400 acres) for services rendered. Today, Glebe accommodates workers' cottages and impressive 19th-century residences on tree-lined streets that meander down to the harbour. It is also home to numerous cafés and restaurants, antique shops, and Sydney's best bookshop Gleebooks, as well as pleasant harbourside parks and the ever-popular Glebe Markets.*

Waterfront tables at the Sydney Fish Market

TOP 10 Sights

1. Sydney Park
2. King Street
3. Camperdown Cemetery
4. Sydney University
5. Glebe Point Road
6. Glebe Markets
7. Sze Yup Buddhist Chinese Temple
8. Jubilee, Bicentennial & Federal Parks
9. Anzac Bridge
10. Sydney Fish Market

 Sign up for DK's email newsletter on traveldk.com

1 Sydney Park

The entrance to Sydney Park is marked by four giant chimneys once used for the huge kilns of the Sydney brickworks. Clever park landscaping incorporated parts of the brick works, so that you walk over a courtyard paved with hand-moulded bricks. The grassy slopes of the park make it a favourite with local dog-walkers and offer a wonderful view of the city from the hills. It is a welcome wide open space, rare in Sydney. ◈ Map C6 • Sydney Park Rd & King St, St Peters

2 King Street

Originally known as Cooks River Road, King Street has been an important thoroughfare since the days of European settlement, when it linked Sydney Town with farms in the Cooks River Basin. Newtown once belonged to a few rich men, but by the late 1800s it had become a thriving township. By then King Street looked much as it does today, bustling and lined with shops. Many stately homes on the streets off King Street have been restored, but most of the houses began as poor workers' cottages. Migrants arrived in the 1960s and '70s, along with rockers, goths and punks, and Newtown is still peopled by an eclectic mix. Above the grungy street level, you'll see that the upper façades of many shopfronts have retained Victorian plasterwork detail. ◈ Map C5

3 Camperdown Cemetery

Sydney's oldest remaining cemetery lies in the grounds of St Stephen's Church. When the cemetery was established in 1848, it was one of three serving all of Sydney. Many historic figures are buried here, including Alexander Macleay (see p86), Colonial Secretary from 1826 to 1837. When the Dunbar sank just outside Sydney Heads in 1857 (see p36), the bodies recovered were buried in a mass grave at Camperdown and a memorial was erected for them. Eliza Donnithorne, thought to be the inspiration for Charles Dickens' Miss Havisham, also lies there. While walking the peaceful paths, note the gravestones lining the walls. These original stones were moved inside when the outer area was turned into a park. ◈ Map B5 • Church St, Newtown • Open daylight hours

4 Sydney University

Australia's first university was founded in 1850. Many of the buildings on the large campus are of little architectural merit, but the Main Quadrangle building makes the university well worth a visit. Designed to mimic the hallowed halls of Oxford and Cambridge, its ornate Victorian Gothic façade is adorned with gargoyles and pinnacles. The Nicholson Museum of antiquities is housed in one wing, and the Macleay Museum is also close by (see p43). ◈ Map C5

Main Quadrangle at Sydney University

Sze Yup Buddhist Chinese Temple

5 Glebe Point Road

Glebe came about as a series of land grants to wealthy free settlers. Two remaining Regency villas, Toxteth Park and Lyndhurst, were designed by celebrated Colonial architect John Verge. Today it is a hippie enclave characterised by New Age and health food shops and laidback locals. Leafy and settled into hills with harbour views, the area has a village atmosphere. Glebe Point Road runs through the centre, from Broadway up to the water at Jubilee Point, and is lined with shops and cafés.

To experience Glebe's bohemian side, pop into Sappho bookshop and café for a latte then head to the Excelsior pub for some eclectic live gigs.
§ Map J5 • Toxteth Park: St Scholasticas College, Arcadia St • Lyndhurst: 61 Darghan St • Excelsior: 101 Bridge Rd • 9552 9700 • Sappho: 51 Glebe Point Rd • 9552 4498

6 Glebe Markets

Every Saturday from 10am–4pm, the grounds of Glebe Public School are used by market stalls selling new and second-hand clothes, records and bric-a-brac. A great source for flares, leather jackets and sunglasses, Glebe Markets offer great bargains. § Map K6

Wares at Glebe Markets

7 Sze Yup Buddhist Chinese Temple

Sydney saw its first influx of Chinese immigrants soon after the discovery of gold in the 1850s. The city's Chinese community, the largest in Australia, built this temple on the site of a former market garden in 1898. It is named after a district in the Chinese province of Kwongtung. The traditional red and green temple was restored in 1978 and the archway added in 1982. The bones of the deceased were once kept here before their return to China for burial. Visitors are welcome, but do remember that this is an active place of worship and not a tourist attraction. § Map B4 • Edward St • Open 9am–5pm daily

Incense burning at the temple

8 Jubilee, Bicentennial & Federal Parks

These three contiguous parks overlooking Rozelle Bay offer fantastic views of the city and the working harbour. A pathway follows the north shoreline overlooking the container terminal on the other side of Rozelle Bay. To the west, just over the footbridge, is a great children's playground. And to the south is the old railway viaduct which threads its way past the historic grandstand in Jubilee Park. The small Pope Paul VI Reserve has one of the best views in Sydney, looking across Blackwattle Bay to the Anzac and Sydney Harbour Bridges. § Map B4

9 Anzac Bridge

This stunning bridge was named in honour of Australia's WWI soldiers: Anzac stands for Australian and New Zealand Army Corps. It spans narrow Johnstons Bay and links Pyrmont with Rozelle and Balmain *(see p108)*. Opened in 1995, this is the longest cable-stayed span bridge in Australia, and many consider it Sydney's finest. A pedestrian path runs beside the inbound lanes and is accessible from Quarry Master Drive, north of the Sydney Fish Market. It offers great views of the city in the distance and the adjacent swing-span 1901 Glebe Island Bridge below. ◈ *Map J3*

Anzac Bridge

10 Sydney Fish Market

The largest market of its kind in the Southern Hemisphere, this complex in Pyrmont is home to the fishing fleet, wholesale and retail fish markets, delicatessens, oyster bars, sushi and sashimi bars, cafés, restaurants, and even a bakery. You can enjoy freshly cooked seafood in one of the restaurants, or have a picnic outside in the sunshine with takeaway fish and chips if you prefer. The Fish Market contains the Sydney Seafood School, which runs a range of culinary classes such as filetting and specialist ethnic cuisines.

◈ *Map K4 • Sydney Fish Market: Bank , Pyrmont • Opens daily at 7am • 9004 00 • Sydney Seafood School: 9004 1111 www.sydneyfishmarket.com.au*

Downhill From Newtown to Glebe

Morning

🕐 Start your day in classic Newtown style with a strong coffee at **Barmuda**, 283 Australia Street. Then follow Australia Street to Lennox Street and turn right. At the end is **St Stephen's Church**, designed by Edmund Blacket *(see p79)*. Beside the church is the entrance to the historic, peaceful **Camperdown Cemetery**. Soak up the Gothic atmosphere before heading back to hectic King Street. Check out the bookshops, cafés and funky clothing stores that run almost as far as Little Queen Street. Turn left, cross over Carillon Avenue and enter the manicured grounds of the **Sydney University**. Turn right into Physics Lane, left into Fisher Road, and right into Manning Road, reaching the archway that leads through to the Main Quadrangle. Pass beneath the Gothic Revival clock tower and wander down University Avenue to the open space of **Victoria Park**. Finally, head to bohemian Glebe Point Road to **Badde Manors** *(see p107)* for lunch.

Afternoon

Follow Glebe Point Road to Pendrill Street, turn left and follow the scent of incense downhill to the **Sze Yup Temple**. Turn right into Edward Street, left into Eglington Lane, and right again into Edward Lane to reach **Jubilee Park**. The **Pope Paul VI Reserve** can be found in the northeast corner. When done, catch a 431 or 434 bus back to town.

Left **Gleebooks** Right **C's Flash Back**

TOP 10 Funky Shops

1 Crumpler
Need a bag that will last your lifetime? That's the guarantee Crumpler gives you on their backpacks, laptop carriers, iPod holders and bean bags. Expect good deals at this store. ✎ *Map B5 • 305 King St • Newtown • 9565 1611*

2 Maple
Cool clothes for men and women, with a large selection of denims and accessories. ✎ *Map B5 • 244 King St, Newtown • 9517 1633*

3 Dragstar
Newtown girls love a bit of retro styling, and this is where they find it. New clothes in the style of traditional favourites include T-shirt dresses, minis, shorts and tanks. ✎ *Map B6 • 535a King St, Newtown • 9550 1243*

4 Gleebooks
This much-loved store is crammed with books, including academic and obscure titles, and holds weekly events such as book launches and poetry readings. ✎ *Map K6 • 49 Glebe Point Rd, Glebe • 9660 2333*

5 C's Flash Back
King Street has a few second-hand clothes shops and this is the best of them, carefully divided for easy browsing. ✎ *Map C5 • 180 King St, Newtown • 9565 4343*

6 Platypus Shoes
If the name doesn't get you, the range of shoes will. Find anything from Aussie Blundstone workboots to the most trendy trainers. ✎ *Map B5 • 275 King St, Newtown • 9557 4599*

7 Yoshi Jones
Simple garments feature Japanese silks, kimono fabrics or Oriental-inspired designs. You can also find obis and quirky accessories. ✎ *Map C5 • 134 King St, Newtown • 9550 1663*

8 Faster Pussycat
In this shrine to all things rock and rockabilly, find punk T-shirts, 1950s skirts, studded belts, magazines, music and much more. ✎ *Map B6 • 431a King St, Newtown • 9519 1744*

9 Florilegium
Most Australians have gardens, and this bookshop specialises in titles to inspire and advise on tending them all. ✎ *Map J6 • 65 Derwent S Glebe • 9571 8222*

10 Industrie
Not so original but highly affordable men's clothes range from smart to casual. Part of a chain, this is the place to go if you want a lookalike of the latest Diesel. ✎ *Map C • 239 King St, Newtown • 9519 7577*

Gleebooks' children's and second-hand bookshop is a few blocks up the road at 191 Glebe Point Road, Glebe; 9552 2526.

Price Categories

For a two course meal for one with a drink (or equivalent meal), plus taxes and extra charges.

$	under $35
$$	$35–$60
$$$	$60–$120
$$$$	$120–$200
$$$$$	over $200

Badde Manors Café

Cheap Eats

1 Twelve
Enjoy food with a northern Italian influence in this buzzing restaurant with an open kitchen. ⊗ Map C5 • 222 King St, Newtown • 9519 9412 • Dinner Tue–Sat • $$

2 Linda's on King St
For many years, Linda's was a well-kept local secret hidden at the back of a hotel. Today, it has been discovered and its modern Australian food is so popular that bookings are essential. ⊗ Map B5 • 341 King St, Newtown • 9550 6015 • Dinner Tue–Sat • $$

3 Sumalee Thai
This one tops Newtown's many great Thai restaurants because it's in an outdoor courtyard. Enjoy the sultry flavours on a balmy summer evening. ⊗ Map C6 • Bank Hotel, 324 King St, Newtown • 8568 1988 • No dis access • $

4 Rice Paper
Classic Vietnamese food with generous servings. You can make your own rolls using the freshly-made rice paper the restaurant takes its name from. ⊗ Map C5 • 131 King St, Newtown • 8065 7271 • Open 11am–10pm Sun–Wed, 11am–10:30pm Thu–Sat daily for lunch and dinner • $$

5 Vargabarespresso
A friendly Newtown café offers good breakfasts, burgers and coffee. ⊗ Map B5 • 10 Wilson St, Newtown • 9517 1932 • $

6 Green Gourmet
Vegan food has never tasted so good as at this Buddhist Chinese restaurant. Lunchtime yum cha is excellent. ⊗ Map C5 • 115 King St, Newtown • 9519 5330 • $

7 Sonoma Bakery Café
Simplicity, authenticity and quality are the hallmarks of this gem. Sonoma serves top-class coffee to wash down delicious muesli, muffins and breakfast and lunch rolls. ⊗ Map C4 • 215 Glebe Point Rd, Glebe • 9660 2116 • Breakfast & lunch 8am–4pm • $

8 Thanh Binh
Vietnamese food is great for meat lovers, who come here for a variety of pho: huge, comforting bowls of noodles and meatballs topped with mint leaves and broth. ⊗ Map C5 • 111 King St, Newtown • 9557 1175 • BYO • $$

9 Badde Manors
Enjoy the bohemian charm of this busy café-cum-meeting spot, but expect haphazard service. ⊗ Map C4 • 37 Glebe Point Road, Glebe • 9660 3797 • $

10 Cantina S, AB Hotel
Enjoy some of Sydney's best grub in this refurbished pub with communal tables and bargain meal deals. The emphasis is on Asian cuisine and steaks. ⊗ Map C4 • 225 Glebe Point Rd, Glebe • 9660 1417 • Lunch Mon–Sat, dinner Tue–Sat • $

Cold drink

Unless otherwise stated, all restaurants are open daily, accept credit cards, serve vegetarian meals, and provide disabled access.

Left **Handmade soaps at the Balmain Markets** Centre **Leichhardt Town Hall** Right **Italian Forum**

Balmain & Leichhardt

WILLIAM BALMAIN, *a surgeon on the First Fleet, was granted 223 ha (550 acres) west of the city in 1800, perhaps in gratitude for having tended to Governor Phillip following his 1790 spearing (see p38). The area was subdivided in the mid-1800s, and grand harbourside residences were erected alongside working-class stone and timber cottages and a multitude of pubs that catered to the employees of the local timber, mining and maritime industries. By the 1960s, Balmain had become a haven for writers, artists and actors, a reputation it still retains today.*

Balmain war memorial

Leichhardt's cultural connections are more tenuous. The suburb was named after the explorer Ludwig Leichhardt (see p79) who disappeared without a trace while crossing the continent in 1848; Patrick White (see p40) immortalised Leichhardt in his 1957 novel, Voss. Now Leichhardt is home to two diverse populations – Sydney's colourful "Little Italy" and a prominent lesbian community.

A café-junkshop in Balmain

🔟 Sights

1. Balmain East
2. Darling Street
3. Elkington Park
4. Birchgrove
5. Cockatoo Island
6. Goat Island
7. Leichhardt Town Hall
8. Leichhardt Post Office
9. Norton Street
10. Italian Forum

Saturday Balmain Markets at St Andrew's

Balmain East
1 At the eastern end of the Balmain peninsula is the Darling Street Wharf, overlooked by manicured Thornton Park. A sign tracing the route of the Balmain History Trail can be found near the bus stop. On Darling Street, check out the former Dolphin Hotel and the Waterman's Cottage. To the south, Peacock Point offers great views over Millers Point, Darling Harbour and the Anzac Bridge. Mort Bay Reserve to the north features two massive ships' propellers and views over the ferry and tugboat maintenance yards in Mort Bay. ◈ *Map C3*

Darling Street
2 Darling Street runs from the wharf in Balmain East to Victoria Road in Rozelle. It's a steady uphill climb from the wharf past narrow Victorian houses until you reach the friendly London Hotel, just before a large roundabout. En route you pass the childhood home of former New South Wales premier Neville Wran, No. 117, and the 1854 Watch House at No. 179, the oldest in Sydney. Find Gladstone Park past the roundabout, and St Andrew's across the road, which hosts the Balmain Markets every Saturday. From here on it's boutiques, cafés, bookshops and salons all the way to the Victorian court house, Town Hall, Fire Station and Library *(see p57)*. ◈ *Map B3*

Elkington Park
3 This lovely reserve on White Horse Point, overlooking Cockatoo Island, is best known for the Dawn Fraser Baths, one of Sydney's oldest municipal pools, built in the 1880s. Dawn Fraser is a local legend, as much loved for her candid take on life and wild streak as she is for having dominated the pool at the 1956, 1960 and 1964 Olympic Games, leaving 41 world records in her wake. Including an outdoor saltwater tidal pool, the baths are open from October to April. ◈ *Map B2 • Dawn Fraser Baths, Fitzroy Ave, Balmain • 9555 1903*

Birchgrove
4 This area has some lovely Colonial homes, a small shopping village on Rowntree Street and Birchgrove Park, the site of Australia's first Rugby League match in 1908. The northern tip of Birchgrove is known as Yurulbin Point, formerly called Long Nose Point, which, along with Manns Point, forms the mouth of the Parramatta River. Yurulbin Park has spectacular views of the Harbour Bridge, and an interpretation board near the ferry wharf provides interesting details on the area's Aboriginal heritage. ◈ *Map B2*

> **Spaghetti Western**
> When the first Italians escaped war-torn Europe to arrive in Leichhardt in 1917, the area was largely populated by Irish free settlers. After WWII many more Italians were drawn by the availability of paid work, fine weather and peace. The Italians, who continued to pour in until the 1960s, introduced Sydneysiders to many new things, perhaps most importantly espresso and spaghetti.

The Leichhardt area once belonged to the Wangal tribe of indigenous people.

Cockatoo Island

5 Since European settlement, the largest of Sydney Harbour's islands has been used variously as a convict prison, granary, girls reformatory and a major shipyard. Convicts from the infamous Norfolk Island penal colony were quartered on the island until 1871. During that time only one prisoner, the bushranger nicknamed "Captain Thunderbolt" escaped, aided by his Aboriginal wife, Mary. Sutherland Dock was completed in 1890 and the island became a major shipyard. It also served as the naval dockyard for the Royal Australian Navy at the outbreak of World War I. The dockyards closed down in 1992 and the Sydney Harbour Federation Trust has opened the island to the public. The trust runs activities, a campground, events and tours on the island (see p15). ☜ Map B2

Goat Island

6 Northeast of Balmain, Goat Island was one of Bennelong's (see p9) favourite picnic spots. In the 1830s it was used as a gunpowder magazine and convict barracks. One prisoner, Charles "Bony" Anderson, tried numerous times to escape the barracks, receiving 1,200 lashes for his troubles. He was chained to a sandstone "couch" for two years. The island later became a base for the Water Police and Fire Brigade, and in 1925 shipyards were built on its western side. In the 1990s it was the film set for the TV series *Water Rats*. Boasting fantastic views of Sydney Harbour, the island is managed by the National Parks and Wildlife Service (see p14). ☜ Map C2

Leichhardt Town Hall

Leichhardt Town Hall

7 Designed by Drake and Walcott and built in 1888, the style of this ornate building is described as Victorian Free Classical. The structure reflects the creativity and craftsmanship applied towards significant buildings of its time. When it opened, the Town Hall was considered the best municipal building outside the city centre. Many of the Italian migrants who settled in Leichhardt became Australian citizens in Town Hall ceremonies between 1920 and 1960. ☜ Map A5 • 107 Norton St

Leichhardt Post Office

8 Designed by James Barnet (see p77), Leichhardt Post Office is no longer in use, but it is possible to admire its strong lines and severe shape from the street. It is a good example of the Victorian Italianate style, popularised in Australia by architectural pattern books and used in many homes. The tower, designed to accommodate a clock that never arrived, provides a formal divide between the public and residential parts of the building. ☜ Map A4 • 109 Norton St

Leichhardt Post Office

There isn't much accommodation in Leichhardt, but if you're keen to stay in the area, try the Pensione Italia at 73 Renwick Street.

9 Norton Street

Named after James Norton, an English attorney who arrived in 1818 and established a thriving legal practice in the colony, Norton Street has long been the heart of this district. Much of the large estate purchased by Norton in 1834 is now the bustling shopping and dining strip that runs from Parramatta Road to Allen Street. You'll find a range of stores with an Italian flavour *(see p62)*, from bridal fashion to books, clothing and shoes, as well as bakeries, delis and butchers. ◈ *Map A4*

10 Italian Forum

This kitsch development evokes reminiscences of Italy, and has a sundial and a statue of Dante based on a similar one in Verona. On the mezzanine level, you'll find boutiques selling imported and local Italian fashion. Descending the stairs finds the piazza, surrounded by cafés and restaurants that offer wonderful, sunny positions for languid lunches. Located on the piazza level is the Leichhardt Library which contains a Local History Section, a rich source of historical photographs and oral histories of the local Italian community. ◈ *Map A6*
● *23 Norton St • Leichhardt Library: open 9:30am–8pm Mon–Fri, 9:30am–4pm Sat, 10am–4pm Sun*

Restaurant at the Italian Forum

A Balmain Stroll

Morning

🕐 Catch a ferry from **Circular Quay** *(see p18)* to the quaint **Darling Street Wharf**. Enter **Illoura Reserve** and walk south beneath she-oaks and other native trees to **Peacock Point**'s views across to **Darling Harbour** *(see p28)*. Johnston Street has great views of **Anzac Bridge** *(see p105)*. Head back to Darling Street and admire some of Balmain's finest residences. Turn into Killeen Street and wander down through **Ewenton Park**. Around the corner is grand **Hampton Villa** overlooking the docklands, home of Sir Henry Parkes *(see p37)*. Back at Darling Street, get a drink at the pleasant **London Hotel**. Then, window-shop all the way to the **Town Hall**. Finally, backtrack to **Go Bungai** at 333 Darling Street for the best Japanese lunch in town.

Afternoon

After lunch, continue back down Darling Street to Mort Street and turn left. At the end is **Mort Bay Park**, site of the former Mort's Dock shipyards, named for Thomas Mort *(see p79)*, which is now open harbourside parkland. Follow the shoreline around to the steps leading up to Wharf Road via Ronald Street. This lovely street leads to **Snails Bay** and the historic **Birchgrove Park**. A path traces the shoreline to Louisa Road, which has some seriously expensive real estate. Turn right and head towards **Yurulbin Park** for some spectacular harbour views before catching the ferry back to Circular Quay.

➔ *The annual Italian Festa on Norton Street draws thousands of visitors every year for food, music and rides.*

Outdoor dining and exterior of Welcome Hotel

TOP 10 Pubs & Bars

1 East Village Hotel
You'll wish the second oldest pub in Balmain was your local after enjoying craf beer, couches to relax in and friendly owners behind the bar. ◎ *Map C3 • 82 Darling St, Balmain East • 9810 3333*

2 London Hotel
Established in 1870, this is one of the most atmospheric pubs in Sydney. Grab a tractor seat on the balcony, sip the west Australian wheat bear, Red Back beer, and enjoy Harbour Bridge views. ◎ *Map C3 • 234 Darling St, Balmain • 9555 1377 • www.thelondonhotel.com.au*

3 Welcome Hotel
The bistro at this Irish pub serves excellent food. Portions are generous and European flavours are infused with an Irish influence. ◎ *Map B3 • 91 Evans St, Rozelle • 9810 1323 • www.thewelcomehotel.com • $$*

4 Town Hall Hotel
Something for everyone with great bar food, a giant screen, lounge area and discrete gaming section. It's the best place for a pick-me-up brunch. ◎ *Map B3 • 366 Darling St, Balmain • 9818 8950 • www.town-hallhotel.com.au • Dis access*

5 Riverview Hotel
This tiny local with much charm and fin-de-siècle interiors is hidden in a backstreet but is certainly worth seeking out. ◎ *Map B2 • 29 Birchgrove Rd, Balmain • 9810 1151*

6 Sackville Hotel
A busy schedule of comedy, trivia and movie nights at this stylish pub, as well as live DJs. It also has an excellent and reasonably priced menu. ◎ *Map B3 • 599 Darling St, Rozelle • 9555 7555 • Dis access*

7 Royal Hotel
An excellent local with entertainment every night, including a pool competition on Mondays. The place really comes alive on Friday and Saturday nights for karaoke sessions. ◎ *Map A4 • 156 Norton St, Leichhardt • 9569 2638 • www.royalhotelleichhardt.com*

8 Martini
Upstairs in the Palace Cinema complex, pop in to sip martinis and mull over the latest flick. Fun atmosphere and tasty food. ◎ *Map A5 • Level 1, 99 Norton St, Leichhardt • 9568 3344*

9 Leichhardt Hotel
More a bar than a pub, with a feisty Italian crowd. In summer the doors fold back to make an outdoor party, and in winter gas heaters keep you snug. ◎ *Map A5 • 95 Norton St, Leichhardt • 9518 3476*

10 Nortons on Norton
A traditional pub revamped with a restaurant and giant screens. The upper level has a clubby feel with DJs and pool tables. ◎ *Map A5 • 1 Norton St, Leichhardt • 9560 3322*

Martini

Price Categories

For a two course meal for one with a drink (or equivalent meal), plus taxes and extra charges.

$	under $35
$$	$35–$60
$$$	$60–$120
$$$$	$120–$200
$$$$$	over $200

Fresh bread at Victoire

Best of the Rest

1 Bar Italia
A no-fuss restaurant with great Italian food and arguably the area's best coffee and gelato. ◈ Map A4 • 169 Norton St, Leichhardt • Open 9am–11pm daily • 9560 9981 • $

2 Il Piave
A refined North Italian *cucina* turns out seasonal and regional delights. Head to the back courtyard. ◈ Map B3 • 639 Darling St, Rozelle • 9010 6204 • Open Tue–Sun • Bookings essential • $$

Chocolate violin at Belle Fleur

3 Kazbah on Darling
At the Kazbah you can fill up on fabulous Middle Eastern food in the middle of Balmain. ◈ Map B3 • 379 Darling St, Balmain • 9555 7067 • $$

4 Blue Ginger
Modern Asian food from Thailand, Vietnam, China and Japan at great prices. There's something for everyone. ◈ Map C3 • 241 Darling St, Balmain • 9010 4002 • Bookings essential • Dis access • $

5 Victoire
Stop in for amazing cakes and pastries, crusty sourdough bread and excellent cheese. ◈ Map B3 • 660 Darling St, Rozelle • 9818 5529

6 Belle Fleur
Handcrafted chocolates and truffles, many with unusual flavours such as wattleseed and lemon myrtle, are exquisitely

decorated and boxed. ◈ Map B3 • 658 Darling St, Rozelle • 9810 2690

7 Berkelouw
At this wonderful bookstore, take your tomes to the café upstairs and settle into a comfy couch. ◈ Map A5 • 70 Norton St, Leichhardt • 9560 3200

8 Palace Cinema
Catch the latest quality films at this small, stylish cinema. ◈ Map A5 • 99 Norton St, Leichhardt • 9550 0122

9 Alfie's Little Brother Carter
A neat shop sells the best local and imported streetwear. ◈ Map B3 • 348 Darling St, Balmain • 9555 5222

10 Rozelle Markets
The best Sydney market for vintage clothes and bric-a-brac. ◈ Map B3 • Rozelle Public School, Darling St, Rozelle • Every Sat & Sun • 9818 5373

The Palace Norton St Cinema offers mothers and babies sessions called "Babes in Arms" at 11am every Thursday.

Left **Decorative gables at Manly** Center **Manly Beach** Right **Detail on New Brighton Hotel**

The North Shore

I F THE EASTERN SUBURBS ARE *"gorgeous"*, and the southern and western *suburbs are "aspirational", the North Shore is best described as "satisfied". For many Sydneysiders the North Shore is not only geographical shorthand for the suburbs north of the harbour, it's equally a state of mind. One that is respectable, well-off and content. From Hunters Hill in the west to Manly in the east, and all points north to Ku-ring-gai Chase National Park, the North Shore is bourgeois to the back teeth. Here you'll find some glorious pockets of remnant bushland nestled around the harbour, stunning ocean beaches,*

quiet harbourside beaches, and plenty of options for those who love the great outdoors, walking, cycling, kayaking, surfing, diving, sailing and parasailing. And then there are always some of Sydney's perennial favourites to tempt you: Luna Park, Nutcote, Taronga Park Zoo, Bradleys Head, Oceanworld Manly and North Head.

A giraffe at Taronga Zoo

🔟 Sights

1 Balls Head Reserve
2 Lavender Bay & Blues Point
3 Milsons Point
4 North Sydney
5 Kirribilli
6 Neutral Bay & Cremorne
7 Mosman & Balmoral
8 Middle Harbour
9 Manly
10 Manly Scenic Walk

Mural on a surf shop

Balls Head Reserve

On the headland east of Manns Point and the Parramatta River *(see p109)* lies this pleasant park, site of Aboriginal rock art and bushwalking trails. It offers stunning views across the harbour to Goat Island *(see p110)* and Balmain *(see p108)*. BBQ facilities are available, and it's easily accessible from Waverton Railway Station. The park is cradled by the dormitory suburbs of Waverton and Wollstonecraft, the latter named after Edward Wollstonecraft, nephew of Mary Wollstonecraft, the author of *Rights of Women*. Edward was an enterprising local merchant who operated a shipping business with his partner Alexander Berry, after whom the bay was named. 🖲 *Map C2*

Lavender Bay & Blues Point

East of Berry's Bay, this cove has great views of the Opera House framed by the Harbour Bridge. It was named after George Lavender, a boatswain who married the daughter of his neighbour Billy Blue *(see p37)*. In 1817 Governor Macquarie granted Billy Blue 32 ha (80 acres) west of Lavender Bay. In 1830, at the age of 82, Billy Blue established a ferry service from Dawes Point *(see p13)* to the headland that now bears his name. There is a small reserve at its end, but the point is dominated by a Harry Seidler *(see p47)* apartment building that many consider an eyesore. 🖲 *Map D2*

Milsons Point

Nestled beneath the Harbour Bridge is a tiny suburb best known for its fun fair. Luna Park *(see p56)*, which is based on New York's Coney Island. Luna

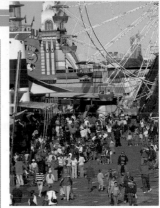

Crowds at Luna Park, Milsons Point

Park's famous laughing clown face set between two Art Deco towers, although remodelled several times over the years, has continuously overlooked the harbour since 1935. The park is built upon a former Sydney Harbour Bridge construction wharf and workshops. Beside the park is the North Sydney Olympic Pool *(see p49)* which opened in 1936. 🖲 *Map D2*

North Sydney

In 1932 John Bradfield *(see p12)* predicted that, with the opening of the Harbour Bridge, North Sydney and Mosman would merge into a second Brooklyn. He was certainly on the money regarding North Sydney's development, as indicated by the area's many skyscrapers. Sydney's second CBD is home to major Australian banking, finance and insurance giants. Its attractions include a small museum, chapel and tomb dedicated to the memory and works of Mary MacKillop (1842–1909), who became Australia's first saint in 2010. 🖲 *Map D1 • Mary MacKillop Place Museum: 7 Mount St • 8912 4878 • www.marymackillopplace.org.au • Open 10am–4pm daily • Adm*

115

Apartments at Kirribilli

Kirribilli

Kirribilli is Australia's most densely populated suburb. But it is better known for two residences that occupy its tip: Admiralty House (1843) and neighbouring Kirribilli House (1855). The former was the residence of the Commander of the British Royal Navy, and is now the Sydney residence of the Governor General, the Queen's representative in Australia. The latter is the official Sydney residence of the Australian Prime Minister. The Gothic Kirribilli House has one of the best views in Australia. ◈ *Map D2*

Neutral Bay & Cremorne

Neutral Bay was named by Governor Phillip, who ordered that all foreign ships entering Sydney Harbour anchor here. The area includes Careening Cove, so named because ships were laid on their sides here for refitting. Now this tranquil bay is home to the Royal Sydney Yacht Squadron, the Ensemble Theatre *(see p65)*, and the Sydney Flying Squadron. May Gibbs' *(see p40)* residence, Nutcote, is on the eastern slope. Further east is Cremorne, a long, narrow peninsula with a popular harbourside reserve. ◈ *Map D1*
- Nutcote: 5 Wallaringa Ave, Neutral Bay
- 9953 4453 • www.nutcote.org
- Open 11am–3pm Wed–Sun • Adm

Mosman & Balmoral

Mosman Bay was named after Archibald Mosman, who established a whaling business nearby in 1830. The suburb is best known for Taronga Zoo *(see p32–3)* and Bradleys Head *(see p50)*. Lieutenant William Bradley arrived with the First Fleet and later served in the Napoleonic Wars, before he was found guilty of fraud and exiled to France in 1814. Headland Park, unites the former military lands at Chowder Bay, Georges Heights and Middle Head, offers harbourside walking tracks and several restaurants. Balmoral *(see p48)* has three beaches, including Chinaman's Beach. ◈ *Map F1*

Middle Harbour

The entrance to the northern arm of the harbour is marked by Middle Head and Dobroyd Head. North of Chinaman's Beach is the Spit Bridge, which can be raised allowing boats to pass beneath. Castlecrag, northwest of the Spit Bridge, was home for a period to Walter Burley Griffin (1876–1937), the US architect who designed Australia's capital, Canberra. Much of Middle Harbour's shoreline is parkland, with calm waters perfect for kayaking *(see p54)*. To the north is Garigal National Park *(see p50)*. ◈ *Map T3*

Krishnamurti's Amphitheatre

An amphitheatre was built in Balmoral in 1924 by Theosophists who anticipated a Second Coming under their spiritual leader, Jiddu Krishnamurti (1897–1986). This structure was one of several worldwide dedicated to the "World Teacher", who had been discovered as a boy in Madras. Krishnamurti renounced the Theosophists in 1929.

 Mosman's Military Road contains the best shops for picnic supplies, gifts, cheese, chocolates, seafood and more.

Walking along Manly Beach

9 Manly

This peninsula was so named because Governor Phillip felt the Aborigines he met here in 1788 were "manly". In 1853, businessman Henry Smith purchased 121 ha (300 acres) on the formerly remote peninsula, and set about creating a seaside pleasure resort. Today, Manly is a very popular and lively destination. Home to lovely beaches, it also features attractions such as Oceanworld Manly (see p118) and October's Manly Jazz festival (see p73). Catch the enjoyable harbour ferry ride from Circular Quay and make a full day of it (see p39).

○ Manly Visitor Information Centre: The Forecourt, Manly Wharf • 0076 1430
Open 9am–5pm Mon–Fri, 10am–4pm Sat, Sun & public holidays

10 Manly Scenic Walk

A 10-km (6-mile) walk, one of Sydney's best, traces North Harbour's shoreline from Manly to the Spit Bridge. The walk passes by coastal heathlands, past sandy beaches and sub-tropical rainforest. Highlights on the way include pretty Forty Baskets Beach, rugged Dobroyd Head, the 1911 Grotto Point lighthouse, Clontarf Beach (see p48), and Aboriginal shell middens east of the Spit Bridge. The NPWS (see p14) offers a useful map of the route, available at the NPWS and Manly Visitor Information Centres.

A Beach Crawl Around Manly

Morning

⏱ Pack a picnic lunch and catch the ferry to Manly Wharf. Cross **The Esplanade** and follow **The Corso** down to **Manly Beach** (see p118). After paying homage to William Gocher (see p39), head south and follow the path around to **Cabbage Tree Bay**, where you'll find the delightful **Fairy Bower** rockpool and **Shelly Beach** (see p118), both of which are perfect for children. Then take some time out to enjoy a picnic on the protected beach before wading in to wet your feet in the calm water or messing about in the rockpool.

Afternoon

Leave the beach via Bower Street and follow this around to College Street, past the million-dollar mansions overlooking Manly Beach. Turn right into Reddall Street, left into Addison Road, and left again into Darley Road. Head uphill and take a peek over the stone walls at the **Former St Patrick's Seminary** (see p118). Continue past the hospital and take the right fork leading into **Sydney Harbour National Park** (see p14). Pass beneath the sandstone arch and take Collins Beach Road on your right. This winds down through a lovely shaded gully to the **Police College**. A small path on your right leads to the secluded **Collins Beach** (see p.38), one of Sydney's hidden secrets. A path at the end of the beach leads to Stuart Street, which takes you back to Manly.

Left **Oceanworld** Centre **Shelly Beach** Right **Former St Patrick's Seminary**

TOP 10 Manly

1 Manly Cove
The ferry wharf houses boutiques and cafés, a Visitor Information Centre *(see p117)*, Manly Boat and Kayak Hire, Oceanworld and the Manly Art Gallery and Museum. Ⓢ *Map U3 • ManlyBoat and Kayak Hire: 0412 622 662 • Manly Art Gallery and Museum: 9976 1420*

Brass band at The Corso

2 Oceanworld Manly
Dive with sharks, giant turtles and rays on Oceanworld's Shark Dive Xtreme. For the less courageous there are live shows and guided tours. Passes allow multiple entry. Ⓢ *Map U3 • West Esplanade • 8251 7877 • Open 10am–5:30pm daily • www.oceanworld.com.au • Adm*

3 The Corso
This lively pedestrian avenue runs from The Esplanade to Manly Beach. The Manly Deli is a good place to stock up for a picnic lunch. Ⓢ *Map U3*

4 New Brighton Hotel
Built in 1926, this Egyptian Classical Revival Style pub on The Corso is a popular summer watering hole. Ⓢ *Map U3*

5 Manly Beach
Backed by a reserve lined with Norfolk Island pines and a busy esplanade, this ocean beach *(see p48)* is a Sydney favourite. There are rock baths at the northern end. Ⓢ *Map U3*

6 Cabbage Tree Bay
A lovely bay that features shallow crystal waters, wind-sculpted sandstone cliffs, the magical Fairy Bower rockpool and protected Shelly Beach. Ⓢ *Map U3*

7 Former St Patrick's Seminary
A prominent 1885 seminary for Catholic priests was the setting for Thomas Keneally's *(see p41)* novel *Three Cheers for the Paraclete*. It is now a college of hospitality and tourism. Ⓢ *Map U3*

8 North Head
This windswept, heath-covered highlight of the Sydney Harbour National Park *(see p14)* is home to the former North For Artillery Museum. The museum has re-opened as an ecological sanctuary. Ⓢ *Map U3 • 8969 2100 for museum information)*

9 Old Quarantine Station
Until 1984, Sydney's infecte arrivals were quarantined at this bulwark against infectious diseases. Ⓢ *Map U3 • North Head, Sydney Harbour National Park*

10 Collins Beach
The site where Governor Phillip was speared in 1788 is a peaceful spot nowadays *(see p38)*. Steps lead to a secluded rock diving platform.

Price Categories

For a two course meal for one with a drink (or equivalent meal), plus taxes and extra charges.

$	under $35
$$	$35–$60
$$$	$60–$120
$$$$	$120–$200
$$$$$	over $200

Nilgiri's

≈10 Places to Eat

1 Nilgiri's
A low-key Indian restaurant with a small, well-chosen menu. On Sunday they have regional buffets for lunch and dinner. They also offer private cushion rooms and cooking classes. ✆ Map T3 • 81 Christie St, St Leonards • 9966 0636 • www.nilgiris.com.au • $$

2 Mosman Rowers
This club is a short walk from Mosman Bay wharf. The views from the balcony are spectacular. ✆ Map F1 • 3 Centenary Ave, Mosman Bay • 9953 7966 • www.mosmanrowers.com.au • $$

3 Sushi Studio
Authentic and traditional Japanese food. Sit at the sushi bar and order a deluxe plate to witness the chef's slicing prowess. ✆ Map E1 • 75 Military Rd, Neutral Bay • 9953 7317 • No dis access • $

4 Hugo's at Manly Wharf
Enjoy one of Sydney's most spectacular waterfront locations along with contemporary Italian cuisine, in particular the varied pizza menu. ✆ Map U3 • Shop 1, Manly Wharf, East Esplanade, Manly • 8116 8555 • www.hugos.com.au • $$

5 The Little French Patisserie
Mosman has wonderful food shops and delicatessens. This bakery and patisserie offers pots of tea, savoury pies and sweet treats. ✆ Map U3 • 840 Military Rd, Mosman • 9969 4599 • $

6 Out of Africa
You don't need a safari suit to indulge in North African delicacies, such as tagines, while leaning back against the zebra-skin banquettes. Map U3 • 43–45 East Esplanade, Manly • 9977 0055 • www.outofafrica.com.au • No dis access • $$

7 Ripples at Chowder Bay
Enjoy harbour views and savour contemporary Italian-inspired food in a historic naval building. Stylish bistro menu in a serene location. ✆ Map U3 • Deck C, Chowder Bay Rd, Mosman • 9960 3000 • www.rippleschowderbay.com.au • $$$

8 Ormeggio at The Spit
It's worth booking to enjoy the sunset and the north Italian cuisine here, overlooking Middle Harbour. Great value set price lunch. ✆ Map U3 • d'Albora Marinas, Spit Rd, The Spit, Mosman • 9969 4088 • Closed Mon • www.ormeggio.com.au • $$$

9 Pilu at Freshwater
This listed timber beach house catches a gentle ocean breeze. Sardinian-inspired cuisine includes oven-roasted suckling pig. ✆ Map U3 • End of Moore Rd, Freshwater • 9938 3331 • Closed Mon • www.piluatfreshwater.com.au • $$$

10 Szechuan Garden
When this restaurant moved loyal customers followed in droves for the authentic northern Chinese dishes. ✆ Map T3 • Shop 1, 599 Pacific Hwy St Leonards • 9438 2568 • www.szechuangardenrestaurant.com.au • $$

➤ Unless otherwise stated, all restaurants are open daily, accept credit cards, serve vegetarian meals, and provide disabled access.

Grose Valley from Govetts Leap, considered the best view of the Blue Mountains

Beyond Sydney

THE REGION SURROUNDING THE CITY OF SYDNEY *offers a wealth of natural attractions, historic towns and villages, restaurants with million-dollar views, and endless options for outdoor activities. All regions covered in this section are accessible by public transport, but hiring a car will give you far greater flexibility. To the north of Sydney is Ku-ring-gai Chase National Park, the Hawkesbury River, the Central Coast and Hunter Valley. To the west are the famous Blue Mountains and historic Parramatta and Windsor, while to the south is the gorgeous Royal National Park and the Southern Highlands. All are only a day's trip away from the city centre, but try combining neighbouring attractions into an overnight or weekend trip, for each area offers a diverse and unique set of attractions. Accommodation options range from luxury guesthouses in the Blue Mountains to houseboats on the Hawkesbury River to beach campsites at the Royal National Park.*

Berrima, a Georgian village in the Southern Highlands

Attractions

1. Blue Mountains
2. Hunter Valley
3. Central Coast
4. Hawkesbury River
5. Pittwater & Broken Bay
6. Ku-ring-gai Chase National Park
7. Northern Beaches
8. Parramatta
9. Royal National Park
10. Southern Highlands

120

Left **Hope Estate winery in Hunter Valley** Right **The picturesque Hawkesbury River**

Blue Mountains

These World Heritage-listed mountains are named for their constant bluish haze, the result of evaporating eucalyptus oil. The lovely mountains offer numerous bushwalks and plenty of natural attractions, including the Three Sisters, the Jenolan Caves and Wentworth Falls *(see p126)*. When the explorers Gregory Blaxland, William Lawson and WC Wentworth *(see p37)*, crossed the 1,100-m (3,600-ft) range in 1813, they opened up the continent's grassland interior to white settlement. The main township of Katoomba *(see p128)* is about 107 km (56 miles) west of Sydney.

Hunter Valley

Grapes have been grown in this region since the 1830s. Now there are more than 60 vineyards and countless providores producing condiments, cheese and other gourmet delicacies; some also contain restaurants or cafés. Most of the wineries surround Pokolbin and neighbouring Cessnock, which is the regional township closest to Sydney. Beautiful Hunter Valley is also a popular area for outdoor activities such as cycling, golf, horseriding and hot air ballooning. Numerous tour operators in Sydney offer attractive day, overnight and weekend packages to the area.

Central Coast

The coast from Broken Bay *(see p122)* to Newcastle offers glorious ocean beaches, national parks and several lakes and water-ways. The main regional town is Gosford, at the head of Brisbane Water. This large waterway runs out to Broken Bay past Woy Woy and the pleasant townships of Hardy's Bay in Killcare, Pretty Beach and Wagstaffe. Behind Wagstaffe is Bouddi National Park *(see p127)*, which extends north to pleasant McMaster's Beach. Pearl Beach *(see p128)* and the tiny fishing village of Patonga, surrounded by Brisbane Water National Park *(see p127)*, overlook Broken Bay. ◈ *Map U1*

Hawkesbury River

This broad river runs from Windsor *(see p124)* in the west to Broken Bay *(see p122)* in the east, passing massive sandstone escarpments, historic riverside towns, national parks, mangrove islands, fishing villages and holiday homes, as well as the spectacular Berowa Waters and Cowan Creek *(see p128)* coves and Pittwater *(see p122)*. Berowa Waters is home to the famous Berowa Waters Inn. Cowan Creek peters out near pretty Bobbin Head. Although parts of the river are popular with water-skiers, it's actually best enjoyed at a leisurely pace. ◈ *Map U1*

5 Pittwater & Broken Bay

Pittwater is a long, slender waterway running from Newport to Palm Beach *(see p48)*, Ku-ring-gai Chase National Park and Broken Bay. Exclusive houses, private wharves and public marinas populate its eastern shoreline. Housing on the western shoreline thins out as you head north, until you reach Ku-ring-gai Chase National Park, north of isolated Towlers Bay and exclusive Scotland Island. Pittwater's sheltered waters have long been a favourite haunt with yachties. Broken Bay is a beautiful, wide and sometimes wild expanse of water dominated by Lion Island, an uninhabited rocky outcrop. ✪ *Map U1*

6 Ku-ring-gai Chase National Park

Bounded by the Hawkesbury River to the north and Pittwater to the east, this gorgeous native bushland is a bushwalker's and kayaker's delight. There are numerous walking trails, picnic areas, The Basin campsite, lookouts, hundreds of Aboriginal rock art sites, secluded beaches, a tucked-away restaurant overlooking the water at Cottage Point and marinas at Akuna Bay and Bobbin Head. Cycling and horseriding are allowed in certain sections of the park. Flora and fauna highlights include banksias, waratahs, Sydney red gums, wallabies, flying foxes, pelicans, platypus, blue-tongued lizards, cockatoos and parrots. The information centre runs activities and provides maps and useful tips. ✪ *Map T1*
• *Information Centre: via Bobbin Head* • *9472 8949*
• *Open 10am–4pm daily*

Palm Beach peninsula's Whale Beach

7 Northern Beaches

This stretch of stunning ocean beaches runs from Manly to Barrenjoey Head. Palm Beach *(see p48)* is a haven for Sydney millionaires, as well as being the outdoor location for the popular TV soap opera *Home and Away*. The Barrenjoey Lighthouse overlooks Broken Bay, the Central Coast and the Hawkesbury River *(see p121)*. Behind Palm Beach lies lovely Pittwater. ✪ *Map U1*

8 Parramatta

Parramatta is part of Greater Sydney, just 20 km (13 miles) west of the city centre and easily accessible by the suburban train network. The fertile soil found here in the 1780s spared the fledgling colony from probable starvation and spawned Sydney's original satellite township. It was a rural retreat for Governor Phillip, who built a cottage here in 1790. Old Government House *(see p125)*, which replaced Phillip's cottage in 1799, is one of Sydney's most historic sites. Other highlights include Experiment Farm Cottage, Elizabeth Farm, Hambledon Cottage *(see pp124–5)* and Australia's oldest cemetery, St John's. ✪ *Map S3*
• *St John's Cemetery: O'Connell St, Parramatta*

Rock art at Ku-ring-gai Chase National Park

9 Royal National Park

Proclaimed in 1879, this is Australia's oldest national park and the world's second oldest. The 15,074-ha (37,248-acre) park is 32 km (19 miles) south of Sydney. Here you'll find subtropi-cal rainforests, deep valleys, cycle and walking trails, rugged ocean beaches, sandstone clifftops, heathlands, mangroves and inland lagoons.

There are several picnic- and campgrounds, and if you're lucky you could spy a swamp wallaby, a

Waratah satin bowerbird, a pied oystercatcher or the endangered tiger quoll. A tram from Loftus Station connects with the visitors centre on Sundays and public holidays.
Map S6 • Visitors Centre: Farnell Ave, Audley Heights • 9542 0648 • Open 9.30am–4:30pm Mon–Fri, 8:30am–7:30pm Sat–Sun and public holidays

10 Southern Highlands

The coastal hinterland and the city of Wollongong, one or two hours south of Sydney, is a popular weekend getaway destination. With no shortage of antiques and crafts shops, galleries, B&Bs, English-style pubs, ivy-clad Georgian buildings and cottage gardens, this region is reminiscent of the English countryside. Since 1993, a major attraction has been Bundanon, the former estate and studio of artist Arthur Boyd, who bequea-thed his property to the nation. Other popular attractions include the historic townships of Bowral *(see p125)*, Berrima, Kiama *(see p127)*, Berry and Kangaroo Valley. The movie *Babe* was filmed in nearby Robertson.

A Scenic Drive by Hawkesbury River

Morning

Head north across the **Harbour Bridge** and follow the signs to **Windsor** *(see p124)*. After a pit stop at the 1815 **Macquarie Arms Hotel** on George Street, backtrack to Pitt Town Road and follow this northwards. It becomes Cattai Road and then the Wisemans Ferry Road, passing through farmland and bush before dropping down to Wisemans Ferry on the **Hawkesbury River** *(see p121)*. Take the southern ferry across the Hawkes-bury and follow the incredibly scenic road that tracks the **Macdonald River** as far as **St Albans** *(see p124)*, where you can enjoy lunch at the 1848 **Settlers Arms Inn**.

Afternoon

Head back towards Wisemans Ferry along the other side of the Macdonald River until it meets the Hawkesbury River. Follow the river beneath its sandstone escarpments and through the isolated riverside townships of **Gunderman** and **Spencer** before climbing up through the forest to **Central Mangrove**. Drop down to **Calga** via Peats Ridge and take the Old Pacific Highway south to the Hawkesbury again. Cross the river and take the turnoff to the small fishing and boating township of **Brooklyn**. Enjoy an ale at the **Anglers Rest Hotel** or take a 15-minute ferry trip across to Dangar Island's idyllic **Island Shop** for homemade cake and coffee overlooking the water.

Left **Settlers Arms Inn, St Albans** Centre **Elizabeth Farm garden** Right **Hambledon Cottage**

Historic Sites & Townships

1 Windsor

Governor Macquarie established five towns in 1810 on the fertile land around the upper Hawkesbury River, one of which was Windsor, now a weekend tourist haven. The town's wonderful Colonial buildings include one of Australia's oldest pubs, the 1815 Macquarie Arms Hotel, as well as the 1823 St Mathew's Anglican Church and Rectory, designed by Francis Greenway *(see p23)*.

Macquarie Arms Hotel, Windsor

2 Rouse Hill House and Farm

Richard Rouse (1774–1852), Superintendent of Public Works and Convicts at Parramatta, once occupied this estate in Western Sydney and was succeeded by seven generations of descendants. The 1813 Historic Houses Trust property features a Georgian residence and gardens. The furniture dates from the 1830s to the 1960s.
⊗ Guntawong Rd, Rouse Hill • 9627 6777 • Open 9:30am–4:30pm Wed–Sun • Adm; guided tours only • Bookings advisable

1810 medicine chest at Experiment Farm

3 St Albans

The highlight of this quaint historical village is the charming Settlers Arms Inn. Built by convict labour between 1836 and 1848, this National Trust-classified pub overlooks the Macdonald River and offers good food and accommodation. ⊗ Settlers Arms Inn: 1 Whar St • 4568 2111 • www.settlersarms.com.a

4 Experiment Farm Cottage

Emancipated convicts James and Elizabeth Ruse established Australia's first self-sufficient farm in 1789. In the colony's first land grant, Governer Phillip gave then a further 12 ha (30 acres) for thei efforts. The charming Colonial bungalow was built by the farm's next owner, the surgeon John Harris. The property is owned by the National Trust. ⊗ Map S4 • 9 Ruse St, Harris Park • 9635 5655 • Open 10:30am–3:30pm Tue–Fri (from 11am Sat Sun) • Adm • www.nsw.nationaltrust.org.a

5 Elizabeth Farm

Built by John and Elizabeth Macarthur *(see p37)*, this 1793 estate was once an important social, politica and cultural centre. The farm's cottage is the oldest surviving building in Australia, and is carefully furnished with reproductions of the original interiors. ⊗ Map S4 • 70 Alice St, Rosehill • 9635 9488 • Ope 9:30am–4pm Fri–Sun • Adm • www.hht.net.au

Drawing room at Old Government House

6 Hambledon Cottage

Close by Elizabeth Farm, this cottage was named after a village in Hampshire, England. The Macarthurs built this cottage in 1824 as a retirement home for their governess, Penelope Lucas. The furnishings of the rendered sandstone cottage reflect the 1820s to the 1850s. ✪ *Map S3 • 63 Hassall St, Parramatta • 9635 6924 • Open 11am–4pm Wed, Thur, Sat & Sun • Adm*

7 Old Government House

Overlooking the Parramatta River, this distinguished plastered brick residence *(see p39)* is located on 105 ha (260 acres) of parkland. Australia's oldest public building, it was built by Governors Hunter and Macquarie between 1799 and 1818. The porch is credited to Francis Greenway. The interior faithfully reflects the Macquaries' era, and houses one of Australia's finest collections of 19th-century furniture. Tours explore the people who lived here as well as the eras they lived in. ✪ *www.nsw.nationaltrust.org.au*

8 Rock Art in Ku-ring-gai Chase National Park

Prior to white settlement, the area from Broken Bay to Sydney Harbour was inhabited by the Kuringai people. However, by the 1840s, most had been wiped out by smallpox or driven away. Over 800 sites record the Aboriginal culture and their bond with the land, including rock engravings, axe-grinding grooves, burial sites, cave shelters, middens (sea-shell mounds) and ochre hand stencils. ✪ *Map T1*

9 Norman Lindsay Gallery

Artist and writer Norman Lindsay (1879–1969), much loved for his 1918 classic children's book *The Magic Pudding* and his paintings and sculptures of satyrs, nymphs and sirens, occupied this Blue Mountains property from 1912 until his death. The National Trust property is now a museum and gallery with an extensive collection of Lindsay's work, including novels, watercolours and sculptures. ✪ *14 Norman Lindsay Crescent, Faulconbridge • 4751 1067 • Open 10am–4pm daily • Adm • www.normanlindsay.com.au*

10 Bowral

The Southern Highlands' main town began life in the 1860s when John Oxley, an early Colonial explorer, subdivided his land grant and a small township emerged. Bowral has an arty, old-world feel. It is probably best known as the former home of the famous cricketer Sir Donald Bradman *(see p92)*. The Bradman Museum honours the game and its greatest batsman, while the Bradman Walk is a self-guided tour of the historical sites in the town. ✪ *Bradman Museum: St Jude St, Bowral • 4862 1247 • Open 10am–5pm daily • Adm • www.bradman.com.au*

Antiques shop in Bowral

The Three Sisters in the Blue Mountains

TOP10 Natural Attractions

Jenolan Caves

1 Jenolan Caves

Discovered in 1838, this striking complex of underground limestone caves lies southwest of Katoomba *(see p128)* in the Blue Mountains *(see p121)*. Renowned for their icy underground rivers, huge caverns and intriguing limestone formations, they are surrounded by an extensive wildlife reserve. *6359 3911 • Tours daily • Adm • www.jenolancaves.org.au*

2 Mount Annan Botanic Gardens

On display at this amazing Botanic Garden is 404 ha (1,000 acres) of Australian plant life. Drive through gardens displaying the bizarre and colourful plants that make their home on the great southern continent. On the hillsides and near the lakes there is an abundance of bird life. Kangaroos can also be seen here. *Mt Annan Drive, Mt Annan • 4648 2477 • Open Apr–Sep: 10–4pm daily; Oct–Mar: 10am–6pm daily • Adm*

3 Three Sisters

The most popular landmark of the Blue Mountains is this spectacular rock formation, which derives its name from an Aboriginal Dreamtime legend. The story relates that the leader of the Gundungurra people, concerned for the safety of his three beautiful daughters, turned them into stone to protect them from enemies but died before being able to reverse his spell. The Three Sisters stand at the entrance to the long climb into Jamison Valley.

4 Wentworth Falls

These impressive 300-m (1,082-ft) falls mark the start of some of the Blue Mountains' most challenging walking trails down to neighbouring Jamison Valley. The Wentworth Falls Reserve lies near the village of Wentworth, named for one of the first Europeans to explore the region *(see p37)*.

Wentworth Falls

Mount Tomah Botanic Gardens

5 Kiama Blowhole

A large fishing and resort town, Kiama is one of the most attractive coastal spots south of Sydney. Discovered by explorer George Bass in 1797, this 25-m (82-ft) blowhole originates in a natural fault in the cliffs. It erupts whenever a wave hits with enough force, which can be every few minutes. Water can be thrown as high as 60 m (200 ft).

6 Illawarra Coast

A massive sandstone escarpment traces the coastline south of Royal National Park and north of Wollongong. A string of small towns nestled beneath the escarpment all offer spectacular ocean views.

7 Mount Tomah Botanic Gardens

Covering 28 ha (60 acres), these alpine gardens are located on a summit of the Blue Mountains. The rich basalt soil lies 1,000 m (3,281 ft) above sea level. Along with stunning views, the gardens feature an excellent collection of cool-climate plants. To reach the gardens, follow the Botanists' Way trail into the Blue Mountains. ⊗ Bells Line of Road via Bilpin • 4567 2000 • Open Mar–Oct: 10am–4pm daily; Oct–Mar: 10am–5pm daily • Adm • www.mounttomahbotanicgarden.com.au

8 Bouddi National Park

With clifftop walks overlooking the ocean and Broken Bay, secluded beaches, heathlands and banksia forests, this tiny coastal park is a gem. It extends from Box Head to McMaster's Beach on the Central Coast (see p121), and offers good bushwalking trails and camping facilities. ⊗ NPWS: 207 Albany St North, Gosford • 4320 4200

9 Wollemi National Park

This scenic national park is the largest wilderness area in NSW at 492,976 ha (1,217, 650 acres). The rugged terrain is composed of a maze of canyons and gorges that traverse rainforested mountains. Other features include riverside beaches, whitewater rafting and camping.

10 Brisbane Water National Park

Aboriginal rock art and spring wildflowers are the highlights of this 12,000-ha (39,640-acre) park overlooking Broken Bay and the Hawkesbury River. There are great views over the Hawkesbury from the path leading from Pearl Beach to tiny Patonga, accessible by ferry from Palm Beach (see p48). ⊗ Map U1

Left **Yachts in a creek at Pittwater** Centre **Palm Beach** Right **Seaplane at Rose Bay**

TOP 10 Things to Do

1 Swim at Pearl Beach
This National Trust hamlet is cradled by Brisbane Water National Park *(see p127)*. The calm waters and rockpool are simply magical. ◈ *Map U1*

2 Sail Pittwater & Cowan Creek
Hire a yacht and pack a picnic lunch to explore these isolated coves. ◈ *Map U1 • Hardy's Bay Yacht Charters: 46 Fisherman's Pde, Daleys Point • 4360 1442 • www.hbyc.com.au*

3 Hitch a Ride with the Riverboat Postman
Join this unique postal service as it delivers mail to isolated Hawkesbury River settlements. ◈ *Map T1 • Riverboat Postman: Dangar Rd, Brooklyn • 9985 7566 • 9:30am–1:15pm Mon–Fri • Adm*

4 Surf at Palm Beach
There may be better waves to the south, but it's hard to beat the setting. ◈ *Map U1*

5 Seaplane to Lunch
For a romantic lunch, take a seaplane from Rose Bay *(see p17)* to the Cottage Point Inn restaurant on Cowan Creek, or enjoy a picnic at Pittwater.

6 Australian Reptile Park
Crocodiles, alligators, snakes, spiders and friendly, hand-fed kangaroos are all here. ◈ *Pacific Highway, Somersby (next to Gosford exit on the F3) • 4340 1022 • Open 9am–5pm daily • Adm • www.reptilepark.com.au*

7 Visit Katoomba
Katoomba is the site of Echo Point, which offers superb views. Take a bushwalk around the clifftop paths or head down the Giant Stairway, across Jamison Valley *(see p126)* and back up on the Scenic Railway. ◈ *Echo Point Visitors Centre: Echo Point Road, Katoomba • 1300 653 408*

8 Overnight Trip to Canberra
Highlights of Australia's capital include the Parliament Houses, the National Gallery, the War Memorial, the National Library, Lake Burley Griffin and Black Mountain.

9 Southern Highlands
A quaint English-village feel permeates towns such as Bowral and Mittagong. Their main streets are lined with teahouses and antiques shops.

10 Premier's Walk
Bob Carr, former NSW premier, is a Coast Track enthusiast. This 26-km (16-mile) route through the Royal National Park *(see p123)* offers ocean views and seasonal glimpses of migrating whales. You can walk a section or go for the whole two-day stretch.

Kangaroo

→ *Brochures advertising coach tours are available in hotel lobbies. For small groups, try Red Carpet Custom Tours at 9971 0796.*

Price Categories

For a two course meal	**$**	under $35
for one with a drink	**$$**	$35–$60
(or equivalent meal),	**$$$**	$60–$120
plus taxes and extra	**$$$$**	$120–$200
charges.	**$$$$$**	over $200

Solitary

🔟 Places to Eat

1 Darley's
Flawless Modern Australian cuisine is served in a listed homestead with original fireplaces and breathtaking views. ◈ *Lilianfels Resort & Spa, Katoomba • 4780 1200 • Open brunch daily, lunch Sun, dinner Tue–Sat • $$$ • www.lilianfels.com.au*

2 Bell's at Killcare
Beach house-style cottage overlooking lush lawns. Great modern Italian food. ◈ *107 The Scenic Rd, Killcare • 4360 2411 • Open lunch Fri Sun, dinner daily • $$$$*

3 Letterbox Restaurant
Tasty Mod Oz food in a delightful converted post office. Try the saltimbocca with grilled polenta. ◈ *4 Ash St, Terrigal • 4385 4222 • Open Tue–Sun, Mon group bookings only • No dis access • $$$*

4 Solitary
Serving modern Australian food often made with ingredients from its own organic garden, Solitary offers a beautiful view of the Jamison Valley. ◈ *90 Cliff Drive, Leura Falls • 4782 1164 • Open 11:30am– 2pm daily, also for dinner Fri & Sat • $$$*

5 Esca Bimbadgen
Let the staff match the winery's delicious Bimbadgen wines to your selection from the tasty Moz Oz menu. ◈ *790 McDonalds Rd, Pokolbin • 4998 4666 • $$$$*

6 Paragon
Get a sense of Katoomba in its heyday at this atmospheric Art Deco café. Sit snug in a booth, choose from handmade chocolates on display, and be sure to check out the lovely back rooms. ◈ *65 Katoomba St, Katoomba • 4782 2928 • No dis access • $$*

7 The Chairman & Yip
Long considered one of Canberra's best restaurants, with a good value, modern Asian fusion menu. ◈ *108 Bunda St, Civic • 6248 7109 • Open Mon–Sat • $$*

8 Harbourside Brighton
Overlooking the Kiama harbour, this café and restaurant offers great views and an extensive menu stretching from breakfast to dinner ◈ *4–6 Terralong St, Kiama • 4232 2799 • Dis access • Open 8am–10pm daily • $$*

9 Vulcan's
Join the Sydney foodies who head to Vulcan's to enjoy chef Phillip Searle's food. ◈ *33 Govetts Leap Rd, Blackheath • 4787 6899 • Open dinner and lunch Fri–Sun • $$$*

10 Coffee Culture
It's a local secret that the best coffee in the Southern Highlands comes from this aromatic shop, hidden behind a cinema on Bowral's main street. ◈ *Shop 6, Empire Cinema Complex, 327 Bong Bong St, Bowral • 4862 2400 • $*

Coffee Culture

Unless otherwise stated, all restaurants are open daily, accept credit cards, serve vegetarian meals, and provide disabled access.

STREETSMART

Planning Your Trip
132

Getting to Sydney
133

Getting Around
134

Sources of Information
135

Banking &
Communications
136

Security & Health
137

Things to Avoid
138

Shopping Tips
139

Sydney on a Budget
140

Dining Tips
141

Accommodation Tips
142

Places to Stay
143–149

SYDNEY'S TOP 10

Left **Casual dress at a beachside café** Right **All non-Australians need passports**

TOP 10 Planning Your Trip

1 When to Go
Late spring (October–November) and early autumn (March–April) are the best times to visit Sydney. The days are warm and the evenings mild. Sydney's winters are cool to mild, but summer can be hot and unbearably humid with the occasional downpour.

2 What to Bring
Sydney fashion is casual, so a selection of light mix-and-match clothing should suffice. Be sure to pack beach gear and walking shoes.

3 How Long to Stay
One week will allow you to cover all the top 10 sights, in two weeks you'll be able to explore the Around Town section, and three weeks will be enough time to experience the national parks and outlying regions.

4 Media
Sydney has three major dailies. *The Sydney Morning Herald*, *The Daily Telegraph* and *The Australian*, all of which have websites.

5 Websites
The New South Wales (NSW) government portal is an informative site, and its Culture and Recreation section is useful for planning a holiday, as is the website of the state government tourism department, Destination NSW. The Australian Tourist Commission site provides information on various events and lists worldwide Australian travel agencies.

6 Passports & Visas
All foreign visitors to Australia must have a valid passport. If you are a New Zealander you will receive an electronic visa. If you are from any other country, you will require an entry visa or ETA (Electronic Travel Authority). Visa forms are available from travel agencies and the Australian government's immigration website.

7 Australian Consulates & Embassies
Australian consulates, embassies and missions are found in almost every country's capital city. They can provide inform-ation about Sydney and answer questions regarding visas. To locate the consulate in your city, visit the site listed under "Consulates".

8 Insurance
Although travel in Australia is generally straightforward, and hospitals won't turn you away if you're uninsured, it's always advised to be well insured when travelling. Before any challenging outdoor activity, read the fine print to ensure that you will be covered in an emergency.

9 Driver's Licenses
Drivers with a valid overseas license in English can drive in Australia. Carry your license at all times if you are driving. Seat-belts are compulsory.

10 Customs
Customs regulations are strictly enforced and prohibit the unauthorised import of goods made from plant or animal products, weapons or firearms, protected wildlife, amounts exceeding $10,000 and non-prescription drugs. If you require medication, carry your prescription.

Directory

The Sydney Morning Herald
• www.smh.com.au

The Daily Telegraph
• www.dailytelegraph.news.com.au

The Australian
• www.theaustralian.news.com.au

NSW Government
• www.nsw.gov.au

Destination NSW
• www.sydney.com

Australian Tourist Commission
• www.australia.com

Australian Immigration
• www.immi.gov.au

Consulates
• www.embassy.gov.au

Customs
• www.customs.gov.au

Previous pages: **View from Harbourside Shopping Centre looking east towards the city** _oft **Flight arriving at the airport** Centre **Passenger train** Right **The QEII passenger ship**

10 Getting To Sydney

1 Kingsford-Smith International Airport

Sydney's only international airport is 9 km (5.6 miles) south of the city centre. All domestic flights also arrive and depart from here. The international (T1) and domestic terminals (T2 and T3) are far apart, so you'll need to catch a taxi, bus or train to travel between them. Airport Link takes 2 minutes, but first check if your airline offers a free shuttle.

2 Airport Link

Trains provide a fast and easy way to get into the city, particularly at peak hour when traffic is heavy. The trip takes only 13 minutes. Use the elevators to get to the stations, directly below the terminals.

3 Airport Buses & Shuttles

Though very cheap, government-owned buses are only a good option if you are heading to Randwick, Coogee and Bondi Junction. Private shuttles such as Sydney Airporter, Airport Connect and Airbus Sydney are more expensive, but can be booked for specific times and will take you right to your destination.

4 Help Desks

Visit the NSW Tourism Information Desks at the airport and at Central Station if you need any help.

5 Taxis

A taxi (see p134) from T1 to the CBD costs about $30. There are ranks outside each terminal. A $3.50 toll has to be paid if you take a taxi from any of these. Taxi queues are longest on weekdays at 7–9am and 5–7pm, the airport's peak hours.

6 Car Hire

Car companies (see p134), have desks at the airport. Hiring a small car will cost $40–$80 per day, so it is advisable to shop around.

7 Central Station

All interstate and regional trains terminate on the upper level of this station. Many coach services drop passengers here, at the Sydney Coach Terminal. Suburban train services run from the lower level, buses to the eastern suburbs leave from Eddy Avenue, and those to the inner-west suburbs from nearby Railway Square. There is a taxi rank at the upper level entrance.

8 Passenger Ship Terminals

Both passenger ports, the Overseas Passenger Terminal (OPT) at West Circular Quay and Wharf 5 at Darling Harbour, are excellent places to arrive, centrally located and close to many hotels. The OPT is spectacular as it faces the Opera House.

9 Left Luggage

Due to security policies, lockers are not available at the airport. Luggage can be left in the baggage storage areas of the arrivals hall in each terminal. There are no left luggage facilities at Central Station or at the ports.

10 Lost Property

Collect lost property from Sydney Airport Reception at T1. Contact your airline if your luggage goes missing or is left on the baggage carousel, or if you lose an item in T2 or T3. Items lost on a train or at a station can be found at Cityrail's lost property office at Central Station.

Directory

Airport Connect and Air Bus Sydney
• 9557 7615

Airport Link
• Runs every 10 mins on weekdays, every 15 mins on weekends

Sydney Airporter
• 9666 9988

NSW Tourism Information Desks
• Airport: T1 level 1; open 6am–11pm
• Central Station: main concourse, 6am–10pm

Lost Property
• Sydney Airport Reception: T1 level 3; 9667 9583 • Cityrail: Central Station, main concourse; 9379 3341

Left **The City Sightseeing bus** Right **Circular Quay**

⑩ Getting Around

1 Buses
Bus services run frequently and are a good, cheap way to get around. Routes with an "L", "E" or "X" indicate services that travel a greater distance between stops. Buy your ticket before boarding buses in the city. Single or multi-trip pre-pay tickets are sold at kiosks, convenience stores and newsagents.

2 Trains
Trains to most areas leave from the Town Hall, Wynyard and Central stations. Services run frequently from 6am until after midnight.

3 Ferries
Sydney Ferries (see pp16–17) run services from Circular Quay to 39 wharves. The 30-minute ride from Circular Quay to Manly is extra special, but those who find it too long can catch the Fast Ferry. Though not cheap, ferries are a great way to see Sydney and to experience the harbour.

4 Light Rail
A pleasant and fast way to get around, this is easily the best direct transport from the CBD to the Fish Market.

5 Free City Shuttle
Sydney Buses operates free shuttle bus services that run every 10 minutes, travelling in a loop between Central Station and Circular Quay via Elizabeth and George Streets. Board the bus at stops marked with the green shuttle logo.

6 Taxis
Make bookings if you want to arrive at an exact time, especially at peak hours and on weekend nights. If drivers don't know the way, you are entitled to have them turn off the meter while they look up the street directory. Fares are regulated and cost more after 10pm. Smoking is not allowed and a driver may refuse to take you if you are drunk.

7 Water Taxis
Running from most piers, they'll pick you up from anywhere they can navigate. Prices vary, but expect to pay a flagfall of about $45 and an additional cost per person. Look for them at Circular Quay, or call to book one. Confirm the price before you board.

8 City Sightseeing Buses
Great value tickets allow you to get on and off the buses at will, and frequent services run the loop. A one or two-day twin ticket allows you to travel on both Sydney and Bondi Sightseeing Buses.

9 Car Hire
While the public transport network is excellent, having a car in Sydney makes getting around easy, particularly in the outer suburbs.

10 Bicycles
There are some cycle lanes in Sydney but the roads are very crowded. Download a cycle map and hire a bike from Cheeky Monkey or Woolys Wheels.

Directory

Light Rail
• Runs 24 hours from Central to Star City

Taxis
• Taxis Combined: 133 300
• Legion Cabs: 131 451

Water Taxis Combined
• 9555 8888

City Sightseeing Buses
• one-day ticket: $40; two-day twin ticket: $60

Car Hire Companies
• Hertz: 133039
• Bayswater 9360 3622
• Europcar: 1300 131 390

Bicycle Information
• Maps: www.rta.nsw. gov.au
• Cheeky Monkey: 28 Clovelly Rd; 9399 3370
• Woolys Wheels: 82 Oxford St; 9331 2671

Transport Infoline
• www.131500.com.au
• 131500

Free City Shuttle
• www.sydneybuses. info/free-shuttles

Streetsmart

For discounted travel passes for buses, City Sightseeing buses, ferries, airport train transfers and harbour cruises, see p140.

Left **Sydney Visitors Centre** Centre **Information kiosk at Central Station** Right **Children playing**

10 Sources of Information

1 Tourist Offices
The Sydney Visitors Centre at The Rocks (see p140) and Darling Harbour offer information and maps. You'll find City Host information kiosks at Circular Quay, Sydney Square and Martin Place. The Visitors Centre at Sydney Airport handles accommodation and travel bookings.

2 Embassies & Consulates
Several nations have consulates in Sydney, which can be located in the Yellow Pages telephone directory.

3 Disabled Travellers
Travellers with disabilities will find the Access Foundation's site an excellent resource for news, entertainment, travel, accommodation, transport and links to community resources.

4 Gay & Lesbian Travellers
The Gay and Lesbian Tourism site provides accommodation information, while the Sydney Star Observer has news and entertainment listings. Lesbians on the Loose has information, contacts and classifieds.

5 Travelling with Children
Sydney's Child is a free monthly magazine with tips for parents. You can pick one up at many chemists, tourist venues and child-friendly facilities like public pools. Many venues also host kids' programmes.

6 Older Travellers
The Senior Card and Seniors Information Service sites offer event listings, news and links to relevant organisations. Get Up and Go magazine contains information on travel agencies.

7 Websites
The City of Sydney, Tourism NSW and City Search websites cover sports, festivals, music, tours, the arts and more.

8 Radio & TV
Five free TV networks include SBS and ABC. Triple J (105.7 FM) is an alternative music station, and 2SER FM (107.3) and FBI FM (94.5) are also worth checking out. 702 ABC (702 AM) serves up current affairs and drive-time formats while Radio National (570 AM) presents current affairs, music and culture.

9 Free Publications & Listings
City Weekly is a weekly newspaper covering entertainment and leisure. The Sydney Morning Herald's Metro section offers information on Sydney events.

10 Bookshops & Café Windows
Many independent bookshops and cafés have noticeboards with local advertisements, especially around Glebe Point Road, Crown Street, King Street and Campbell Parade.

Directory

Sydney Visitor Centre
• 9240 8788 or freecall 1800 067 676; www. sydney.com

Consulates
• New Zealand: 8256 2000 • Canada: 9364 3000 • India: 9223 9500 • Ireland: 9264 9635 • UK: 9247 7521 • USA: 9373 9200

Yellow Pages
• www.yellowpages. com.au

Access Foundation
• www.accessibility. com.au

Sydney's Child
• www.sydneyschild. com.au

City Sites
• www.cityofsydney. nsw.gov.au
• sydney.citysearch. com.au
• www.visitsydney.com

Gay & Lesbian Sites
• www.galta.com.au
• www.ssonet.com.au
• www.lotl.com

Seniors Sites
• www.seniorscard. nsw.gov.au
• www.getupandgo. net.au

Radio & TV
• www.abc.net.au

Left **50-cent and $1 coins** Centre **$20 bill** Right **Phone card**

⁜10 Banking & Communications

1 Money, Taxes & Refunds

The Australian dollar is divided into 100 cents. There are $5, $10, $20, $50 and $100 plastic notes. A 10 percent tax is levied on most goods and services (GST), but tourists may be entitled to refunds from Customs through the Tourist Refund Scheme (TRS). Be sure to ask for a "tax invoice" for purchases over $300, just in case.

2 Banks & Post Offices

Most banks are open from 9:30/10am–4/5pm Monday to Friday. Australia Post branch hours vary, but most are open from 9am–5pm Monday to Friday. The GPO is open from 8:15am–5:30pm Monday to Friday and 10am–2pm Saturday. Poste Restante mail should be addressed to the GPO, 1 Martin Place, Sydney 2000.

3 Public Holidays

Banks, post offices and most government agencies are closed on these public holidays: New Year's Day, Australia Day (26 January), Good Friday and Easter Monday, Anzac Day (25 April), Queen's Birthday (2nd Monday in June), Bank Holiday (1st Monday in August), Labour Day (1st Monday in October), Christmas Day and Boxing Day (26 December). The summer school break extends from late December to late January. There are usually two-week breaks in April, July and October.

4 Currency Exchange

Bureaux de change at the airport open between 5am and 6am and close between 9:45pm and 11pm daily. There are numerous bureaux de change in the CBD.

5 Traveller's Cheques

Traveller's cheques are still accepted by major hotels, banks and the like, but personal cheques from foreign accounts are not.

6 ATMs

Most ATMs are located outside banks, and can also be found in many pubs, clubs and some convenience stores. If your bank's debit card is linked to an international system such as Cirrus, you can use your card at retail outlets. Make sure your PIN applies to Australian ATMs.

7 Credit Cards

MasterCard and Visa are the two major credit cards in Australia; some establishments also accept American Express and Diners Club. Cash advances against your credit card are also possible. In most cases you'll need a credit card to hire a car in Sydney.

8 Telephones

Public telephones accept coins, phone cards and sometimes credit cards. A local call costs 50 cents. Phone cards are available at newsagents and convenience stores; make sure the card allows international calls before buying one. You may be able to use a pre-paid SIM card in your own mobile phone.

9 Internet Access

Most hotels are set up to allow you to log on the net. There is also no shortage of Internet cafés across the city.

10 Tipping

While tipping is not compulsory, it is always appreciated – 10 per cent of the total bill is appropriate for good service, while cafés have a tip jar at the counter. It is common to round up taxi fares, and hotel staff may expect a gratuity.

Directory

Customs
• www.customs.gov.au

Stolen Credit Cards
• MasterCard: 1800 120 113 • Visa: 1800 450 346
• Amex: 1300 132 639
• Diners Club: 1300 360 060

Mobile Phone Sales
• Vodafone Sales: Sydney Airport: 9700 7788

The International prefix to dial Australia is 61. The area code for Sydney is 02. Ten-digit numbers preceded by 04 are mobile numbers.

Left **Police vehicle** Centre **Pharmacy in The Rocks** Right **Lifesaving sign**

10 Security & Health

1 Theft
Sydney is a safe destination, but the usual Big City" rules apply. Don't leave valuables in cars, avoid ATMs late at night, and be alert to pickpockets at train stations. Baggage storage is available at the airport, and lockers at the State Library, most swimming pools and at Bondi and Manly.

2 Dangerous Areas
It's sensible to avoid parks, barren areas and the back-streets of Kings Cross late at night. If you're travelling on a train alone at night, sit near the guard's compartment (marked by blue light).

3 Hospitals & Medical Centres
Sydney Hospital, St Vincent's Hospital, RPA Hospital and the Sydney Children's Hospital Randwick are the most central facilities that accept emergency admissions. If you require an ambulance, call 000. Make sure your travel insurance covers ambulance fees, which can be expensive.

4 Pharmacies
Pharmacies are found all over Sydney. In most suburbs they open weekends as well as weekdays. It's advisable to carry your prescription if you require regular medication.

5 Women Travellers
Sydney can be "blokey" (macho), but women travellers mostly find it a relaxed and casual city. The WIRS (Women's Information and Referral Service) has information on women's services and organisations. The Rape Crisis Centre can also help in an emergency.

6 Things that Bite & Sting
Sydneysiders are obsessed with creatures that bite and sting, such as sharks and funnel-web spiders, but you'd be unlikely to encounter them. Blowflies and "mozzies" can be annoying in summer, but they don't carry malaria. Do wear sturdy shoes and long trousers if walking in bushland.

7 Ticks
Bush ticks are small insects that crawl from foliage and burrow into your skin; check your scalp, neck and ankles if you have been bushwalking. Sodium bicarbonate can help to remove ticks.

8 Sunburn
Take precautions against the strong Australian sun, for even overcast days can have a high UV rating. When swimming or sailing, keep in mind that water amplifies the intensity of UV rays.

9 Swimming
Unless an experienced open-water swimmer, stick to beaches patrolled by lifeguards. Always swim between the red and yellow flags. If caught in an undertow (see p138), don't try swimming against the current; wait until help arrives or the rip peters out.

10 Bushfires
Bushfires are part of Sydney life in the bushy outer suburbs. "Total Fire Ban" days are often declared in summer. If you're in trouble, don't try to outrun the fire: seek shelter immediately to avoid the most common cause of death, which is radiant heat.

Directory

Hospitals & Clinics
• Sydney Hospital: 8 Macquarie St
• St Vincent's Hospital: Victoria St, Darlinghurst
• Sydney Children's Hospital: Randwick
• RPA Hospital: Camperdown

Women's Resources
• WIRS: 1800 817 227 www.women.nsw.gov. au • Rape Crisis Centre: 24 hrs daily; 9819 7357; freecall 1800 424 017

Emergencies
• Fire, Police, Ambulance: freecall 000
• Lifeline: 131 114
• Poisons Information Line: 131 126

Left **Lifesaving flag** Right **Central Railway Station**

TOP 10 Things to Avoid

1 Swimming Outside the Flags

Although Sydney beaches are idyllic, their unpredictable rips (undertows) can be hazardous. Always swim between the red and yellow flags and ensure that you are being watched by a lifeguard. If you get into trouble, try to relax and raise an arm to alert the lifeguards.

2 Bushwalking Alone

Bushwalking is a great way to see a different part of the city, but never go alone. Let someone know where you are going and your expected time of return. Stick to walking tracks, take a map, mobile phone, plenty of water and snacks.

3 Age Restrictions

Age restrictions apply to entry to licensed premises and gambling venues, 18 years in both instances. Cigarettes are not sold to under 18-year olds and there are penalties if caught buying for minors. There are also penalties if caught with illicit drugs.

4 Walking into Traffic

If you're fresh off the plane from Los Angeles or New York and feeling a little jetlagged, look both ways before stepping off the pavement (sidewalk): Australian cars drive on the left-hand side of the road, not the right.

5 Beggars & the Homeless

Like any big city, Sydney has its share of homeless beggars, most of whom present no danger. Some of them are registered street vendors of *The Big Issue*; purchase a copy if you'd like to support those trying to get back on their feet. They get half the proceeds and it's a good read.

6 Drink Driving

Drink driving is a problem in Australia and police are equipped to test drivers for alcohol. The legal limit is 0.05 in NSW. "Booze buses" (police teams with testing equipment) randomly target locations at odd hours. If caught, your car keys will be confiscated and you will face a hefty fine. It's just not worth the risk, so catch a taxi.

7 City Circle Train Stations at Peak Hour

Sydney's central underground railway stations are frantic at peak hour. Not just busy, they can be stiflingly hot, especially in summer. Like all congested city venues they are frequented by pickpockets, so be careful.

8 Arguments with Drunks

Some young local men who have had too much alcohol on a night out can get into arguments that sometimes turn physical. This is not common but it does happen. If you are confronted in this way don't argue back, just walk away.

9 You say Bond-ee, I say Bond-eye

North Americans and other English-speakers are particularly prone to stumbling into this minefield. Listen careful to local pronunciation ar follow suit – or just ask. Bondi is pronounced "Bond-eye", not "Bond-ee". For some reason Sydneysiders fin this mistake particularly irksome. Some other pronunciation pitfalls include "Mel-born" instead of "Mel-bun" for Melbourne, and "Coo-gee" instead of "Could-gee" for Coogee Beach.

10 Bluebottles

Strong winds can bring bluebottles onto beaches: they look like small, clear jellyfish with blue veins and hav long stinging tentacles. Their sting is painful but they are only dangerous for people with asthma. Dead bluebottles stranded on the sand can still sting. Avoid swimming near them, don't rub a sting and if no medical attention is available, treat stings with ice packs.

 Peak hours run between 7–9am and 5–7pm on weekdays.

Left **Paddington Market** Centre **Darling Harbour** Right **The Strand**

Shopping Tips

1 Trading Hours

Most stores are open daily 9am–5:30pm, with some closing at 4pm Sundays. Late-night shopping on Thursdays sees shops open until 9pm. In areas such as Paddington, Balmain and Double Bay, shops open between 10 and 11am and close at 6pm. Many shops in Chinatown are open until 7pm daily.

2 Sales

While boutiques no longer stick to a firm schedule of sales, department stores have huge sales in January and again in June. There are great bargains, especially in homewares. Sales are usually advertised in newspapers and on TV.

3 GST

A Goods and Services Tax (GST) of ten percent is applied to most items. If you spend more than $300 at any one shop within 28 days of leaving Australia, you are entitled to reclaim the GST. Take your receipts to the booth at Sydney Airport.

4 Payment

All stores accept credit cards, though some claim a surcharge on credit card purchases. Some larger stores, souvenir shops and duty free stores may accept traveller's cheques as long as you have passport identification.

5 Warehouse Outlets

Many local chain stores and manufacturers have warehouse outlets in inner city suburbs such as Alexandria. The best way to check them out is on a day tour. Try Sydney Shopping tours, which has six city pick-up points and includes lunch.

6 Souvenirs

For stuffed koalas, you can't beat the discount shops on Pitt and Park Streets. Most attractions offer quality keepsakes; try the Museum of Sydney (see p42) and Opera House Store (see p81). Buy opals and boomerangs in The Rocks (see p81), swimwear and T-shirts at surf shops (see p94) and sheepskins in the QVB (see p80). Try the weekend market at The Rocks for handmade items.

7 Fashion & Accessories

You'll find high-end designer fashion in Double Bay, Paddington (see p94) and the Westfield Bondi Junction (WBJ) (see p100). A younger crowd shops in The Galeries (see p80), Surry Hills (see p94) and Woollahra for casual and party clothes. Try Newtown (see p106) for alternative and secondhand shops, including Enmore Rd. Find kids' clothes at David Jones (see p81) and WBJ.

8 Design & Homewares

The best of Australian and international design can be found in Surry Hills and Alexandria. A stroll around the streets near Central station will unearth gems. Crown Street between Foveaux and Devonshire is also a great strip (see p94). The Object store (see p44) has a great range of Australian design crafts.

9 Food

The big supermarkets are mostly found in the suburbs, but there is a Woolworths at Town Hall station and a Coles at Wynyard. Delicatessens offer great sandwich fillings, small goods and cheese. David Jones' food hall offers gourmet goodies as well as pre-cooked dinners. Grower's markets, advertised in *The Sydney Morning Herald* on Tuesdays, are a wonderful way to shop.

10 Going Green

A current campaign to reduce the quantity of plastic bags that end up as landfill has caused shops to introduce many eco-friendly options. Buy a sturdy, reusable green bag – fast becoming trendy – from Coles or Woolworths supermarkets, department stores and even smaller shops, or pack your purchases into your backpack.

Contact Sydney Shopping Tours at 1800 673 709 or www.sydneyshoppingtours.com.au – a day's tour costs $50.

Left **Sydney Harbour Youth Hostel roof terrace** Centre **Picnic basket** Right **Laundromat**

🔟 Sydney on a Budget

1 Discount Plane Tickets
There are often cheap tickets to Australia in the low season, from mid-April to end-September. If flying in from elsewhere in Australia, check out the websites of discount air carriers Virgin Blue, Tiger Airways and Jetstar for good deals.

2 Hotel Deals
Look for packages that offer free or very cheap accommodation when you buy your flights. You can also find cheap rates by booking hotels online, or by making week-long reservations *(see p142)*.

3 Youth Hostels
Staying in hostels is not just for backpackers, as most have comfortable double and twin rooms available for modest prices. You'll also benefit from the use of the kitchen, fridge, laundry and lounge areas. Some hostels have swimming pools.

4 Concessions
An International Student Identification Card, available from STA travel agents, will get you a concession entry into most attractions, galleries and museums, but not the concession rate on public transport.

5 Travel Passes
Weekly and day passes for unlimited trips on buses, trains and ferries can save plenty of money. My Multi 1 weekly pass is great value, particularly if you're planning on making more than two trips on public transport a day. A My Multi 3 pass will even get you to the Blue Mountains by train. However, these passes cannot be used on the monorail and light rail services or at the airport train stations. Every Sunday, Family Funday tickets allow unlimited travel on Government buses, trains and ferries for $2.50 per person. There should be at least one adult and one child in the group.

6 Phone Cards
Convenience stores all over the city sell international calling cards, so shop around for one with good rates. Buy a Telstra phone card to use for local calls.

7 Cheap Eats
Sydney has myriad cheap and cheerful restaurants. The best are often small ethnic diners offering Thai, Chinese, Indian or Lebanese food. To save more money, bring your own wine or beer and stop by a gelataria for an ice cream or gelato dessert.

8 Coupons and Online Discounts
There are often vouchers for Sydney's top restaurants among the brochures in high-end hotel lobbies. More coupons may be available at the Sydney Visitors' Centre. Many attractions offer significant discount for online bookings and ticket purchases via their websites.

9 Picnics
Buying lunch every day can be expensive. Instead, buy staples such as bread, fruit and cheese and store them in the fridge at your hostel or hotel room. Make a picnic lunch and pack it for the day. Sydney's tap water is good quality, so buy a bottle of water and keep refilling it.

10 Laundromats
Hostels usually have coin-operated washing machines, but if you're staying somewhere without one, avoid the cost of laundering by going to a laundromat to use the coin-operated machines.

Directory

STA Travel
841 George St, Sydney; 9212 1255

Sydney Visitors' Centre
• Cnr Argyle & Playfair Sts, The Rocks; 9240 8788

Laundromats
Laundrette on King: 409 King St, Newtown • Soap Sud City: 56 Bays-water Rd, Kings Cross

Left **Wine bottle label** Centre **Fresh produce** Right **Making coffee at Bar Colluzi**

TOP 10 Dining Tips

1 Mod Oz

Modern Australian cuisine is generally a fusion of Asian and Eastern flavours with European technique. Experimental Australian chefs draw on the highly multicultural population and a diverse climate that ranges from tropical to cool-region conditions.

2 Menu Jargon

The quest for the exotic generates menus loaded with foreign terms and regional Australian names. Bangalow and Barossa refer to regions; Wagyu and Hiramasa to quality; assiette, confit and panacotta to French and Italian techniques and dishes. Chinese restaurants often have an English and a Chinese menu.

3 Courses

Pre-dinner nibbles are called hors d'oeuvres or canapés. The first course is the entrée, and the second is the main course. These are followed by dessert and coffee, or sometimes by a cheese platter.

4 Dégustation

This French word means to take a small amount into the mouth and test its quality. A Sydney trend, dégustations offer 7–12 small set courses instead of orders from the menu. These courses allow chefs to take advantage of the freshest ingredients and to show off their skills.

5 Bookings

The more expensive the restaurant, the further ahead you'll need to make your reservation. Sydney's top restaurant, the dégustation-only Tetsuya's (see p58), takes bookings three months in advance. Vegetarians and those with special dietary requirements should book at least a day ahead. Some restaurants don't take bookings but will send you to a nearby bar and call you when your table is ready.

6 Tipping

Usual but voluntary, tipping is a way to express your enjoyment of or dissatisfaction with a restaurant meal. If the food and service are of good quality, leave about 10 per cent. You may want to leave more for extraordinary service, and less or no tip if service has been shoddy.

7 Wine

Most expensive restaurants have helpful sommeliers who are experts at matching food and wine, so you can leave the choices up to them. You might tell them that you wish to taste a variety of Australian wines. When buying wine from a bottle shop, be aware that Australian names refer to the grape variety and not the region. You can take your own wine to some restaurants but you may have to pay a small charge for corkage.

8 Beer

Some types of food are highly spiced and do not go well with most wines. Choosing a beer to go with Thai, Indian and Chinese food is a good option. Good Australian beers include Boag's, Cascade, Hahn Premium, James Squire, Cooper's and Redback.

9 Coffee

The ubiquitous espresso coffee comes in various forms. A flat white is a shot of coffee with milk but no froth while the popular latte has additional milk and is often served in a long glass. Try a macchiato, a shot topped with a burst of froth. Decaf, soy and light milks are common.

10 Dining With Children

Some restaurants specifically cater to kids with dedicated menus. Others will suggest entrée-sized dishes that might appeal to children. The large Chinese and Italian restaurants and places by the beach are usually used to kids running around. Some have paper napkins and provide crayons so that kids can draw on them.

> Some restaurants which are not licensed have a policy of BYO, or "bring your own" alcohol; at some others, BYO is optional.

Left **Hotels at Darling Harbour** Right **Comfortable hotel room**

Accommodation Tips

1 Choosing Hotel Locations

Staying at the beach means a refreshing dip is only moments away. Hotels on the fringe of the CBD, especially those with harbour views, are a relaxing option for business travellers. Those with children might avoid areas around Potts Point and Darlinghurst, which necessitate walking through the red light district of Kings Cross.

2 Making Reservations

It is advisable to make reservations. Book well in advance when Sydney is busiest, from mid-December until the beginning of February, during Mardi Gras in early March, and in school holidays – the first two weeks of April, July and October. Reservations can be made via the hotel directly or through your travel agent.

3 Discount Rates

Some hotels offer significant discounts for last minute bookings and walk-ins. Hotel websites sometimes offer great rates. If you are prepared to make a non-refundable booking, you might get as much as a 50 per cent discount on rooms.

4 Longer Stays

Some hotels, particularly hostels, budget and boutique hotels, reward guests for lengthy stays with reduced weekly rates. Many hostels set a limit of a 14-day stay. Serviced apartments may offer incentives for stays of up to a month.

5 Frequent Flyers

Most airline frequent flyer programmes have lists of hotels where members can accrue points. Existing points can usually be used for room upgrades or special packages. Airline bookings sometimes offer a discount.

6 Water Views

While many hotels are situated at the water's edge, the standard room rate usually applies to a room without a view. Expect to pay a premium of about $50–$100 above the standard rate. You might find better value in the best room of a smaller or lower-rated hotel.

7 Extra Costs

Even the most basic breakfast can be expensive in the large CBD hotels, so head to a nearby café or bakery. Drinks and snacks provided in the minibar are often double their retail cost, so check the prices first. Avoid surcharges on phone calls by using a public phone in the lobby. Other services, such as late checkouts, parking, laundering, Internet access, in-house movies and receiving faxes usually incur a fee.

8 Travelling with Children

Children under 12 usually stay for free using existing bedding. This can be a good arrangement in twin rooms that offer a double and single bed, or in studios that include sofa beds. Where offered, there is a fee of approximately $30 for rollaway beds. Many hotels can arrange interconnecting rooms.

9 Disabled Travellers

Regulations force larger hotels to offer rooms with full disabled access, and some hotels have as many as ten such rooms. The same rules don't apply to small hotels and B&Bs in converted mansions or heritage buildings. It's best to enquire about facilities when making reservations and to check that there is room to manoeuvre a wheelchair.

10 GST

GST *(see p139)* is charged on hotel rooms and on other services that hotels may provide for you. The tax is usually included in the room rate and will be clearly marked on any accounts. It is not possible to reclaim GST incurred on accommodation.

Exterior of Park Hyatt Sydney

Price Categories

For a standard double room per night (with breakfast if included), taxes and extra charges.

$	under $80
$$	$80–150
$$$	$150–250
$$$$	$250–350
$$$$$	over $350

⁰10 Harbourside Hotels

1 Blue Sydney
This modern boutique hotel is one of the coolest in Sydney. Sip fabulous cocktails at the award-winning Water Bar and enjoy the luxury robes and Aveda bath products. ◈ Map P3 • The Wharf at Woolloomooloo, Cowper Wharf Rd • 9331 9000 • $$$$ • www.tajhotels.com/sydney

2 The Sebel Pier One Sydney
In a restored wharf building in the Walsh Bay World Heritage precinct, look right into the water through the lobby's glass floor. Luxurious rooms incorporate original features and contemporary design. ◈ Map M1 • 11 Hickson Rd, Walsh Bay • 8298 9999 • $$$$ • www.sebelpierone.com.au

3 Vibe Hotel Rushcutters
Between the CBD and Bondi, this stylish hotel neighbours a harbourside park and overlooks the Cruising Yacht Club marina. A brisk walk up the hill takes you to Kings Cross and Darlinghurst. ◈ Map J5 • 100 Bayswater Rd, Rushcutters Bay • 8353 7988 • $$$$ • www.vibehotels.com.au

4 Park Hyatt Sydney
Many rooms in this luxurious six-star hotel have Opera House views, as does the rooftop heated swimming pool. Perfectly equipped for business travellers, the hotel offers high-speed Internet access in every room and a dedicated business centre. ◈ Map M1 • 7 Hickson Rd, The Rocks • 9256 1234 • $$$$$ • www.sydney.park.hyatt.com

5 Four Seasons Hotel Sydney
You'll be able to spot this superbly-located high-rise hotel from many vantages. Inside, the higher the floor number, the better the view. Corner rooms have a full harbour panorama. The marble-clad lobby leads to lovely lounge areas and two fine restaurants. ◈ Map M2 • 199 George St, The Rocks • 9250 3100 • $$$$ • www.fourseasons.com/sydney

6 Quay Grand Suites
Next door to the Opera House at one of Sydney's premier addresses, apartments are tastefully furnished with kitchen facilities. Try ECQ, the hotel's dress circle bar. ◈ Map N1 • 61 Macquarie St, East Circular Quay • 9256 4000 • Some dis access • $$$$$ • www.mirvachotels.com

7 Star City
A first-rate hotel with stylish rooms and an endless list of facilities. Drawcards include king beds in the standard rooms, 20 restaurants, cafés and bars, 24-hour entertainment and a health club with a pool. Choose between hotel and apartment-style accommodation. ◈ Map K3 • 80 Pyrmont St, Pyrmont • 1800 700 700, 9777 9000 • $$$$$ • www.star.com.au

8 Novotel Darling Harbour
Enjoy the benefits of staying in a very large hotel by choosing one of many different room configurations. This hotel is at the top end of the four-star range. ◈ Map L4 • 100 Murray St, Pyrmont • 9934 0000 • $$$$ • www.novoteldarlingharbour.com.au

9 Ibis Darling Harbour
The pleasant three-star Ibis hotel is close to all the Darling Harbour attractions, and is a good alternative for a water view without the usual hefty charge. ◈ Map L4 • 70 Murray St, Darling Harbour • 9563 0888 • $$$ • www.ibishotels.com.au

10 Holiday Inn Darling Harbour
The location's great and so is the refurbished, Heritage-listed woolstore that houses the hotel. They offer good facilities for business travellers in the executive suites. ◈ Map L5 • 68 Harbour St, Darling Harbour • 9291 0200 • $$$$ • www.holidayinndarlingharbour.com.au

⮞ *Unless otherwise stated, all hotels accept credit cards, have en-suite bathrooms and air conditioning and provide dis access.*

Left **Dive** Right **Sebel Manly Beach**

Beachside Accommodation

1 Coogee Sands Hotel & Apartments
Close to the sand, surf and park, Coogee Sands has clean, comfortable rooms with optional business facilities and a spacious rooftop terrace. ◎ *Map U4 • 161 Dolphin Street, Coogee • 9665 8588 • Dis access • $$$ • www.coogeesands.com.au*

2 Ravesi's
Each room of this lovely boutique hotel has a stunning ocean view. Split-level suites cost more but each is unique and opens on to a private terrace. There is also a popular bar and a restaurant downstairs. ◎ *Map H5 • 118 Campbell Parade, Bondi Beach • 9365 4422 • $$$$ • www.ravesis.com.au*

3 Dive
A stylish hotel featured in design magazines, its rooms have high ceilings and designer bathrooms. Complimentary breakfast and unlimited tea and coffee are available. The two front rooms have spectacular views. ◎ *Map U4 • 234 Arden St, Coogee • 9665 5538 • No dis access • Some air conditioning • $$$ • www.divehotel.com.au*

4 Crowne Plaza Hotel Coogee Beach
Located right beside the bustling beach filled with families and backpackers, Crowne Plaza offers lovely ocean views. Relax in modern rooms, which have Internet access and flat-screen TVs, or take a dip in the pool – assuming you can drag yourself away from the beach. ◎ *Map U5 • 242 Arden St, Coogee • 9325 7600 • $$$$ • www.crowneplazacoogee.com.au*

5 Sebel Manly Beach
Choose a lovely ocean view room or suite at this four-star hotel. The Sebel is close to Fairy Bower Beach and a delightful coastal walk (see p118). ◎ *Map U3 • 8–13 South Steyne St, Manly • 9977 8866 • $$$$ • www.mirvachotels.com*

6 Periwinkle Guesthouse
A striking Federation-era mansion has been converted into a B&B with antique furniture and tasteful colour schemes. Rooms with a view attract only a small premium. ◎ *Map U3 • 18–19 East Esplanade, Manly • 9977 4668 • No dis access • No air conditioning • $$$ • www.periwinkleguesthouse.com.au*

7 Rydges Cronulla Beach
Most rooms in this great value hotel have views of the ocean. A great place to use as a base when exploring the Royal National Park, Cronulla is also packed with groovy restaurants and bars. ◎ *Map T6 • 20–26 The Kingsway, Cronulla • 9527 3100 • $$$$ • www.rydges.com*

8 Quest Cronulla
This apartment-style hotel offers fabulous ocean views. Rooms have Internet connections, fully equipped kitchens and laundries, and the hotel can arrange to stock up your pantry or to have dinner at a local restaurant charged to your room. ◎ *Map T6 • 1 The Kingsway, Cronulla, • 8536 3600 • $$$$ • www.questcronullabeach.com.au*

9 Sydney Beachouse YHA
At this hostel on the northern beaches, spend days lounging by the pool, surfing, cycling or playing beach volleyball. There is a cinema next door, and Manly is only a bus ride away. ◎ *Map U2 • 4 Collaroy St, Collaroy • 9981 1177 • Some air conditioning • $$ • www.sydneybeachouse.com.au*

10 Jonah's
Have dinner at Jonah's and stay at their wonderful guesthouse. Each of the ten deluxe rooms has a private balcony with ocean views, a king bed and Jacuzzi. ◎ *Map U1 • 69 Bynya Road, Palm Beach • 9974 5599 • $$$$$ • www.jonahs.com.au*

Unless otherwise stated, all hotels accept credit cards, have en-suite bathrooms and air conditioning and provide dis access.

Price Categories

For a standard double room per night (with breakfast if included), taxes and extra charges.

$	under $80
$$	$80–150
$$$	$160–250
$$$$	$250–350
$$$$$	over $350

Left **Sofitel Sydney Wentworth** Right **The Westin Sydney**

Traditional Hotels

1 InterContinental Sydney

A beautiful 1851 Treasury building offers five-star luxury. The soaring foyer has a lovely lounge. All rooms have window seats, a chaise longue and views of the city or harbour and Botanic Gardens. ⊗ *Map N2 • 117 Macquarie St • 9253 9000 • $$$$$ • www.sydney. intercontinental.com*

2 The Westin Sydney

In this glorious heritage building, rooms in the restored main building feature antique fittings, although the majority of rooms are in the modern tower section. Find great restaurants and a food store in the GPO.
⊗ *Map M3 • 1 Martin Place • 8223 1111 • $$$$$ • www.westin.com.au*

3 Shangri-La Hotel

Take in stunning views of the Harbour Bridge and Opera House at this luxurious, award-winning hotel in the heart of The Rocks district. Dining at the hotel's Altitude restaurant will complete the experience. ⊗ *Map M2 • 176 Cumberland St, The Rocks • 9250 6000 • $$$$ • www.shangri-la.com*

4 The Observatory Hotel

Book a package at the renowned day spa when you stay at this absolute luxury hotel. The hotel caters especially well to business travellers, and runs one-way transfers into the central business district daily from 7–10am. ⊗ *Map L2 • 89–113 Kent St • 9256 2222 • $$$$$ • www. observatoryhotel.com.au*

5 Sheraton on the Park

Enjoy all the facilities you'd expect at a fine hotel, such as marble bathrooms, stylish furnishings, data ports, 24-hour room service, helpful concierges, baby-sitting services and lounges. ⊗ *Map M5 • 161 Elizabeth St • 9286 6000 • $$$$$ • www.sheraton. com/sydney*

6 Sofitel Sydney Wentworth

This building is a Sydney classic thanks to its curved, copper-clad façade. Inside, modern chandeliers feature hundreds of glass tear-drops, and throughout the hotel pale wood and rich, dark fabrics are used to maximum effect. ⊗ *Map N3 • 61–101 Phillip St • 9228 9188 • $$$$ • www. sofitelsydney.com.au*

7 Hilton

The Hilton Sydney is one of the city's premier landmarks. Alongside super chef Luke Mangan's glass brasserie and New York designer Tony Chi's Zeta bar, there are luxurious guest rooms and relaxation suites that are divided into Zen-like zones. ⊗ *Map M4 • 488 George St • 9266 2000 • $$$$$ • www. hiltonsydney.com.au*

8 Castlereagh Boutique Hotel

Full of character, this well-located hotel is great value. The rooms here, full of period furniture and patterned upholstery, offer essentials such as TVs, bars, fridges and tea and coffee facilities. ⊗ *Map M4 • 169 Castlereagh St • 9284 1000 • Limited dis access • $$$$ • www. thecastlereagh.com.au*

9 The Grace Hotel

You couldn't be closer to the action than at The Grace. The restored hotel dates from the 1930s and its refurbishment has retained the building's original Art Deco style. ⊗ *Map M3 • 77 York St • 9272 6888 • $$$–$$$$$ • www.gracehotel.com.au*

10 The Russell

A lovely old-fashioned hotel sits above a historic pub, the Fortune of War. The Russell offers complimentary breakfast, a quaint guest sitting room, well-stocked library and sunny rooftop garden overlooking the busy Rocks area. Some rooms have shared bathrooms. ⊗ *Map M2 • 143a George St, The Rocks • 9241 3543, • No dis access • Some air conditioning • $$$$ • www.therussell.com.au*

Room rates may vary with season, availability, specials and promotions. All prices listed are high-season rates.

Left **Medusa's courtyard** Centre **Establishment** Right **Kirketon**

Boutique Hotels

1 Kirketon

This boutique hotel is an oasis of style, glamour and comfort in the heart of the vibrant suburb of Darlinghurst. The Kirketon Dining Room and Bar offers a contemporary dining experience inspired by the iconic brasseries of Paris. ◈ *Map P5 • 229 Darlinghurst Rd, Darlinghurst • 9332 2011 • No dis access • $$$ • www.kirketon.com.au*

2 Medusa

Medusa makes its own rules as only a boutique hotel can, and traditional room fittings have been replaced by a strong modernist look. Lindt chocolates and Aveda toiletries are complimentary, as is use of a neighbouring gym. There's also a business room available and dogs are allowed in some rooms. ◈ *Map P5 • 267 Darlinghurst Rd, Darlinghurst • 9331 1000 • No dis access • $$$$ • www.medusa.com.au*

3 Establishment

This is one of the most fashionable and desirable places in town. Two suites and 33 rooms offer a choice of lively or tranquil colour schemes, marble or stone bathrooms with separate baths and showers, thick sheets, and CD and DVD players. ◈ *Map M2 • 5 Bridge Lane • 9240 3100 • $$$$$ • www.merivale.com.au*

4 L'Otel

A large terrace house has been converted into a stylish hotel with small but lovely rooms. There's a hip bar and restaurant downstairs, and the hotel is close to Oxford Street's cafés and bars. ◈ *Map P5 • 114 Darlinghurst Rd, Darlinghurst • 9360 6868 • No dis access • $$$$ • www.lotel.com.au*

5 Crown Hotel

The spacious rooms have luxurious touches at this boutique accommodation above a friendly pub that has been a landmark in inner Sydney for more than 100 years. Close to the city, it's also surrounded by top restaurants and night spots. ◈ *Map D5 • 589 Crown St, Surry Hills • 9699 3460 • $$$ • www.crownhotel.com.au*

6 Kathryn's on Queen

In a National Trust-listed Victorian terrace, this charming boutique B&B accommodation is in one of Sydney's most peaceful and beautiful streets. Close to designer and antique stores, as well as Paddy's Markets. ◈ *Map F5 • 20 Queen St, Woollahra • 9237 4535 • $$$$ • www.kathryns.com.au*

7 Vulcan Hotel

A high-class hotel for businessmen when it opened in 1894, the Vulcan had a stint as a student jazz bar until it was refurbished. The minimal rooms are fabulous value. Breakfast at Hummingbird restaurant is great. ◈ *Map L6 • 500 Wattle St, Ultimo • 9211 3283 • $$$ • www.vulcanhotel.com.au*

8 Lord Nelson

Get a taste of Colonial Sydney in the pretty rooms at this famous sandstone pub. The accommodation includes modern necessities such as dataports. Breakfast is included. ◈ *Map P5 • 19 Kent St • 9251 4044 • No dis access • $$$ • www.lordnelsonbrewery.com*

9 Altamont

At this fun budget hotel, all rooms have cable TV and solid, comfy wooden furniture. There are discount weekly rates and a few top-quality backpacker rooms: they fill up quickly, so book them early. ◈ *Map P5 • 207 Darlinghurst Road, Darlinghurst • 9360 6000 • No dis access • $$$ • www.altamont.com.au*

10 Tricketts B&B

At this grand old gentleman's residence, large bedrooms are lovingly restored. The house is furnished with antiques and Persian carpets. ◈ *Map C4 • 270 Glebe Point Rd, Glebe • 9552 1141 • No dis access • $$$ • www.tricketts.com.au*

Unless otherwise stated, all hotels accept credit cards, have ensuite bathrooms and air conditioning and provide dis access.

Price Categories

For a standard	**$** under $80
double room per	**$$** $80–150
night (with breakfast	**$$$** $150–250
if included), taxes	**$$$$** $250–350
and extra charges.	**$$$$$** over $350

A room in Hughenden Manor

🔟 Gay & Lesbian Friendly Hotels

1 De Vere
A boutique-style, budget B&B, located close to the city so offering a friendly and professional service within easy reach of excellent cafés and restaurants. Rooms are comfortable and good value for money. ⬡ Map Q4 • 44–46 Macleay St, Potts Point • 9358 1211 • $$$ • www.devere.com.au

2 Hughenden Manor
This former gentleman's mansion is a Woollahra institution. Writers' groups meet and artists exhibit their work within its walls, providing a connection to the surrounding arty community. ⬡ Map E5 • 14 Queen St, Woollahra • 9363 4863 • No dis access • $$$ • www. thehughenden.com.au

3 Simpsons
A charming B&B at the "Paris" end of Potts Point, where the complimentary breakfast is served in a glass-roofed conservatory. Guests staying in the romantic Cloud Suite enjoy chocolates, flowers and champagne when booked under the Honeymoon package. ⬡ Map P3 • 8 Challis Ave • 9356 2199 • No dis access • $$$ • www.simpsonshotel.com

4 Arts Hotel Sydney
Standard rooms at this friendly hotel face the bustle of Oxford Street. It's worth paying a tiny bit more for a garden room which overlooks the courtyard and swimming pool. Guests can use the Internet, pool, gym, in-house movies and bicycles. ⬡ Map P6 • 21 Oxford St, Paddington • 9361 0211 • $$$$ • www.artshotel.com.au

5 Diamant Hotel Sydney
A a short walk away from Oxford Street, this luxury botique hotel is surrounded by cafés, bars and restaurants. Elegant rooms with city views make this a stylish and comfortable choice. ⬡ Map P4 • 14 Kings Cross Road, Potts Point • 9295 8888 • Dis access • $$$$ • www.8hotels.com

6 Cambridge Hotel Sydney
This well-located hotel is close to many gay bars and clubs. Rooms are great value and amenities include 24-hour room service, a heated pool, gym, spa and sauna. ⬡ Map N6 • 212 Riley St, Surry Hills • 9212 1111 • $$$ • www. cambridgehotel.com.au

7 Victoria Court
Historic 1881 buildings have been transformed into a delightful B&B. Most rooms have marble fireplaces, some have four poster beds and all are decked out in authentic period furniture. In winter, snuggle up by the fire in the guest lounge. ⬡ Map P4 • 122 Victoria St, Potts Point • 9357 3200 • No dis access • $$ • www.victoriacourt.com.au

8 BIG Hostel
This hostel offers dorm rooms, doubles and triples, and is a great place to meet people. BIG has great facilities, including a slick kitchen, lounge area, projector screen and complimentary breakfast. ⬡ Map M5 • 212 Elizabeth St, Surry Hills • 9281 6030 • $$ • www.bighostel.com

9 Rydges Camperdown
One of the few hotels in the gay and lesbian enclaves of Camperdown. The hotel is also near Parramatta Road, where buses leave for the city and Leichhardt. Relax in the pool or sauna. ⬡ Map B5 • 9 Missenden Rd, Camperdown • 9516 1522 • $$$ • www.rydges.com/camperdown

10 Macleay Apartments
There are excellent value weekly rates available at this hotel. The clean apartments have well-equipped kitchenettes and are a great choice for busy travellers. There's a rooftop pool and barbecue area. ⬡ Map Q3 • 28 Macleay St, Potts Point • 9357 7755 • Limited dis access • $$$$ • www.themacleay.com

Room rates may vary with season, availability, specials and promotions. All prices listed are high-season rates.

Left **Studio Apartment** Right **Manly Bungalow**

🔟 Budget Hotels & Hostels

1 Y Hotel
Expect less of the party crowd at this peaceful backpacker spot since all dorm rooms have just four single beds and are single-sex. There's coffee, tea and breakfast included in the room price. Standard double rooms are basic but clean. ◎ Map N5
• 5–11 Wentworth Ave
• 9264 2451 • Dis access
• Air conditioning • $$$
• www.yhotel.com.au

2 Sydney Harbour YHA
This is the only backpacker hostel in The Rocks. There are great views from the roof terrace, where you can take in the sunset over the harbour as you eat at the picnic tables.
◎ Map M2 • 110 Cumberland St • 8272 0900
• Air conditioning • $$
• www.yha.com.au

3 wake up!
If your plan for Sydney is all action, this is the place for you. It offers special cushion rooms for watching TV, colour-coded dorm walls and many other facilities.
◎ Map M6 • 509 Pitt St
• 9288 7888 • Limited dis access • Air conditioning
• $$ • www.wakeup.com.au

4 Ibis Budget Kings Cross
You can count on rooms being spick and span at this reliable budget motel chain. All accommodate three people for the flat room rate, most with a queen and single bunk bed. There's a TV but not much else. ◎ Map P4
• 191–201 Williams St, Kings Cross • 9326 0300
• Dis access • En-suite
• Air conditioning • $$

5 Verona Guest House
Located at the quiet end of Glebe's main street, this two-storey property has an old-world charm and is just a short walk away from the cafés, shops and waterfront parklands at Rozelle Bay. ◎ Map J5 • 224 Glebe Point Rd, Glebe • 9660 8975 • Dis access • Air conditioning • $$$ • www. verona-guesthouse.com

6 Noah's Bondi
Spectacular views come at only a tiny premium at this friendly, welcoming hostel. The rooms and bathrooms are clean and Noah's staff speak both Japanese and Hebrew. ◎ Map H5
• 2 Campbell Parade, Bondi Beach • 9365 7644 • $ • www.noahsbondibeach.com

7 Billabong Gardens
Billabong offers both motel and hostel accommodation, a great kitchen and a swimming pool. The amiable owners also specialise in helping backpackers to find work. ◎ Map C5
• 5–11 Egan St, Newtown
• 9550 3236 • $$ • www. billabonggardens.com.au

8 Sydney Central YHA
Housed in a Heritage-listed building opposite Central Railway Station, this hostel offers panoramic views of the city from the rooftop and outdoor area. It also has a pool, bistro and convenience store. ◎ Map M6
• 11 Rawson Place • 9218 9000 • Air conditioning • $$
• www.yha.com.au

9 Manly Bungalow
A classic Manly house has been converted into an eight-room guesthouse, surrounded by tropical plants and an outdoor entertaining area. It's close to the ocean beach and to the ferry wharf. Each room has a kitchenette, there's a shared laundry, and week-long rates are available. ◎ Map U3
• 64 Pittwater Rd, Manly
• 9977 5494 • $$ • www. manlybungalow.com

10 Waldorf Woolloomooloo
Studio apartments in this serviced complex are excellent value and good for families. They can sleep up to five people and have full kitchens and living areas. The walk to the city through the Botanic Gardens is lovely. ◎ Map P4 • 88 Dowling St, Woolloomooloo Bay
• 8837 8000 • Dis access
• En-suite • Air conditioning
• $$$ • www. woolloomooloo-waldorf-apartments.com.au

Unless otherwise stated, these hotels accept credit cards but do not provide dis access, en-suite bathrooms or air conditioning.

Price Categories

For a standard double room per night (with breakfast if included), taxes and extra charges.

$	under $80
$$	$80–150
$$$	$150–250
$$$$	$250–350
$$$$$	over $350

Lobby at Medina Executive Sydney Central

TOP 10 Serviced Apartments

1 Quay West Suites Sydney

Luxurious, fully-equipped apartments with five-star service. Spacious suites have all the standards plus two TVs, stereos, fax and modem ports, deluxe minibar, valet and 24-hour room service. Choose from city or harbour views. ⊛ Map M2 • 98 Gloucester St, The Rocks • 9240 6000 • No dis access • $$$$$ • www.mirvachotels.com

2 Medina Executive Sydney Central

Housed in one of Sydney's most beautiful buildings, the former Parcel Post Office, Medina's apartments are stylishly furnished. There are work areas as well as living and dining spaces, great kitchens, cable TV and stereos. ⊛ Map M6 • 2 Lee St, Haymarket • 8396 9800 • $$$$$ • www.medina.com.au

3 Waldorf

Reasonably priced and well-located, the Waldorf has facilities such as a rooftop pool, spa and sauna, complimentary in-house movies and a shopping service. ⊛ Map M5 • 57 Liverpool St • 9261 5355 • No dis access • $$$$$ • www.waldorf-apartments-hotel-sydney.com.au

4 The York

This hotel is ideally located close to several tourist attractions and transport links. Its refurbished apartments have balconies and good facilities. ⊛ Map M2 • 5 York St • 9210 5000 • No dis access • $$$ • www.theyorkapartments.com.au

5 Adina Sydney Crown Street

Close to the Crown Street shops and restaurants, Sydney Cricket Ground and Fox Studios, this hotel is also right above the legendary restaurant Bills (see p60). ⊛ Map N6 • 359 Crown St, Surry Hills • 8302 1000 • $$$$$ • www.medina.com.au

6 Hotel Stellar

This hotel is ideal for families, there is no extra charge for kids under 12, and two bedroom apartments have a queen and four bunk beds. The rooms are large but only three apartments have fully equipped kitchens. ⊛ Map N5 • 4 Wentworth Ave • 9264 9754 • No dis access • $$$$ • www.hotelstellar.com

7 Morgans of Sydney

Situated on one of Darlinghurst's prime eat streets, this art deco boutique hotel is walking distance to Potts Point and Paddington. Check out the roof terrace for views to the Opera House and Harbour Bridge. ⊛ Map F4 • 304 Victoria St, Darlinghurst • 9360 7955 • No dis access • $$$$ • www.morganshotel.com.au

8 Meriton Bondi Junction

Built above the Bondi Junction bus and train interchange, these bedroom apartments have views of Sydney Harbour or the ocean. Great features include full-sized kitchens and laundries, pools and tennis courts. ⊛ Map F5 • 95–97 Grafton St, Bondi Jnctn • 8305 7600 • No dis access • $$$ • www.meritonapartments.com.au

9 Quest Grande Esplanade

A smart, modern apartment hotel, where many rooms look over a row of pine trees onto Manly's harbour beach. It is also close to dozens of restaurants and cafés. ⊛ Map U3 • 54a West Esplanade, Manly • 9976 4600 • $$$$ • www.questgrandeesplanade.com.au

10 Manly Seaside Holiday Apartments

This agency rents 134 fully self-contained apartments in a range of buildings around Manly. Perfect for longer stays, this is a great way to feel at home. Various types of accommodation are available, many with views, from budget to deluxe in all sizes. ⊛ Map U3 • 2/39 East Esplanade, Manly • 9977 5213 • No dis access • Some air conditioning • $$–$$$ • www.manly-seaside.com

Unless otherwise stated, all apartments accept credit cards, have en-suite bathrooms and air conditioning and provide dis access.

General Index

A

ABC Shop, The 81
A Fish Called Coogee 59
Access Foundation 135
accommodation tips 142
activities for children **56–7**
Adina Sydney Crown Street 149
Admiralty House 116
age restrictions 138
Airport Link 133
Akira 94
Alfie's Little Brother Carter 113
Allen, Peter 11
Alliance Française French Film Festival 73
Allianz Stadium 47, 92
Allphones Arena 53
Altair 46
Altamont 146
Andrew "Boy" Charlton Pool 20, 49
Andrew McDonald 94
Anegawa Enterprises 62
Anglers Rest Hotel 123
Annandale Hotel 67
ANZ Stadium 52
Anzac Bridge 105, 111
Anzac Memorial 50, 78
architectural highlights **46–7**
Argyle Stores 80
Aria 59
Army Museum 92
ARQ Sydney 88
art galleries **44–5**
Art Gallery of NSW 7, 21, **24–5**, 26, 44, 56
culture vultures 56
fundays 24, 56
gallery shop 81
Sydney artists **26–7**
Arthouse Hotel 68
Arthur McElhone Reserve 86
Arts Hotel Sydney 147
Artspace 44
Arup, Ove 10
Assiette 95
Astor, The 22
ATMs 136
Auburn 62
Aurora Place 46
Aussie Stadium see Sydney Football Stadium

Australia Square 46
Australian, The 132
Australian Ballet 8
Australian Centre for Craft and Design 44
Australian Centre for Photography 45
Australian Chamber Orchestra 64, 66
Australian Galleries 93
Australian Festival of Jewish Cinema 73
Australian Hotel 18
Australian immigration 132
Australian Institute of Architects 86
Australian Museum 42, 57
Australian National Maritime Museum 15, 17, 28, 42, 56, 80
Kids' Deck 56
Australian Reptile Park 128
Australian Theatre for Young People 65
Australian Tourist Commission 132
Axel Mano 100

B

Backen, Robyn 21
Badde Manors 105, 107
ballooning 55
Balls Head Reserve 15, 115
Balmain & Leichhardt 15, 65, 105, **108–113**
best of the rest 113
pubs & bars 112
Balmain East 109
Balmain library 57
Balmain markets 108, 109
Balmain, William 108
Balmoral Beach 48, 116
Bambini Trust Café 79
Bangarra Dance Theatre 64
Bank Hotel, The 70
banking & communications 136
Bar Cleveland 69
Barefoot Bowls & Beer 55
Bar Europa 83
Bar Italia 62, 113
Barmuda 105
Barnes, Jimmy 17

Barnet, James 21, 77, 85, 99, 110
Barzura 101
Basement, The 66
Bathers' Pavilion Café, The 61
BBQ King 69
beaches **48–9**
beachside accommodation 144
Beare Park 86, 87
Becker Minty 100
Bell Shakespeare 65
Belle Fleur 113
Bell's at Killcare 129
Belvoir Street Theatre 65
Bennelong 9, 110
Bennelong Point 8, 9
Berkelouw 113
Berowa Waters 121
Berrys Bay 115
Beyond Sydney **120–129**
historic sites & townships 124–5
natural attractions 126–7
places to eat 129
things to do 128
Bicentenary 28, 47, 92
Bicentennial Park 104
bicycles 134
BIG Hostel 147
Big Day Out 72
Bigge, Commissioner JT 23
Bikini Island 34
Bill & Toni's 60
Billabong Gardens 148
Bills Surry Hills 60
Billy Kwong 60
Birchgrove 109, 111
Blacket, Edmund 19, 79, 105
Black Sunday 35
Blanchett, Cate 17
Blaxland, Gregory 37, 121
Blue Ginger 113
Blue Mountains 20, 32, 54, 55, 121, 127
Blue Sydney 143
Blue Water Café 61
Blue, William "Billy" 23, 37, 115
Bluebottles 138
Blues Point 115
Boathouse on Blackwattle Bay 59

Bookshop Darlinghurst, The 71
Bondi Beach 7, **34–5**, 48, 63, 65, 73
Bondi Icebergs 35, 49, 69
Bondi Junction 92
bookings 141
Boomerang 15, 86, 87
Botany Bay 30, 38, 90
Bottoms Up 87
Bouddi National Park 121, 127
Boulevarde, The 63
Bourke St Bakery 61
boutique hotels 146
Bowral 123, 125, 128
"Boy" Charlton, Andrew 20, 21
Boyd, Arthur 25, 123
Bradfield, John 12, 115
Bradleys Head 50, 114, 116
Bradman Museum 125
Bradman, Sir Donald 92, 125
Brass 87, 89
Brett Whiteley Studio 44, 93
Brighton Up Bar 88
Brisbane Water 121
Brisbane Water National Park 38, 121, 127, 128
Broken Bay 121, 122, 125
Bronte Beach 35, 49
Brooklyn 123
Brown Sugar 61
Brown, Bryan 65
budget hotels & hostels 148
budget tips 140
Bukhara, Le 101
Bungalow 8 83
Buon Ricordo 89
Busby, John 86
buses 133, 134
bushfires 137
bushwalking 55, 138
Buttrose, Ita 37
BYO 82, 141

C
C'o Flesh Book 106
Cabbage Tree Bay 51, 117, 118
Cadigal people 42
Cadman's Cottage 14, 18, 19, 39
Café Hernandez 69

Café Lounge 71
Café Mint 61
Café Sopra 61, 83
Café Sydney 83
Café West 9
Café Zoe 61
Cahill, Joseph 10
Cambridge Hotel Sydney 147
Camp Cove 14, 98, 99
Camperdown Cemetery 103, 105
Canberra 116, 128, 129
Cantina S, AB Hotel 107
Capital L 94
Capitol Theatre 29, 78
Captain Cook 36, 38
   landing place 38
"Captain" de Groot, Francis 13
car hire 133, 134
Careening Cove 65, 116
Carey, Gabrielle 41
Carey, Peter 41
Carmel Bakery 63
Carousel Club 85
Castlereagh Boutique Hotel 145
Castlereagh Street 80
casual dining **60–61**
Cat & Fiddle Hotel, The 66
Catalina 101
Catamarans 16
CBD 40, 54, 55, 62
Centennial Park 16, 39, 50, 54, 57, 90
   Federation Pavilion 26, 39
Central Coast 120, 121, 127
Central Station 31, 76, 133, 138
Ceviche 101
Chairman & Yip, The 129
Chat Thai 82
Cheeky Monkey 134
children, travelling with 135, 142
Chinaman's Beach 116
Chinatown 7, 28, 62, 76
Chinese Noodle, The 82
Chinta Ria The Temple of Love 83
Chisholm, Caroline 37
Circular Quay 7, 13, 16, 18, 19, 32, 38, 76, 79, 99, 111, 117, 134

Circus Oz 56
City Centre **76–83**
   chinatown eateries 82
   city shopping centers 80
   one of a kind shops 81
   pubs & restaurants 83
City Recital Hall 66
City Sightseeing Buses 134
Civic Hotel 69
Clock Hotel 95
Clontarf Beach 48, 117
Cloth 94
Clovelly Beach 35, 49
Coast 59
Cockatoo Island 15, 109, **110**
Coffee Culture 129
Collette Dinnigan 100
Collette, Toni 65
Collins Beach 38, 51, 117, 118
Colombian, The 70, 88
Company B Belvoir 65
concessions 140
consulates & embassies 132, 135
Coogee Bay Hotel 67
Coogee Beach 35
Coogee Sands Hotel & Apartments 144
Cook & Phillip Park Pool 49
Cooper, Robert 91
Corelli's Cafe 61
Corris, Peter 40
Corso, The 73, 117, 118
Cossington-Smith, Grace 13, 25, 26, 27
Cowan Creek 121, 128
Cox, Phillip 47, 92
Crawford, Michaelie 47
credit cards 136
Cremorne 116
Crescent, The 99
Croft, Brenda 47
Cronulla Beach 48
Crossley, George 23
Crowe, Russell 15, 17, 65, 86
Crown Hotel 146
Crown Street 63, 92, 139
Crowne Plaza Hotel Coogee Beach 144

Cruise Bar & Restaurant 68, 83
Crumpler 106
currency exchange 136
Cusack, Dymphna 41
customs 132, 136
Customs House 18
cycling 54

D

Daily Telegraph, The 132
Daly Male 71
Danks Street Depot 61
Dark, Eleanor 41
Darley's 129
Darling Harbour 7, 15, **28–9**, 30, 42, 56, 59, 68, 76, 80, 111, 139, 142
Darling Point 15, 51
Darling Street 109, 111
Darling Street Wharf 111
Darlinghurst 84, 90
Darlinghurst Court House & Old Darlinghurst Gaol 85, 93
Darlinghurst Road 85
Darlo Bar 69
David Jones 81, 139
Davis, Judy 17, 65
Dawes Point 13, 115
Dawes, William 19
Dawn Fraser Baths 49, 109
dégustation 141
Del Rio 84, 86, 87
De Vere 147
design & homewares 139
Destination New South Wales 132, 135
Devine, Tilley 37
Diamant Hotel Sydney 147
dining tips 141
dining with children 141
Dinosaur Designs 78, 81
disabled travellers 135, 142
discount plane tickets 140
discount rates 142
Dive 144
Domain, The 7, 20, 21, 24, 76
Dome Lounge & The Attic 68
Done Art & Design 81
Done, Ken 27
Double Bay 96, 97, 139
Dragstar 106

drink driving 138
driver's licenses 132
Dunbar 36, 99, 103
Dupain, Max 26, 27

E

Eagar, Edward 23
East Ocean 82
East Sydney TAFE College 85, 88
East Village Hotel 112
Eastern Suburbs 16, 48, 90, **96–101**
  luxe 100
  relaxed dining 101
Easton Pearson 94
Eco, Umberto 18
El Alamein Fountain 85, 86
Eleni's at Civic 83
Elixir Espresso 79
Elizabeth Bay 51, 84, 86
Elizabeth Bay House 86
Elizabeth Farm 122, 124
Elkington Park 109
emergencies 138
Emperor's Garden, The 82
Emperor's Garden BBQ & Noodles 82
Endeavour 38
Engelen Moore 46
Enmore Theatre 67
Ensemble Theatre 65, 116
Entertainment Quarter, The 93
Eora 6, 19, 21, 36, 87
Esca Bimbadgen 129
Esplanade, The 117
est. 58
Establishment Hotel 58, 68, 146
Experiment Farm Cottage 122, 124

F

Fairy Bower Pool 49, 117, 118
fashion & accessories 139
Faster Pussycat 106
ferries 15, 16–7, 134
Festival of German Cinema 73
Festival of the Winds 73
festivals & events **72–3**
Fig Tree Baths, The 21
film festivals 73
First Fleet 6, 18, 36, 42, 72, 77, 79, 108, 116
Fish Shop, The 89

Fishface 59
Fitzroy Gardens 86
Five Ways 90, 93
Flame Opals 81
Flat White 61
Flickerfest 73
Florilegium 106
Flying Fish 59
Flying Squirrel 69
Foley, Fiona 47
Forresters, The 95
Fort Denison 15, 16, 19, 20, 38, 50, 92
Forty Baskets Beach 49, 117
Four Seasons Hotel Sydney 143
Fox Studios 47, 93
Franklin, Miles 41
Fraser, Dawn 109
Fratelli Paradiso 89
free city shuttle 134
free publications 135
Freeman, Cathy 37
frequent flyers 142
Friels, Colin 17
Fu-Manchu 89
Funkis 78

G

Gale, Megan 65
Galeries, The 80, 139
Gallery Bar 68
Gallery Kids 56
Gap, The 99
Garfish 59
Garigal National Park 50, 116
Garrison Church 18, 19
gay & lesbian friendly hangouts **70–71**
gay & lesbian friendly hotels 147
gay & lesbian travellers 135
George Street 18, 77
getting around 134
getting to Sydney 133
Gibbs, May 17, 40, 116
Ginn, Henry 19
Glebe Island Bridge 105
Glebe Markets 102, 104
Glebe Point Road 104
Gleebooks 102, 106
Gloria's Café 62
Goat Island 15, 16, 110
Gocher, William 39, 117
going green 139
Golden Century 82

golf 54
Goosens, Eugene 10
Gosford 121
Government House 21, 46
Governor Bligh 36
Governor Gipps 21
Governor Hunter 39, 125
Governor Macquarie 20,
   22, 36, 99, 116, 124,
   125
Governor Phillip 7, 9, 18,
   19, 20, 36, 38, 51, 98,
   102, 108, 116, 117, 118,
   122, 124
Governor Phillip Tower 46
GPO 38, 77, 79
Grace Hotel, The 145
Graham, Anne 22
"Granny" Smith Memorial
   Park 39
great depression 6, 13, 90
Great Irish Famine
   Memorial 22
Green Bans 37, 85
Green Gourmet 107
Green Park 85
Green Park Hotel 70
Green Point 99
Greenway, Francis 9, 12,
   21, 22, 23, 42, 99, 124
Greer, Germaine 22
Greycliffe House 51, 97,
   98, 99
GSI 136, 139, 142
Guillaume at Bennelong 9,
   58
Gunderman 123
Guringai people 125
Gusto 93

H
Haigh's 81
Halvorsen, Lars 37
Hambledon Cottage 122,
   125
Hampton Villa 111
Han, Jisuk 47
Harbour Foreshore
   Vigilance Committee 15,
   97
Harbour View Hotel 12
Harbourside Brighton 129
harbourside hotels 143
Hargrave, Lawrence 31,
   73, 97
Harry's Café de Wheels 86
Hawkesbury River 36, 55,
   120, 121, 123, 124, 128

Hayes, Sir Henry Browne
   97
Headquarter 88
helicopters 16
Helyer, Nigel 47
Hemmesphere 68
Henry Wilson, John 70
Hermit Point 97
Hero of Waterloo 18
Hilton 145
Historic Houses Trust 23,
   42, 87, 124
historic sites & buildings
   38–9
HMAS Kuttabul 15
HMAS Sydney 13, 50
HMS Sirius 79, 98
Holiday Inn Darling
   Harbour 143
Home 66
Homebush Bay 39
Homebush Train Station
   47
Honeymoon Patisserie 62
Hornby Lighthouse 51, 98
horseriding 54
hospitals & clinics 137
hotel deals 140
Hotel Stellar 149
Howard, John 17
Howe, George 23
Hughenden 147
Hugo's Bar Pizza 89
Hugo's Lounge 69, 89
Hugo's at Manly Wharf
   119
Hunters Hill 114
Hyde Park 50, 70, 78, 79
   Archibald Fountain 50,
   79
   Pool of Reflection 78
Hyde Park Barracks
   Museum 22, 23, 42

I
Ibis Budget Kings Cross
   148
Ibis Darling Harbour 143
Icebergs Club 69
Icebergs Dining Room 58
Iguana Bar 69
Il Barotto 05
Il Piave 113
Il Porcellino 22
Illawarra Coast 127
Illoura Reserve 111
images of Sydney 27
Imax Theatre 56

Imperial Hotel 70
Industrie 106
insurance 132
InterContinental Sydney
   145
Internet access 136
Ireland, David 41
Island Shop 123
Italian Festa 111
Italian Film Festival 73
Italian Forum 108, 111
Ives Steps Wharf 57
Ivy 67

J
Jacob's Ladder 99
James, Florence 41
Jamison Valley 126, 128
Jan Logan 100
Japan Foundation, Sydney
   – Cultural Section 73
Japanese Film Festival
   73
Jasmin1 63
Jenolan Caves 121, 126
Jetty Bar 69
Jimmy Liks 89
Joh Bailey 100
Johnson, Reverend
   Richard 102
Johnstons Bay 105
Jonah's 144
Jubilee Park 104, 105
Juniper Hall 91
Justice & Police Museum
   42

K
Kable, Henry 23
Kate Owen Gallery &
   Studio 45
Kathryn's on Queen 146
Katoomba 121, 126, 128
Katzy's 63
kayaking 54
Kazbah on Darling 113
Kemp, J 91
Keneally, Thomas 41, 118
Kiama 123, 127
   Kiama Blowhole 127
Kidman, Nicole 17, 65
King Street 103, 105
Kings Cross &
   Darlinghurst 84–9
   gay bars 88
   places to eat 89
Kingsford-Smith
   International Airport 133

Kinokuniya 80
Kirketon 146
Kirribilli 116
Kirribilli House 116
Krishnamurti, Jiddu 116
Ku-ring-gai Chase National Park 38, 114, 120, 122, 125

L
L'Otel 146
La Campana 62
Lady Bay Beach 14, 98, 99
Lakemba 63
Lands Department Building 79
Lane Cove National Park 50
Lang, JT 13
late-night haunts 69
laundromats 140
Laurence, Janet 47
Lavender Bay 115
Lavender, George 115
Laws, John 17
Lawson, Henry 41, 49
Lawson, William 37, 121
Le Petit Crème 61
Lee, Ben 65
left luggage 133
Leichhardt Hotel 112
Leichhardt, Ludwig 79, 108
Leichhardt 62, 108–113
Leigh, Kate 37, 90
Lesley McKay's Bookshop 100
Lette, Kathy 41
Letterbox Restaurant 129
Lewis, Mortimer 85
Lieutenant William Bradley 116
Life's An Adventure 54
Light Brigade Hotel 95
Linda's on King St. 107
Lindsay, Norman 125
Little French Patisserie, The 119
Living Room, The 83
local advertisements 135
Locke Elliot, Sumner 41
Lo-Fi 95
Loft, The 68
London Hotel 109, 111, 112
London Tavern 93
Long Nose Point 109
longer stays 142
Longrain 60
Lord Nelson 18, 146

Lord, Simeon 23
lost property 133
Luna Park 56, 114
Lush Bucket 30
Lush on Bondi 61

M
Macarthur, John & Elizabeth 37, 124
Macdonald River 123
Macleay Apartments 147
Macleay Museum 42, 103
Macleay, Alexander 86, 103
Macquarie Arms Hotel 123, 124
Macquarie Lighthouse 23, 51, 96, 99
Macquarie Street 79
Macquarie, Elizabeth 20, 23, 84
Mado 62
Mahjong Room 95
Maisys 69
Major George Barney 92
Major Mitchell 79, 97
making reservations 142
Mallard, Henri 13, 27
Mandela, Nelson 11
Manly 14, 15, 16, 39, 48, 72, 73, 114, 117, 118
cove 14, 16, 118
jazz festival 73, 117
Manly Bungalow 148
Manly Fast Ferry 16–17, 134
Manly Seaside Holiday Apartments 149
Manly Wharf Hotel 69
Manns Point 109, 115
Manta Seafood 59
Maple 106
Marchetta, Melina 41
Mardi Gras 37, 70, 71, 73
events 71
film festival 71, 73
Marigold 82
Market City 29, 80
Maroubra Beach 48
Marque 58
Marrickville 63
Martin Place 22, 25, 77, 79
Martini 112
Mary MacKillop Place Museum 115
Maunsell Wickes 45
Maya 63
McElhone Stairs, The 86
McEwen, Sandra 30

McIver's Baths 49
McMaster's Beach 121, 127
Mecca Cosmetica 94
Media 132
Medina Executive Sydney Central 149
Medusa 146
Melbourne 59, 89
Mercantile Hotel 18
Meriton Bondi Junction 149
Metro Theatre 66, 87
Middle Harbour 16, 54, 116
Middle Head 116
Midnight Shift Hotel 88
Military Road 38, 62, 116
Milsons Point 115
Mint Museum 22
MLC Centre 80
Mobbs, Michael 31
mobile phone rental 136
Mod Oz 141
Mohr Fish 59
moments in history **36–7**
money, taxes & refunds 136
Mooks 81
Moore Park 54, 57, 90
Moorhouse, Frank 40
Morgan, Francis 38
Morgans of Sydney 149
Mort Bay 109, 111
Mort, Thomas 79, 111
Mosman 15, 115, 116, 119
Mosman, Archibald 116
Mosman Rowers 119
Mother Chu's Vegetarian Kitchen 82
Mount Annan Botanic Gardens 126
Mount Tomah Botanic Gardens 127
Mr Eternity 85
Mrs Biggs' Bathing Machine 21
Mrs Macquarie's Chair 8, 20
Mundey, Jack 37
Museum of Contemporary Art 19, 26, 44
Museum of Sydney 42, 46, 77, 139
Museum of Sydney Café 60
museums **42–3**
Muum Maam 95

N

NAIDOC Week 72
Napoleon Perdis 100
Neutral Bay 62, 116
New Brighton Hotel 114, 118
Newtown & Glebe 67, 70, 90, **102–107**
    cheap eats 107
    funky shops 106
Nicholson Museum 42, 103
Nielsen Park 15, 49, 51, 97, 99
Nielsen, Juanita 85
nightlife & live music **66–7**
Nilgiri's 119
Nina's Ploy Thai 101
Noah's Bondi 148
Norman Lindsay Gallery 125
Norrie, Susan 26
North Bondi Golf Course 38
North Bondi Italian Food 101
North Fort Artillery Museum 118
North Harbour 117
North Head 50, 114, 118
North Shore 12, 39, 50, 56, 62, **114–19**
    Manly 118
    places to eat 119
North Sydney Olympic Pool 12, 40, 115
Norton Street 62, 111
Norton, James 111
Nortons on Norton 112
Novotel Darling Harbour 53, 143
NPWS 14, 15, 55, 98, 110, 117, 118
NSW government 132
NSW tourism information desks 133
Nutcote 40, 114

O

O'Grady, John 41
O'Hare, Sarah 17
Object 44, 139
Observatory Hotel, The 145
Observatory Park 50
Oceanworld Manly 114, 117, 118
Old Government House 39, 122, 125

Old Quarantine Station 51, 118
older travellers 135
Oliver, Bronwyn 47
Olley, Margaret 26
Olsen, John 26, 45
Opera Australia 8, 64
Opera Bar 9, 68
Opera House Store 81, 139
Ormeggio 119
Orson & Blake 94
Out of Africa 119
Overseas Passenger Terminal 19
Oxford Arts Factory 88
Oxford Hotel 88
Oxford Street 69, 70, 72, 90, 92
Oxley, John 125

P

Paddington & Surry Hills **90–95**
    fashion & homewares 94
    hot spots 95
Paddington Bowling Club 55
Paddington private galleries 45
Paddington Town Hall 91
Paddington Village 91
Paddy's Markets 29, 80
Palace Norton St Cinema 113
Palm Beach 48, 122, 127, 128
Paragon 129
Parkes, Sir Henry 37, 111
Park Hyatt Sydney 143
Park, Ruth 41, 90
parks & gardens **50–51**
Parliament House 22
Parramatta 16, 120, 122
Parramatta River 14, 109, 115
Passion Flower 82
passports & visas 132
Patrick, James 15
Patyegarang 19
Pavarotti, Luciano 11
payments 139
Peacock Point 109, 111
Pearl Beach 121, 127, 128
Pemulwy 37
Perama 63
performing arts companies **64–5**

Periwinkle Guesthouse 144
Phamish 89
pharmacies 137
Phoenix Bar 88
phone cards 140
Piano, Renzo 46
Pier 59
Pilu at Freshwater 119
Pitt Street Colonnade 79
Pittwater 16, 48, 121, 122, 128
Pizza Mario 60
Planet 94
planning a trip 132
Platypus Shoes 106
Point Piper 65, 97
Pompei 101
Pope Paul VI Reserve 104, 105
Porter, Dorothy 41
Port Jackson 38, 98
Potts Point 65, 84, 86
Powerhouse Museum 7, 29, **30–31**, 42, 80
Premier's Walk 128
Preston, Margaret 26
Prokofiev 8
public holidays 136
pubs & bars **68–9**, 112
Punchbowl 63
Pyrmont 105
Pyrmont Bridge 28

Q

Quay 58
Quay Grand Suites 143
Quay West Suites Sydney 149
Queen Street 92, 97
Queen Victoria Building 79, 80, 139
Queen's Square 22
Quest Cronulla 144
Quest Grande Esplanade 149

R

radio & TV 135
Ravesi's 144
Realm Restaurant 129
Red Chilli 82
Red Eye Records 81
Red Lantern 95
Redfern, William 23
Rees, Lloyd 26
Reiley, Mary 23
Republic 2 47
restaurants **58–9**

Rex Hotel 87
Rice Paper 107
Ripples at Chowder Bay 119
Ripples at Milson's Point 61
Riverboat Postman 128
Riverview Hotel 112
Roberts-Goodwin, Lynne 18, 47
Robeson, Paul 11
Rockpool 59
Rocks, The 7, 18, 19, 37, 76, 81, 139
Rocks, The & Circular Quay, **18–19**
Rose Bay 16, 51,97, 128
Rose Seidler House 47
Rouse Hill House & Farm 124
Royal Botanic Gardens 7, 15, 20, 21, 47, 76
Royal Botanic Gardens & The Domain **20–21**
Macquarie Street Precinct 22
Royal Hotel 112
Royal National Park 38, 54, 120, 123, 127, 128
Royal Randwick Racecourse 52
Rozelle 104, 105, 109
Rozelle markets 113
Rum Corps 36
Rum Hospital 22
Ruse, James & Elizabeth 124
Rushcutters Bay 15, 51, 84, 87
Russell, The 145
Rydges Camperdown 147
Rydges Cronulla Beach 144

S
Sackville Hotel 112
sailing 16, 17, 55
Sailors' Home 19
Saint Albans 123, 124
Saint Andrew's Cathedral 79
Saint James Church 22
Children's Chapel 22
Saint Mary's Cathedral 77
Saint Patrick's Seminary 117, 118
Saint Stephen's Church 103, 105
sales 139

Sappho Bookshop 104
Savion 63
Scanlan & Theodore 94
Sculpture by the Sea 35
seafood 59
Sea Life Sydney Aquarium 28
Sean's Panaroma 59
seaplanes 16, 97
Seasalt 101
Sebel Manly Beach 144
Sebel Pier One Sydney 143
security & health 137
Seidler, Harry 46, 47, 115
Selinas at Coogee Bay Hotel 67
Senbergs, Jan 17
Sepia 59
serviced apartments 149
Settlers Arms Inn 123, 124
SH Ervin 44
Shangri-La Hotel 145
Shark Beach 14, 51, 97, 99
Shark Island 15, 16, 97
Shelly Beach 48, 51, 117, 118
Sheraton on the Park 145
shopping tips 139
Shostakovich 11
Showgrounds Exhibition Building 53
Sidewalk Café 9
Silvas 62
Simpsons 147
Slessor, Kenneth 40
Slide Bar 88
Slip Inn 83
Sloane 94
Smart, Jeffrey 27, 45
Smith, Henry 117
Smith, James 33
Snails Bay 111
Sofitel Sydney Wentworth 145
Sofra 62
Solitary 129
Sonoma Bakery Café 107
sources of information 135
South Head 23, 50, 98, 99
Southern Highlands 120, 123, 129
souvenirs 139
Spanish Club, The 62
Spanish Film Festival 73
Spencer 123
Spit Bridge 17, 116
sporting venues & Olympic sites **52–3**
Spring Espresso 89

STA Travel 140
Stace, Arthur 85
Star City 143
State Library of NSW 11, 22, 45
State Theatre 78
Steki Taverna 63
Stonewall 88
Store 88 44
Strand, The 139
Strand Arcade 78, 79, 80
Strand Hatter's 80
Studio Café 9
Sumalee Thai 107
surfing 54
Surry Hills 41, 63, 67, 90–5, 139
Susannah Place Museum 42
Sushi Studio 62, 119
Sutherland, Joan 11, 65
swimming 54, 137, 138
swimming pools 49
Sydney Beachouse YHA 144
Sydney Central YHA 148
Sydney Cricket Ground 53, 90, 92
Sydney Dance Company 8, 64
Sydney Festival 20, 72
Sydney Film Festival 73, 78
Sydney Fish Market 102, 59, 105
Sydney Seafood School 105
Sydney Harbour 6, **14–15**, 16, 33, 36, 38, 51, 99, 116, 125
on the water **16–17**
Sydney Harbour Bridge 6, **12–13**, 16, 17, 20, 49, 51, 54, 56, 72, 115, 123
Sydney Harbour Federation Trust 14, 15, 110
Sydney Harbour National Park 14, 50, 117, 118
Sydney Harbour YHA 148
Sydney Hospital 22, 25
Sydney Jewish Museum 42, 85
Sydney Observatory 18, 19, 51
Sydney Olympic Park 16, 39, 52–3
Aquatic Centre 39, 49, 52
Sydney Olympic Park Golf Centre 53

Sydney Olympic Park
Tennis Centre 52
Sydney Opera House 6,
8–9, 10, 11, 13, 27, 19,
20, 46, 57, 58, 64, 66
Kids at the House 57
Opera House Store 81,
139
raising the roof **10–11**
The Studio 9, 57
Sydney Park 103
Sydney's Child 57, 135
Sydney Heritage Walk 47
Sydney Showgrounds 39
Sydney Stadium 73
Sydney Symphony 64
Sydney Theatre & Walsh
Bay 46, 64
Sydney Theatre Company
64
Sydney to Hobart Yacht
Race 14, 17, 51, 73
Sydney Tower 77, 79
Sydney Writers' Festival 72
Sylvia Rhodes 100
Sze Yup Buddhist Chinese
Temple 104
Szechuan Garden 119

T
tall ships 16, 72
Tamarama Beach 35, 65
Tank Stream 18, 38, 77
Taronga Zoo 7, **32–3**, 114,
116
taxis 133, 134
Taylor Square 70, 71, 95
telephones 136
Tench, Watkin 27
Tennant, Kylie 40
Terry, Samuel 23
Tetsuya's 58
Thanh Binh 107
theft 136, 137
things to avoid 138
Three Blue Ducks 61
Three Sisters 121, 126
Tilbury, The 68
Tillers, Imants 26, 47
Tim Olsen Gallery 93
tipping 136, 141
Tomislav 89
Toolshed 71
Torres Deli 62
Tosca 11
tourist offices 135
Tourist Refund Scheme
136

Town Hall 79, 111
Town Hall Hotel 69, 112
Toxteth Park Villa 104
Trademark Hotel 70, 87
trading hours 139
traditional hotels 145
trains 134
Transit Lounge 66
travel passes 140
traveller's cheques 136
Tricketts B&B 146
Tropfest 73
Tsuchiya, Kimio 47
Turpin, Jennifer 47
Tusculum & Rockwall
Villas 86, 87
2 Danks Street 45
Twelve 107
Tzannes, Alexander 47

U
Uchi Lounge 95
University of Sydney 19,
43, 103, 105
Utzon, Jørn 8, 10–11, 46

V
Valhalla Cinema 104
Vamps Bistro 101
Vanguard, The 67
Vargabarespresso 107
Vaucluse 97
Vaucluse House 98, 99
Verge, The 67
Verge, John 86, 104
Verona Guest House 148
Victoire 113
Victoria Barracks 90, 92
Victoria Court 147
Victoria Park 105
Victoria Room, The 69
Victoria Street 85
Victorian terrace houses 91
Von Guérard, Eugene 27
Vulcan Hotel 146
Vulcans 129

W
wake up! 148
Wakelin, Roland 27
Waldorf 149
Waldorf Woolloomooloo
148
Walkor, Stephen 18
Wangal tribe 109
Wardell, William 77
water taxis 16, 134

waterskiing 55
Watson, Robert 98
Watsons Bay 14, 16, 96, 98
Pilot Station 99
Waverley Cemetery 49
Waverton 115
Weaving, Hugo 65
websites 135
Welcome Hotel 112
Wenham, David 65
Wentworth Falls 121, 126
Wentworth Mausoleum 99
Wentworth, William
Charles 37, 98, 121
Werrington 87
Westfield Bondi Junction
100, 139
Westfield Sydney 80
Westin Sydney, The 145
White, Henry 78
White, Patrick 40, 41, 108
Whiteblue 101
Whiteley, Brett 26, 27, 25,
44, 45, 47, 93
Wildfire 69
Wild Life Sydney 29
Windsor 120, 123, 124
Saint Mathew's Anglican
Church & Rectory 124
Wollemi National Park 127
Wollemi Pine 20, 126
Wollongong 123, 127
Wollstoncraft 115
Wollstoncraft, Edward 115
women travellers 137
Woodward, Robert 86
Woollahra 92, 96
Woolloomooloo 37, 84, 87
Woolloomooloo Finger
Bay Wharf 65, 86
Woolworths 139
Woolys Wheels 54, 134
world flavours **62–3**
writers **40–41**
Wychbury 87
Wylie's Baths 49

Y, Z
Yang, William 26
Y Hotel 148
Yellow Food Store, The 89
yellow pages 135
York, The 149
Yoshi Jones 106
youth hostels 140
Yurulbin Point 109, 111
Zaaffran 83
Zimmermann 94

Acknowledgements

The Authors
Steve Womersley has lived in Sydney on and off since childhood. He has worked with some of the world's leading travel publishers as a writer and editor and currently lives in country Victoria.

Steve Womersley would like to thank Jane Fuller, Mickey Morelle, Terri Dylan and Terry Harding for their hospitality, Gerry Gallagher, Terry Stuart, Stephanie Holt, Peter Anderson, Rachel Neustein, Loren Polzot and Anita Krivickas for their insider tips, and Sera Jane and Minka for their patience.

Born in Paddington, Rachel Neustein has always lived in inner Sydney and knows all the back alleys and secret spots. She writes about art, fashion, film, food and music for various Australian and international magazines.

Rachel Neustein would like to thank Damien Power, Nell Heard, Alice Addison and David N Reginald.

Photographer Carol Wiley
Additional Photography
Shaen Adey, Max Alexander, Simon Blackall, Andy Crawford, Frank Greenaway, Dave King, Eddie Lawrence, Diana Lynn, David Murray, Michael Nicholson, Siobhan O' Connor, Rob Reichenfeld, Sanjay Sharma, Clive Streeter, Alan Williams

DK INDIA
Managing Editor Aruna Ghose
Art Editor Benu Joshi
Project Editor Anees Saigal
Project Designer Divya Saxena
Senior Cartographer Uma Bhattacharya
Cartographer Suresh Kumar
Picture Researcher Taiyaba Khatoon
DTP Co-ordinator Shailesh Sharma
DTP Designer Vinod Harish
Fact Checker Kelly Adams
Indexer Bhavna Seth Ranjan

DK LONDON
Managing Editor Fay Franklin
Publishing Manager Jane Ewart
Senior Cartographic Editor Casper Morris
Senior DTP Designer Jason Little
Production Linda Dare
DK Picture Library Romaine Werblow, Hayley Smith, Gemma Woodward
Revisions Team Namrata Adhwaryu, Emma Anacootee, Claire Baranowski, Julie Bond, Camilla Gersh, Prerna Gupta, Lydia Halliday, Sumita Khatwani, Priya Kukadia, Helen Partington, Ellen Root, Deborah Soden, Ros Walford, Carol Wiley, Ajay Verma, Hugo Wilkinson.

Bathers, 1913 oil on canvas, 197.5cm x 147.5cm 25cra; Collection: Art Gallery of NSW [accn# 182.1984), 25cra; *Amitabha Buddha*, late 8thC–mid 9thC, andesite, 105 x 88 x 65cm, Purchased with funds provided by the Art Gallery Society of New South Wales 2000, Collection: Art Gallery NSW, photograph: Jenni Carter for AGNSW [accn# 144.2000] 24br. © Wendy Whiteley 1996, *The Balcony 2*, 1975, Brett Whiteley (1939-92), oil on canvas, 203.5 x 364.5cm 27b, Collection: Art Gallery of NSW. © NATIONAL GALLERY OF VICTORIA, MELBOURNE, AUSTRALIA Eugene von Guerard, born Austria 1811, worked in Australia 1852-81, died England 1901, *Sydney Heads* 1860, oil on canvas, 48.5 x 76.3 cm, Purchased through The Art Foundation of Victoria with the assistance of Roslyn and Kerry Packer, Founder Benefactors, 1986 27crb. © AUSTRALIAN NATIONAL MARITIME MUSEUM COLLECTION, reproduced courtesy of the museum 36tl, 42c.

The publishers would like to thank the following individuals, companies and picture libraries for their kind permission to reproduce their photographs.
ALAMY IMAGES: Kerry Dunstone 21cb; Nigel Luckhurst, Lebrecht Music Collection 65tr; Christine Osborne, Worldwide Picture Library 104 br; Sergio Pitamitz 14-15c; Slick Shoots 26cla; David South 77tr. ART GALLERY OF NEW SOUTH WALES: 25cr; 25bc. AUSTRALIAN CHAMBER ORCHESTRA: Photographer: Stephen Oxenbury 64bl, 66t. AUSTRALIAN INFORMATION SERVICE: 37tl. AUSTRALIAN MUSEUM, Sydney: 42tl. AXEL MANO: 100tr.
BARZURA CAFÉ: 101bl. BILLS SURRY HILLS 90bc; NIC BEZZINA: 67tl. courtesy CITY CATALINA: 101tl; courtesy CITY SIGHTSEEING: 134tl; CLOTH: 94bc. CORBIS: P. Caron 52tl; Michelle Chaplow 2clb, 49tr, 52bl; L. Clarke, CRDPHOTO 1c; Graeme Goldin, Corbis Photo Library 34-35c; John Van Hasselt, CORBIS SYGMA 64tc, 71l, 21l; Jose Fuste Raga 4-5; Nick Rains, Corbis Photo Library 17c, 72tr; Bill Ross 28-29c; Royalty Free 73tr; Paul A. Souders 45tr, 26t. GETTY IMAGES: Photolibrary/Andrew Watson 8-19c.

THE HUGHENDEN 147tl;
LUNA PARK SYDNEY: 56t, 115tr.
JACQUELINE MITELMAN 40bl.
By Permission of the NATIONAL LIBRARY OF AUSTRALIA; Portrait of Henry Lawson / Paramount, [190-?], gelatin silver, 27.9 x 20.3 cm, nla.pic-an23351980 40tr;
© Greg Weight,1946-, Portrait of Brett Whiteley (Detail), 1976, gelatin silver on fibre-based paper, image 45.6 x 31 cm, on sheet 50.5 x 40.6 cm, nla.pic-an12090936 26tl; John Olsen with painting "The bath" (Detail), 1997, gelatin silver, image 35.3 x 42.5 cm and 17.9 x 22.5cm, nla.pic-an21100990 26tc;v © Mrs. Ann Mills, Self Portrait (Detail) Grace Cossington-Smith 26tr.
MANLY BUNGALOWS: 148tr. MASTERFILE: R. Ian Lloyd 74-75. MITCHELL LIBRARY, STATE LIBRARY OF NEW SOUTH WALES 36tc, 36tr, 36bc, 37tr, 37br.
NSW POLICE: 137bl; NILGIRI'S: 119tl.
OPERA BAR: 68tr.
POWERHOUSE MUSEUM: 7clb, 30c, 30cla, 30bl, 31cr, 31bl, 42bl.
QUAY RESTAURANT 58tc; QUEEN VICTORIA BUILDING: 80tl;
SOFITEL WENTWORTH SYDNEY: 145tl.
SYDNEYATTRACTIONSGROUP: 20br. Courtesy of the SYDNEY OPERA HOUSE: 3tc, 8-9c, 8tr, 8br, 9bc, 10tl, 10tr, 11t, 11c, 11cr.
SYDNEY WILDLIFE WORLD: 29cr. STATE

Dorling Kinder

Top 10 guides can be purchase
Personalized jackets and excerpts o

To find out more, please contact: (in
com or Special Sales, Dorling Kinder
the United States)–Special Marke
Street, New

Selected Street Index

Street	Grid	Street	Grid	Street	Grid
Albert Street	N2	Dixon Street	M5	Missenden Road	B5
Albion Street	N6	Dobroyd Parade	A4	Moncur Street	F5
Alfred Street	M2	Dowling Street	P4	Moore Park Road	E5
Alice Street	B6	Driver Avenue	E5	Mount Street	K3
Alison Road	E6	Druitt Street	M4	Mrs Macquaries Road	P3
Anzac Parade	E5	Earl Place	P4	Murray Street	L4
Arden Street	G6	Earl Street	P4	Neild Avenue	Q5
Argyle Street	M2	Eastern Distributor	E5	Nelson Street	B5
Art Gallery Road	N3	Eddy Avenue	M6	New Beach Road	R4
Balmain Road	B3	Edward Street	K4	New South Head Road	R5
Bank Street	K4	Elizabeth Bay Road	Q4	Nicholson Street	K1
Barcom Avenue	P5	Elizabeth Street	M3	Norton Street	A4
Barlow Street	M6	Enmore Road	B6	Notts Avenue	H5
Baroda Street	Q4	Erskine Street	M3	O'Connell Street	M3
Bathurst Street	M4	Erskineville Road	C6	Ocean Avenue	F4
Bay Street	F4	Essex Street	M2	Old South Head Road	G5
Bayswater Road	P4	Euston Road	C6	Orwell Street	P4
Beach Road	H5	Experiment Street	K4	Oxford Street	N5
Bedford Street	B5	Fig Street	K5	Pacific Highway	D1
Belmore Street	N6	Flinders Street	N6	Paddington Street	R6
Bent Street	N3	Foley Street	N5	Palmer Street	N5
Birchgrove Road	B2	Forbes Street	P4	Park Street	M4
Birrell Street	F5	Foster Street	M5	Parker Street	M6
Bligh Street	M3	Foveaux Street	M6	Parramatta Road	J6
Bond Street	M3	George Street	N2	Patterson Lane	N6
Bondi Road	G5	Gipps Street	K4	Pelican Street	N5
Botany Road	D6	Glebe Point Road	J6	Phillip Street	N2
Boundary Street	P5	Glenmore Road	Q6	Pier Street	L5
Bourke Street	N6	Gloucester Street	M2	Pirrama Road	K3
Bradfield Highway	M1	Goodhope Street	Q6	Pitt Street	M2
Bradleys Head Road	F1	Gosbell Street	Q5	Prince Albert Road	N4
Bridge Lane	J5	Goulburn Street	M5	Pyrmont Bridge Road	K4
Bridge Road	J6	Grafton Street	L6	Pyrmont Bridge Street	K4
Bridge Street	M2	Greenknowe Avenue	Q4	Pyrmont Street	K3
Brighton Street	H5	Grosvenor Street	M2	Quay Street	K6
Brisbane Street	N5	Gurner Street	Q6	Queen Street	F5
Broadway	L6	Harbour Street	L4	Ramsgate Avenue	H5
Bronte Road	G6	Harrington Street	M2	Reiby Place	M2
Broughton Street	J5	Harris Street	K4	Riley Street	N4
Burton Street	N5	Hay Street	M5	Roscoe Street	G5
Cahill Expressway	M2	Heeley Street	Q6	Roylston Street	R6
Campbell Parade	H5	Hereford Street	J4	St James Road	N4
Campbell Street	N5	Hickson Road	M1	St Johns Road	A6
Canterbury Road	A5	Holdsworth Street	F5	St Marys Road	N4
Carrington Road	G5	Hospital Road	N3	Sir John Young Crescent	N4
Cascade Street	R6	Hughes Street	P4	South Dowling Street	P6
Castlereagh Street	M4	Hunt Street	N5	Stanley Street	N5
Cathedral Road	N4	Hunter Street	M3	Stanmore Road	A5
Cecil Street	R6	James Lane	M4	Sussex Street	L3
Chalmers Street	M6	Jamison Street	M2	Syd Einfeld Drive	F5
Chapel Street	N5	Jersey Road	E5	Sydney Harbour Tunnel	N1
Church Street	B5	Jones Bay Road	K3	Sydney Park Road	C6
Circular Quay East Walkway	N2	Jones Street	K5	The Crescent	B4
City Road	K6	Kellet Street	Q4	Thomas Street	K6
City West Link Road	A4	Kent Street	M3	Ultimo Road	K6
Clarence Street	M3	King Street	M3	Union Street	K4
Cleveland Street	D5	Kings Cross Road	P5	Victoria Road	B3
College Street	N4	Knox Street	F4	Victoria Street	P5
Commonwealth Street	N6	Lachlan Street	D6	Waine Street	N6
Cooper Street	Q6	Lee Street	M6	Warrington Freeway	D1
Cowper Street	K6	Lime Street	L3	Watson Road	M1
Cowper Wharf Roadway	P3	Liverpool Street	M5	Wattle Street	K5
Cross Street	F4	Loftus Road	M1	Wemyss Lane	N6
Crown Street	N4	Macdonald Street	P5	Wentworth Avenue	M5
Cumberland Street	M2	Macleay Street	Q4	West Street	P6
Curtin Place	M3	Macquarie Street	M3	Western Distributor	J5
Dacey Avenue	E6	Manning Street	Q4	William Henry Street	L5
Dalley Street	M2	Margaret Street	M3	William Street	N4
Dangar Street	F6	Market Street	M4	Wilson Street	P4
Darley Road	A4	Martin Place	M3	Womerah Avenue	P5
Darling Drive	L5	McEvoy Street	C6	York Road	F5
Darling Point Road	R5	McLachlan Avenue	Q5	York Street	M3
Darling Street	K1	Military Road	H4	Young Street	N2
Darlinghurst Road	P5	Miller Street	K4	Yurong Street	N5
Devonshire Street	D5	Minogue Crescent Street	J6	Yurong Street Parkway	N4

160